THE SAUCE
BIBLE

Guide to the
Saucier's Craft

David Paul Larousse

John Wiley & Sons, Inc.

New York • Chichester • Brisbane • Toronto • Singapore

"There's no sauce in the world like hunger."
—Miguel Cervantes (1547–1616)

Publisher: Tom Woll
Senior Editor: Claire Thompson
Managing Editor: Jacqueline A. Martin
Design and Editorial Supervision: Laura Cleveland, WordCrafters Editorial
  Services, Inc.
Copy Editor: Karen Verde
Photography: Marshall Gordon

This text is printed on acid-free paper.

#ANF 4-8-14

This publication is designed to provide accurate and authoritative
information in regard to the subject matter covered. It is sold with the
understanding that the publisher is not engaged in rendering legal,
accounting, or other professional services. If legal advice or other expert
assistance is required, the services of a competent professional person
should be sought. FROM A DECLARATION OF PRINCIPLES JOINTLY
ADOPTED BY A COMMITTEE OF THE AMERICAN BAR ASSOCIATION
AND A COMMITTEE OF PUBLISHERS.

Library of Congress Cataloging-in-Publication Data

Larousse, David Paul
  The sauce bible : guide to the saucier's craft / David Paul
Larousse.
      p.   cm
    ISBN 0-471-57228-4
    1. Sauces. I. Title
TX819.A1L37   1993
641.8'14—dc20   92-37388
                                                                    CIP

Printed in the United States of America

20   19   18   17   16   15   14   13

CONTENTS

RECIPES

●●

Contemporary Innovations

𝒞REAM (WHITE) SAUCES

Traditional Derivatives

Contemporary Innovations

ADDITIONAL RECIPES

FOREWORD

I first met David Larousse in the Spring of 1975, while working at the Waccabuc Country Club in South Salem, New York. I was in my last year of school at the Culinary Institute of America in Hyde Park, New York, and was employed as a garde manger (pantry cook) at the club. David, a recent graduate, was the sous-chef.

Our paths crossed next in San Francisco. Through the Chef's Professional Agency, managed by the eccentric and delightful Maxine Lockley, we both found gainful employment, and we secured a comfortable two-bedroom apartment in the Richmond District. What an exciting time this was for me, recently graduated from the premier culinary school in the world and living in one of the great food cities. And our lives were full of food (as they still are), cooking for a living and cooking up great feasts at home. We talked Escoffier and Pellaprat and Bocuse. We shopped at Asian and Hispanic and natural food markets. We ate, and drank, and debated all the great culinary debates that needed to be debated. It was during this time that I focused on a discrepancy between what I was cooking professionally and what I really liked to eat.

In San Francisco my friend David introduced me to Nancy, now my wife and the mother of our two beautiful children, for which I am forever grateful. Five years later, Nancy and I found ourselves in New England and my food philosophy came full circle from classical to regional. I traded in Auguste Escoffier and Henri Pellaprat for James Beard and Fanny Farmer. I began to concentrate on the real cuisine of the region, the food and cooking styles that had evolved from indigenous New England foods. My departure from the classics (always essential in any culinary training) was sometimes difficult and misunderstood, but I was determined to follow my intuition. In the hodgepodge melting-pot cuisine of modern America, classical cuisine was defined as upscale, fancy, expensive, high end. And the restaurant business seemed to devote itself to providing what it believed the high-end market wanted, often a slavish, heavy-handed interpretation of classical cooking.

Then, in the 1980s, like a breath of fresh air, the commercial food scene began to change dramatically: Pacific Rim, Southwest, Cajun, Creole, Southern, Tex-Mex, Shaker, and Quaker—whole new regions of cooking styles were being rediscovered. I watched my colleagues throw out their classical references and begin pursuing James Beard and Fanny Farmer.

A friend once said that there are two kinds of food: good and bad. This may be the single most important dictum in the evolution of North American cooking styles. Even with the revival of regional cuisines, quality food preparation is not so much a matter of personal or regional style as one of seeking out the best local ingredients, and applying simple cooking techniques to bring out the best flavors, colors, and textures of those ingredients. Quality ingredients (I have been called fanatical on this subject) and a foundation in classic fundamentals are still the most important elements in good American cooking. I am pleased to report that *The Sauce Bible* reflects the very essence of my own transformation as a chef and restaurateur. Chef Larousse shares my belief in the importance of classical techniques and simple expression in contemporary cookery. In this book he has adhered to the traditional sauce system we all learned, while including contemporary innovations that go beyond the traditional sauces. In this one reference book, the reader will see the foundation classics, essential in any contemporary regional style, combined with examples reflecting the honest culinary offerings based on native North American ingredients.

I must point out that David Paul Larousse and I differ on the function of art in food. My good friend (I believe he likes to call himself "the artist trapped inside the body of a chef") has also addressed the subject of sauce painting, something that I do not subscribe to in my style and approach to cooking. But I will allow him that artist's indulgence. In all, I commend him for bringing the complex subject of sauces into focus, and updating this important fundamental for yet another generation of culinary professionals.

Jasper White
Boston, Massachusetts

PREFACE

· ·

The Sauce Bible began as simply a study of the subject of sauce painting, a technique of food presentation that has been in vogue in the restaurant trade for some years. Over time it has developed into a much more extensive work on stocks and sauces.

Hering's *Dictionary of Classical and Modern Cookery* states that "good fonds and sauces are the foundation of fine cuisine. Their preparation is considered the most important business in every large kitchen." In teaching culinary students, I have always been aware of the great importance of establishing good fundamental skills. This is part of a chef-instructor's responsibility to his students—something that in an age of rapidly changing culinary trends will stand them in good stead no matter where the times lead. Accomplishing this task has always been, for me, a source of satisfaction. In cooking, nothing is more basic than stocks and sauces. This has been reinforced in me by my own professional experience and teaching. Leading a different group of students through this curriculum every three weeks refined and deepened my own understanding.

It is easy for culinary students to become bored when faced with the details and routine of stocks, sauces, and basic knife skills. I tried to augment these studies with anecdotes, miniature biographies of those who have contributed to modern cooking techniques, and historical and linguistic footnotes to specific dishes. These, too, have been added to *The Sauce Bible* as side notes. Not only do they bring added insights to the contents, but I believe it is of great importance to tell and retell these stories to keep them alive. These stories bring a special insight to dishes created in the names of persons, places, and historical events, and they become all the more significant as modern cooking styles continue to evolve and change.

The subject of "sauce painting" is an area of considerable fascination for me. Art and cooking, and where the two intersect, has always been of particular philosophical interest in my pursuit of the culinary craft. Though often referred to normally as an "art," cooking in its most essential and primary function is more accurately a craft. The arrangement of two or more sauces on a serving dish, manipulated into a visually stunning design, represents the sole juncture where art and cuisine truly meet—in a practical, truthful, and stunning way. I firmly believe that this is the purest and most basic presence of art within the craft of cooking. It was in seeking a way to describe and teach this phenomenon that I began referring to the technique of sauce painting as *Arabesque*.

Fine sauciers are a rare breed. Brillat-Savarin once wrote, "On devient rôtisseur, mais on nait saucier." ("Sauciers are born; rotisseurs are made.") They attain their level of expertise through years of hard work, endless hours, and lifelong study. And although I have worked deliberately toward simplifying and demystifying the subject of sauces, I have discovered that it is not quite as simple as that. Recipes, like written music, are only a guide to the real thing. The reality is in the performance. While cooking does have scientific, systematic elements, no recipe can represent the human creativity and complexity. But if one aspires to learn the saucier's craft one must begin somewhere. The advantage to using a book such as *The Sauce Bible* is that it includes not only the traditional basics, but a comtemporary distillation of several generations of development.

In all, *The Sauce Bible* is intended to be a complete reference to one of the most important fundamental areas in the culinary profession. As Raymond Oliver wrote, "A sauce is not only the fluid part of a cooked dish, but the very soul of cooking." And while most of the foundation sauces herein are of the classical, or traditional, mode, certain techniques and approaches are distilled through the experience of the author, which brings contemporary modifications into focus. In addition, numerous sauces and accompaniments created by other culinary practitioners are also included. Through their innovations they have demonstrated a distinctive ingenuity—a crab wonton embellished with plum chutney; blackberry ketchup served with lamb loin; a cranberry relish enhancing a dish of dry-cured salmon. Some of these innovations were created by colleagues who graciously permitted me to include their creations. Others were researched through a variety of sources and are included with permission. Where any of these recipes includes a step that is an integral part of a subsequent sauce, the complete recipe is included. All of the work of these culinary practitioners has helped to make this book a complete, contemporary reference. I humbly acknowledge my debt to them, and hope that this book will serve adequately as a guide for future sauciers.

David Paul Larousse
San Francisco, California

ACKNOWLEDGMENTS

I wish to acknowledge Marshall Gordon, photographer, and prop stylist Susan Neuer for their exceptional work in creating the extraordinary photography for *The Sauce Bible*. I also thank the following individuals for permitting the use of specific information in this book: Jan Marie Schroeder, the Oregon Caneberry Commission, for information on Oregon berries; George Lang, author of *Lang's Compendium of Culinary Nonsense and Trivia* (New York: Clarkson N. Potter, 1980), for historical information on Alexis Soyer; Harold McGee, author of *On Food and Cooking*, for use of information on the New York State Supreme Court case on tomatoes, rhubarb leaf poisoning, peppercorns, pine trees, origin of the word *gravy*, Taillevant's recipe for "gravy of small birds," and a quote by Auguste Escoffier; Prosper Montagne, author, and Jennifer Harvey Lang, editor, of *Larousse Gastronomique*, 1988 edition, for numerous historical and biographical anecdotes; Raymond Oliver, author of *Classic Sauces* (London: Pitman Publishing, 1989), for "a sauce is not only the fluid part of a cooked dish, it is the very soul of cooking; Waverly Root, *Food* (New York: Simon & Schuster, 1980), for information on crayfish and the longest homing run of a sea trout.

The following individuals also permitted the use of recipes in the compilation of *The Sauce Bible*: Giuliano Bugialli, author of *Bugialli on Pasta* (New York: Simon & Schuster, 1988) (Pasta Aglio E Olio, and information on the use of Parmesan cheese); Dan Callahan, sous-chef, The Olympic Club, San Francisco (Crimson Sauce); Gloria Ciccarone-Nehls, chef de cuisine, The Big Four, San Francisco (Golden Pepper Coulis and Papaya-Mint Relish); Craig Claiborne and Pierre Franey (Chicken Liver Mousse, Creamed Tomato Sauce); Jon Cohen and Paola Scaravelli, authors of *Cooking from an Italian Garden* (Orlando: Harcourt Brace Jovanovich, 1984) (Asparagus Sauce); Marcel Desaulniers, chef-proprietor, The Trellis, Williamsburg, Virginia, author of *The Trellis Cookbook* (New York: Weidenfeld & Nicolson, 1988); (Chocolate Rum Sauce and Pear Custard Sauce); Christian DeVos of ARA Services, Inc., who was instrumental in developing many of the recipes which originally appeared in *A Taste for All Seasons* (Boston: Harvard Common Press, 1990); Alan R. Gibson, Food and Beverage Director, Sheraton Hotel, Needham, Massachusetts (for numerous sauce innovations; Fred Halpert, Chef, Brava Terrace, St. Helena, California (Grilled Pork Tenderloin, Pickled Grapes); Timothy T. Hanni, Master of Wine, Beringer's Vineyards, St. Helena, California (Szechewan Grilling Marinade); Gordon Hammersley, chef-proprietor, Hammersley's Bistro, Boston (Smoked Shrimp Butter); Marcella Hazan, author of *Marcella's Italian Kitchen* (New York: Knopf, 1991) (Melanzane Conservate a Crudo and Goat Cheese Pesto); Steve Karapatakis, proprietor of Le Greque, Providence, Rhode Island (Tzakiki); Waldy Malouf, chef de cuisine, Hudson River Club, New York City (Bourbon Sauce); Franz Mitterer, author and publisher of the *Art Culinaire* series (New York: Culinaire, Inc.) (Black Bean Sauce and Beggar's Purses, Avocado Sauce); Wolfgang Puck, chef de cuisine, Spago, Los Angeles (Creamed Chicken Sauce); Thierry Rautureau, chef de cuisine, Rover's Restaurant, Seattle (Grilled Chicken Breast with Black Beans and Goat Cheese); Mary Taylor Simetti, author of *Pomp and Sustenance* (New York: Simon & Schuster, 1989) (Pesto Trapanese); Edouard Walder, chef-instructor, City College of San Francisco (Sauerbraten Marinade); Jonathan Waxman, chef de cuisine, Table 29, Napa, California; Jasper White, chef-proprieter, Jasper's Restaurant, Boston (Oyster Mignonette, Apple Cider Mignonette, Juan's Sauce for clams, Green Clam Sauce, Tuscan Green Sauce); Susan Wilkens, chef de cuisine, Little City Antipasti Bar, San Francisco (Coriander-Lime Vinaigrette and Toasted Cumin Vinaigrette).

CHAPTER 1

A BRIEF HISTORY OF SAUCES

Sauce: n. 1. Any flavorful soft or liquid dressing or relish served as an accompaniment to food. 2. Stewed or puréed sweetened fruit, often served with other foods. 3. Anything that adds zest, flavor, or piquancy to something.[1]

*A*lthough there was a considerable body of literature on the subject of cooking and gastronomy in ancient Greece, little of it survived, possibly due in part to a catastrophic fire that destroyed the library at Alexandria. From the fragments that did survive, we know that one of the earliest cooking treatises was *Art of Cooking*, compiled in Syracuse by Mithaecus in the fifth century B.C.

In the fourth century B.C., Archestratus of Gela (an ancient town in southern Sicily) traveled throughout the Mediterranean as a sort of gastronomic philosopher. He compiled into poetic verse his observations on the eating habits of different nations and his philosophies of gastronomy. Only fragments of his writings survived, but they were incorporated into *Diepnosophistai* (roughly translated to "Sophists of Dining"), a lengthy philosophical work written in the third century A.D. by Athenaeus of Naucratis.

Archestratus's culinary style essentially called for lightness and simplicity. This included the use of fresh, seasonal ingredients; minimal use of fat and salt; the revival of regional cooking styles; innovation and inventiveness; and light sauces, consisting of natural reductions prepared to order. So much for *nouvelle cuisine* and our current "new" and "lighter" cooking styles. It would be easy to say that Archestratus was ahead of his time; it might be more honest to admit that even gastronomic history repeats itself.

FROM APICIUS TO PETRONIUS

Of three notable Romans by the name of Apicius (all known for their gastronomic indulgences), Marcus Gavius Apicius (80 B.C.–40 A.D.), who lived during the reigns of Augustus and Tiberius, was the best known. He was a personality of some note and took his food seriously. He also spent enormous sums on it. According to Athenaeus, Apicius was ". . . very rich and luxurious, for whom several kinds of cheesecake are named. [And] he

[1]*The American Heritage Dictionary.* New York: American Heritage Publishing Co., Inc., 1975.

spent myriads of drachmas on his belly. . . ." The extremes to which wealthy Roman citizens went in their pursuit of gastronomy during the height of Imperial Rome is well known.

———————————— • ————————————

The Emperor Domitian (Roman emperor from 81–96 A.D.) reportedly interrupted a political debate in the Roman senate to ask his colleagues what sauce he should use to accompany a turbot he planned to serve at a banquet that evening.

————————————————————

In spite of the gastronomic excesses which we know were part of the culture of Imperial Rome, the general citizenry believed that paying too much attention to matters of food and drink was a superfluous and even wicked luxury. But the degree to which Apicius himself engaged in hedonistic and self-indulgent debauchery is not clear. He compiled considerable material on the subject of eating and dining, and was famous for creating many original dishes—among them râgouts, cakes, and numerous sauces. He also endowed a school for the teaching and promotion of cooking and culinary ideas. The learned Apicius staged a melodramatic exit from his earthly life, after discovering that he was down to his last 10 million sesterce. Concluding that life would no longer be worth living, he ingested poison at a banquet especially arranged for the event.

Apicius de re Coquinaria, or *The Book of Apicius,* was likely not written by Apicius, but by an unknown author or authors during the latter part of the third century. It has been called a gastronomic bible, consisting of ten different volumes, and it influenced cooking styles on the European continent well into the seventeenth century.

Apician Sauces

Apician sauces were busy eclectic concoctions, containing a dozen ingredients or more. For example, *Cumin Sauce, for shellfish,* contained pepper, parsley, lovage, mint, aromatic leaf (bay leaf), malabathrum (a Middle Eastern leaf), and liquanum. *Ius candidum in elixam,* a white sauce for boiled foods, consisted of pepper, liquanum, wine, rue, onion, pine nuts, spiced wine, a few pieces of bread cut up to thicken, and oil. The nuts and aromatic ingredients were often pounded into a paste, then blended with liquid elements—wine, honey, vinegar, garum, olive oil. Garum consisted of a purée of garus, a small fish as yet unidentified in modern nomenclature—possibly a small mackerel—intestines and all. It was salted and spiced, pounded into a paste, dried in the sun, fermented, blended with wine, honey, vinegar, and/or oil, then the juice was extracted and bottled. It was very popular and expensive, and available commercially in varying degrees of quality and type; the very finest was made from fish livers alone. Historians have pointed to such concoctions as proof of the barbarous and excessive styles of Imperial Rome, while scientists have pointed out that such creations were important sources of vitamin D, particularly when the livers were exposed to the sun.

Liquanum was a general term, referring to stock, brine, marinade, natural juice, and/or a poaching medium. The exact preparation of garum, and the true meaning of liquanum, both remain a mystery. The closest thing we have to garum is anchovy fillets and anchovy paste, and possibly one of the dishes of modern times characteristic of Apician style is the Austrian "Weiner Holstein." This consists of a veal cutlet dipped in flour, eggs, and bread crumbs, then fried, and garnished with a fried egg, anchovy fillets, lemon, and sometimes beets and capers. Joseph Vehling, in his 1936 edition of the Apician book, invokes our own use of bottled sauces as descendants of ancient prototypes, among these catsup, chili, chutney, herbal mustards, and walnut catsup, as well as the brand-named sauces—A-1, Escoffier, Harvey's, Punch, Soyer's, Oscar's, and Worcestershire. It has also been suggested that the Vietnamese *nuoc-mam, nampla* from Thailand, and *patis* from the Philippines, all some form of fish-flavored, fermented soy sauce, may be even more accurate modern equivalents of ancient condiments.

Another important source of information on the styles of cooking and eating at the height of the Roman empire is Gaius Petronius, also known as "Petronius Arbiter" (he was considered an arbiter of fashion). Petronius was a Roman courtier and satirist, and the author of *cena Trimalchionis* (Trimalchio's Dinner). Trimalchio was a braggart, drunk, and wife-beater, given to staging extravagant banquets to show off his transformation from former slave to successful entrepreneur. From Petronius's tale, we learn much about the social excesses at the height of Imperial Rome. Trimalchio too ended his life in dramatic fashion, at a final banquet-funeral, as did Petronius, later on.

As the Roman empire expanded, bringing access to more and more exotic foodstuffs, luxury advanced, and cooks, formerly slaves in the frugal days of the nation, rose to great heights of civic importance. They were treated more as artisans than as servants, and their skills were highly valued. This was followed by a period when professional cooks became vain and arrogant, and "made of their masters their very slaves" (C. Dezobry, *Rome au siècle d'Auguste* [Rome in the century of Augustus]). There was a public backlash of sorts, leading to a custom of severe reprimand when a cook's actions warranted it. Dezobry writes, "If the skill of the artist had failed, if he had served some ill-prepared dish, the cook was put in irons on the spot, or else was led to the triclinium (dining room) by two henchmen and severely flogged in the presence of the guests."

It is important to point out that the fragments of writings based on the Apician style that survived the decline of Rome were preserved through the centuries by various monastic orders. With Gutenberg's invention of the printing press, there was a renewed interest in many works of antiquity, including those of ancient Rome. Between 1498 and 1958, at least 21 different editions of *The Book of Apicius* were published in at least five European languages.

CHARLEMAGNE— FIRST "LORD OF THE TABLE"

The next historical period focuses on the Gauls. Rome's conquering of Gaul brought some refinements, such as the use of spices, and some semblance of table manners, but there were few real gastronomic changes. By modern standards the Gauls ate poorly—meals were long, and meat and fish were often boiled together in cauldrons. The custom to cook these two items separately was developed much later.

When the Franks overran Gaul, Charlemagne (Charles the Great, also known as Charles I), the first "Lord of the Table," introduced some elements of refinement. He was the first to invite women to sit at the table with men, but only on the condition that they did not offend with nauseating odors or noxious perfumes. People ate twice a day—breakfast upon awakening, and a lavish dinner mid-afternoon. Charlemagne introduced a fruit compote as an accompaniment to meats, and at his court people no longer ate with their fingers but with their knifepoints. Still, quantity was preferred to quality. Pyramids of meats, grilled or roasted on a spit, followed one after the other. Stews were of the most elemental nature—chopped meats, boiled with salt, vinegar, and verjuice (unfermented grape juice), then thickened with dates or raisins. With the exception of the monarch's table, hygienic or culinary rules were nonexistent. People drank out of the same goblet, passing it from hand to hand.

The word *sauce* is derived from the Latin *salsus*, past participle of *sallere*, meaning "to salt." The preserving (marinating) of meat, fish, and poultry in salt draws out a liquid essence from the marinating foods that historically was used in both the cooking of a dish and as a liquid to accompany it. During Charlemagne's time, a thick slice of bread, a "trencher," was placed on each diner's plate to soak up the fats and juices from meat, poultry, or game. It is logical to conclude that the evolution of thickened, seasoned liquids used in the cooking of or to accompany a dish may have evolved with the use of a trencher.

A *dodine* was a sort of a sauce made during medieval times that was placed under roasting poultry, mingled with the fat and juices from the roast, and was then served with that roast. There were three classifications of this preparation: white dodine—milk boiled with ginger, egg yolks, and sugar; red dodine—toasted bread soaked in red wine, rubbed through a sieve, then boiled with fried onions, bacon, cinnamon, nutmeg, cloves, sugar, and salt; and verjuice (raw grape juice) dodine—egg yolks, verjuice, crushed chicken livers, ginger, parsley, and stock.

Following Charlemagne's death in 813, French cuisine, along with European culture, slumbered. For the next 500 years, intermittent periods of famine and widespread disease precipitated a dreadful development. According to Raoul Glaber, a ribald monk of the eleventh century, "Cannibalism is rife, particularly in certain sections of the center of France, the most underprivileged areas. On the highroads, the strong seize the weak; they tear them apart, roast them and eat them. Bands of men roam the countryside in groups attacking lonely wayfarers, attacking whole families and strolling minstrels with their children, killing them and selling their flesh in the nearest market." For faithful francophiles this may come as a considerable shock. But it is nevertheless part of a long history that preceded the modern haute cuisine we are familiar with today.

Sometime around the fourteenth century, a more organized cuisine slowly began to develop. At some point, the French made a distinction between *sauce* and *grané*. A grané, from the Latin *granum* (seed), was a meat stew thickened with grains, while sauce was a separate concoction of thickened, seasoned liquid. According to Harold McGee (*On Food and Cooking, The Science and Lore of the Kitchen*), our *gravy* is a corruption of *grané* simply because in a transfer of recipes from one manuscript to another, a transcriber mistook the *n* for a *v.* Taillevent (Guillaume Tirel, 1326–1395), in his *Viandier,* includes a recipe for "Gravy of small birds," as follows: "Grané of fine or such grain as you wish, fry them in clear lard; take white bread, dissolve it in some beef broth and strain; boil with your meat. Grind ginger and cinnamon, dissolve in verjus, boil everything together; it shouldn't be too thick."

CATHERINE DE MEDICI AND THE ITALIAN INFLUENCE

Catherine de Medici's marriage to the Duke of Orléans, the future King Henry II, in 1553, was the next significant development in European culinary history. Exactly how much influence the Italians had on the development of French cuisine is an issue that has been much debated, with strong opinions on both sides. That the French display a steadfast inability to cook pasta and noodles *al dente,* "to the bite," may very well be a reflection of a subtle yet ingrained cultural rejection of the Italian influence on haute cuisine. Could Antoine Carême's comment on the cookery of ancient Rome ("The Roman cuisine was fundamentally barbaric") be further evidence of a refusal by the French to admit any Italian influence on their cuisine? Whether or not de Medici's marriage to the Duke was a catalyst to the birth of haute cuisine, the 14-year-old Catherine did bring with her assorted novelties and a battalion of cooks who demonstrated at least a different style in culinary matters, if not a greater refinement than their French counterparts. And though her entourage reportedly captivated the attention of the aristocracy and the masses, many historians present her as a glutton, with preferences running to cockscombs, kidneys, and artichoke hearts. Further support of the theory of Italian influence can be found on a page from a fifteenth-century Italian manuscript (reproduced in a cookbook by Giuliano Bugialli) describing a roux (flour and fat), which became an indispensable element in French sauces.

THE DEVELOPMENT OF THE FRENCH SAUCE SYSTEM

From the seventeenth century on, the French sauce system really began to take root. Three of the most significant contributors to its development were François Pierre La Varenne, Antoine Carême, and Auguste Escoffier.

François Pierre La Varenne

La Varenne began his career as a marmiton (kitchen boy) in the home of the Duchesse de Bar, sister of Henri IV. The king, observing that La Varenne was a bright lad, entrusted him with negotiations in his romantic affairs. Later, he was put in charge of the kitchens of the Marquis d'Uxelles, the governor of Cahlon-sur-Saône, after whom mushroom duxelle, created by Varenne, was named. His Sauce Robert reflected a trend toward seasoning less likely to overwhelm the tastes of food, and his "flour liaison" (roux) became an official thickening agent.

La Varenne was also the author of the first systematically planned books on cookery and confectionery, and showed how French cuisine had been influenced by Italian cookery during the previous 150 years. His published works include *Le Pâtissier Français* (1653); *Le Confiturier Français* (1664); *Le Cuisinier François* (1651); and *L'École des Ragoûts* (1668).

Antoine Carême

Antoine Carême (1783–1833) was one of the most dynamic of all the culinary practitioners, authors, and gastronomes of his time. He overcame a most traumatic start in the world, when at the age of 11, his father, a handyman, told him, "Go, my boy! In the world there are excellent callings. Leave us to languish! Misery is our lot and we must die of it. This is the day of splendid fortunes. It only needs wit—and you have it—to make one. Perhaps this evening or tomorrow some fine house will open its door to you. Go with what God has given you!" Later, in his memoirs, Carême would write, "Although born into one of the poorest families in France, of a family of twenty-five children, and although my father literally threw me out into the street to save me, fortune smiled very soon upon me. . . ."

He was taken in by the manager of a low-class eating house, where he worked for several years. At the age of 16, he became an apprentice to Bailly, one of the finest pastry cooks in Paris, and the most celebrated caterer of his time. Bailly encouraged him to develop an innate ability to draw, and Carême studied at night in the print room at the National Library. He copied architectural drawings, and from this experience designated confectionery as a form of architecture. One cannot overestimate his role in raising the culinary craft to a higher level of artistic creation. "The fine arts are five in number, to wit: painting, sculpture, poetry, music, architecture—whose main branch is confectionery." His subsequent *pièces montées* created from pastries, puff paste, preserved fruits, creams, and sherbets have influenced centuries of pâtissiers.

Among Carême's employers were Talleyrand, England's Prince Regent (future King George IV), Tsar Alexander I (from this experience he introduced many Russian dishes into French cuisine), the Viennese Court, the British Embassy, Princess Bagration, and during his last years, Baron de Rothschild. Few, however, escaped the sting of his bitter pen, a characteristic perhaps reflecting his traumatic start in life. He died, "burnt out by the flame of his genius and the heat of the ovens."

Carême's published works include *Le Pâtissier Pittoresque* (1815) and *Le Pâtissier Royal Parisien* (1825). In addition to his accomplishment in pastry arts, Carême also classified the sauces of his time into four families—Espagnole, velouté, Allemande, and béchamel—each headed by a basic (or leading) sauce, from which dozens of derivations could be produced. This was the first structure of a system of sauces, which would later evolve into what became known as "the French sauce system."

Carême was the first to classify sauces into four families. They were:

ESPAGNOLE   VELOUTÉ
ALLEMANDE   BÉCHAMEL

Auguste Escoffier

Auguste Escoffier (1846–1935) was born in Villeneuve-Loubet, a small town in the Alpes-Maritimes. He began his career at the age of 13, apprenticing at a celebrated restaurant in Nice owned by his uncle. In 1890, he joined forces with Swiss hotelier César Ritz and opened the Savoy Hotel in London. In 1898, he moved to the Carlton Hotel, then one of the most famous hotels in Europe. He has been called the "King of Chefs, and the Chef of Kings." While on board the steamship Imperator, of the Hamburg-America Line, Emperor William II was so impressed with the food that he personally congratulated Escoffier, saying: "I am the Emperor of Germany, but you are the Emperor of chefs." In 1920, Escoffier was made a Chevalier of the Legion of Honor. He retired from the Carlton in 1921 at the age of 74, and was made an Officer of the Legion in 1928.

Escoffier was tirelessly dedicated to promoting professionalism of the culinary trade. Aware of the rigors and long hours required in the culinary profession, he was known to encourage his employees to pursue their education and individual learning. He was also a man of simple credos and the highest standards of professionalism. Toward that end, he neither drank nor smoked, and was a great believer in the virtue of remaining calm. He is credited with bringing the old opulent style of haute cuisine into the twentieth century. Joseph Donon, who had worked for Escoffier at the Carlton Hotel, once wrote, "He simplified the methods of cooking . . . without sacrificing the quality that distinguishes classical cooking. [He was] A slave of duty, utterly unspoiled by adulation, devoting his working hours to devising new culinary masterpieces, and his scanty leisure to unheralded acts of benevolence."

Donon was later instrumental in establishing *Les Amis d'Escoffier*—a society to promote the appreciation of food and wine—in 1955, and in creating the *Musée de L'Art Culinaire*, in 1966, at Escoffier's birthplace in Villeneuve-Loubet. Escoffier's 62-year career was one of the longest ever recorded in the culinary profession. He died in Monte Carlo at the age of 89, several days after the death of his wife.

Escoffier was famous for several dishes, one of the most notable being *Pêches Melba*, created for the Australian opera diva, Nellie Melba. He penned numerous books, including *Le Guide Culinaire*—first published in 1902 and still in print today as *The Escoffier Cookbook*. Furthermore, he reorganized the sauce tree under the headings of Espagnole, velouté, béchamel, Hollandaise, and tomato. This is the sauce structure that has been taught in professional cookery for the better part of the twentieth century.

Escoffier revised Carême's sauce system, naming the following as the foundation, or *mother sauces:*

ESPAGNOLE   VELOUTÉ
BÉCHAMEL   TOMATE
HOLLANDAISE

SOME OBSERVATIONS AND CONCLUSIONS

Although it is difficult to synopsize twentieth-century cooking, one of the significant trends in the latter half of the century has been nouvelle cuisine, which is characterized by a rejection of complicated dishes, flour-thickened sauces, and overcooked vegetables. Its precepts include avoidance of fatty foods, and a strict adherence to using only the freshest local raw materials, seeking a harmony of ingredients, sauces made with natural reductions, and minimal cooking of all foods, leaving innate character, color, and nutrition intact.

I first encountered nouvelle cuisine in Michel Guérard's *Cuisine Minceur*, published in 1976. While many of my counterparts were touting "the revolutionary way to cook beautiful French food without the calories," I was bemused by the book's inclusion of Sauce Béarnaise along with the caveat that "This sauce and its variations are not to be used in cuisine minceur." In Guérard's subsequent book, *Cuisine Gourmand* (for those who discarded the "nouvelle" approach and preferred to eat whatever they wanted to eat, fat content be damned), a low-calorie Béarnaise was provided, partially thickened with egg yolks and olive oil and further thickened with diced tomatoes and mushroom purée. But, a true Béarnaise has nothing to do with tomatoes or mushrooms. I believe that if you really want a Béarnaise sauce, you first must decide to allow yourself that indulgence. Then, you go out to a local market, locate fresh eggs and tarragon, some fine tarragon vinegar, and unsalted butter, you make an excellent Béarnaise, and that's the end of it. And if you prefer a sauce made with puréed mushrooms and diced tomatoes, you can do that as well. Make sure they are well seasoned, use lots of fresh herbs, and call it *Sauce du Jour* or *Tomato and Mushroom Sauce*, or *The Chef's Secret Sauce*. But to use the name of this classic sauce, and make something completely different, you have effectively cheated yourself out of the pleasure of a splendid egg yolk emulsified sweet butter sauce accented with tarragon.

Fortunately, in the past 15 years or so, we've experienced a culinary revival of sorts. In addition to some very positive changes in our collective culinary and nutritional consciousness, we have a whole generation of media-celebrated culinary practitioners and restaurateurs who embark on regional cooking revivals, using foods indigenous to those regions, and who have reaffirmed many of the most positive elements of our culinary heritage. As a result, restaurant fare in major urban areas throughout North America has greatly improved.

And finally, consider the ten-year epidemiological study conducted by the National Institute of Health and Medical Research in Lyons, France. According to a stunning report in 1991, the annual mortality rate attributed to heart failure among the residents of Toulouse and the surrounding environs (southwestern France) was 80 per 100,000, compared with 145 per 100,000 French males, and 315 per 100,000 in the United States. The shocking part of this discovery was that the diet of the people of Toulouse is higher in saturated animal fats than any other group in the industrialized world. And in spite of additional evidence (also reported) that the fat from fattened geese and duck livers (which comprises the bulk of that fat) is closer in chemical composition to olive oil than butter or lard, it might be wise to consider some of the advice from the Toulousians. One resident, age 95, was quoted as saying, "Always have a salad with your cassoulet, and bread with your foie gras." And another, "We cook everything in duck fat. Everybody knows this is the long-life diet."

Early on, I concluded that the Chinese had been cooking nouvelle cuisine for about 5,000 years. I then learned that about 2,300 years ago, Archestratus developed a gastronomic philosophy, the essence of which was: keep it simple, keep it fresh, and keep it inventive. I concluded once and for all that in the grander context of things, nothing has really changed; culinary and gastronomic history is merely repeating itself. "The secret of success in life is to eat what you like and let the food fight it out inside." (Found by author in a fortune cookie, but actually attributed to Mark Twain.)

CHAPTER 2

THE IMPORTANCE OF CUTLERY

*P*art of the preparatory package incoming students receive at the Culinary Institute of America is a knife kit that contains about a dozen knives and tools. I remember my feelings of excitement upon receiving mine. Unfortunately, by the end of two years of training, all that remained were two grapefruit knives—one was part of my original kit, the other a spare I had picked up from a fellow student who had left it behind. The rest of my tools had been misplaced, left behind, or borrowed—with and without permission.

Most chefs have enormous collections of tools, accumulated over years of working in the trade. I always felt that such large tool chests were unnecessary. One's manual skills, it seemed to me, developed with study and practice and were not dependent on the number of tools one accumulated. This outlook was gleaned from the old southern blues guitarists, who often played on old, hand-made instruments but could produce amazing sound. The music was in their hands and voice, a reflection of a lifetime of singing the six-string acoustic blues.

The culinary trade, however, is not quite the same as singing the blues, and cutlery is important. Some decisions need to be made on just what to work with. During the three years following my graduation from culinary school, I traveled around a bit, using the skills I had learned and building a repertoire. During this time, my mobile "tool chest" consisted of a Chinese cleaver, an eight-inch French (chef's) knife, a paring knife, and a small steel. I somehow always managed to perform all the necessary culinary tasks with those tools. That I traveled solely with these four utensils reflected a personal philosophy—economy of motion and maximum mobility.

The smallwares most important to a saucier are fairly standard in any well-stocked first-class kitchen. There should be numerous saucepans of various sizes, all heavy-guage, and preferably noncorrosive metal: stainless steel or copper with tin-coated interior. Piano-wire (medium weight) whips are also essential, as are wooden spoons, and at least two good fine-meshed strainers (chinois mousseline). A citrus zester and citrus auger (a bulbous hand tool with a sharp point at its end, used to extract juice from a lemon, lime, or orange) are also important if only as time savers. Some sauciers also like to work with a food mill, not so common with the advent of food processors and high speed blenders. They can be essential when one wishes to purée an unfinished sauce before straining, so as to extract every bit of flavor from the ingredients. There are also those who prefer the old-fashioned method of straining with muslin (cheesecloth). The use of these last two utensils, and other individual choices, are matters of personal preference and style, and will vary from practitioner to practitioner.

My students frequently ask what brand of knives to use. The answer is essentially a matter of personal preference, based on experience. For example, once I had the opportunity to meet Francis Dusza, who, for nearly half a century, worked for the Russell Harrington Cutlery Company in Southbridge, Massachusetts. Dusza entered the company's tool-and-die training program at the age of 16, and ultimately was put in charge of all of the company's manufacturing processing. Though now retired, he remains one of the foremost living authorities on professional cutlery. Some years ago, Dusza introduced me to the complex process involved in creating a professional knife, as well as the fascinating history of their company. The present-day Russell Harrington Cutlery Company, Inc., represents a merger of the nineteenth-century John Russell Green River Works and the Henry Harrington Company.

In May 1933, John Russell and Company Green River Works, and the Henry Harrington Company merged to become the present-day Russell Harrington Cutlery Company. The company has changed much since its founding days, but the same care that went into knife making at the original Green River Works is still evident in Russell Harrington's modern manufacturing methods. Modern carbon-steel alloys give knives superior strength, flexibility, and edge-holding characteristics. And cryogenic forging—chilling the blade to 120 degrees below freezing—further reinforces its strength. A forged cook's knife goes through a total of 72 different processes in its construction, and all knives are honed by hand, just as they were in the earliest days of the company. (An eighteen-month apprenticeship is required for a worker to learn this skill.)

CARING FOR PROFESSIONAL KNIVES

The razor-sharp cutting edge of a professional cutting tool has a microscopic burr, or "feather," along its cutting edge. Through repeated use, the feather rolls over and the cutting edge dulls. Stroking the knife on a steel straightens the feather, returning the cutting edge to its original sharpness. Over a period of time, the feather becomes worn away, at which point the knife should be sharpened with a sharpening stone. Sharpening stones come in a variety of shapes, sizes, and grits. A typical Carborundum stone, called a "whet stone," usually has a coarse grit on one side and a fine grit on the other. Any liquid, such as honing oil, liquid soap, lemon juice, or even water, will serve as a lubricant. A tri-stone, consisting of a coarse, medium, and fine stone, resting in a well of honing oil, can be found in most commercial kitchens. A ceramic tri-stone (the Three-Way Knife Sharpener), recently innovated by Russell Harrington, is superior to the former, since it requires no lubricant.

To sharpen a knife, hold the blade at an acute angle to the stone, roughly 15 degrees (the back of the knife should be about a half-inch from the stone's surface). Run the blade simultaneously up and across the entire surface of the stone, with firm even pressure. Flip the knife, and repeat in the reverse direction. Repeat this procedure several times on the coarse surface and on the fine surface. Run the blade down a sharpening steel several times, then test the knife by using it. If the edge is not sharp enough, repeat the procedure.

Once the knife has a sharp edge, keep it sharp by periodically running it down the shaft of a steel. Grasp the steel firmly in one hand, placing the thumb securely behind the handle guard. Hold the steel at a comfortable distance from your body—roughly a 45-degree angle. With the other hand, grasp the handle of the knife. Rest the heel of the knife blade against the top of the steel, with the knife and the steel forming an angle slightly greater than 90 degrees. Keeping the cutting edge pressed against the shaft, lift the back of the blade about a half-inch from the steel (about the same angle when applied to the stone). Maintaining constant, moderate pressure, draw the blade smoothly down and across the upper two-thirds of the steel. Return the knife to the top of the steel, this time on the opposite side, and stroke again. Test the knife after six passes on each side.

With practice, one develops a feel for the proper angles, and pressure, and movement of a knife over a sharpening stone and steel. It is preferable to maintain your own knives, since sharpening services will often over-grind a knife, wearing it down significantly after several applications. All the professionals I have ever worked with were able to maintain the sharpness of their tools by their own hand.

It is also important to store knives properly. When stored in a tool box tray, or kitchen drawer, they should be protected with a hard or soft plastic sheath, to prevent nicking or dulling. Knives should also never be placed in an automatic dishwasher, which can also lead to nicking or damage to the hardwood handle. Wash knives in warm soapy water, dry, and store properly.

With regard to foreign-manufactured knives, there is still some mystique surrounding European knives. Germany, France, and Switzerland all produce exceptionally fine tools, well established in the American market, and all varying considerably in price. Good value is the consumer's ultimate goal, and the best way to discover the value of a company's product is to purchase a small- or medium-sized tool and work with it.

CHAPTER 3

STOCKS

stock: n. The broth from boiled meat or fish, used as a base in preparing soup, gravy, or sauces.

fond: n. The groundwork, foundation, basis. (French, from Latin *fundus,* bottom.)

Good fonds and sauces are the foundation of fine cuisine. Their preparation is considered the most important business in every large kitchen.[1]

The French term for stock is *fond,* which in both English and French also means bottom, or foundation. The application of this word provides a clue to the function and importance of stocks, which are the single most important fundamental preparation in culinary production.

There are some crucial basic guidelines for creating proper stocks, but there is also room for innovation. The Dutch chef with whom I apprenticed would often drop a small piece of mace (the outside shell of nutmeg) into 20 gallons of brown veal stock. In a quantity that large, the mace would hardly be enough to *noticeably* affect the flavor, but it's presence did make a subtle yet distinctive difference on the flavor of final stock. I perceived it as a small yet essential part of that chef's personal signature. Every chef and culinary practitioner has his or her own unique style of cooking, which extends to the preparation of stocks. With an understanding of the basic parameters of good stock production, one is then free to explore variations and innovations as they relate to one's own style.

PREPARING MEAT STOCKS

Stocks are divided into two primary categories: *brown stock* (fond brun) and *white stock* (fond blanc). In a brown stock, the primary ingredients are browned by roasting before they are added to the stock pot (marmite), which adds brown color and a slightly different character than when the bones are simmered raw. Some chefs slice a Spanish onion in half, then place the cut sides down onto the top of a flattop stove or griddle until the sugar in the onion halves caramelizes, turning the onion dark brown. These are then added to the stock. The same procedure can be applied to the bottom three inches of a stalk of celery, or a carrot

[1]*Hering's Dictionary of Classical and Modern Cookery* (London: Virtue & Co., 1991).

split in half lengthwise. A more careful approach to caramelizing the aromatics for a brown stock is preferable: Roast the mirepoix in the fat and residue remaining in the pan in which the bones were roasted. This creates a more uniform browning.

Ingredients

The ingredients of a stock are divided into three elements: *nutritional, aromatic,* and *liquid.* The nutritional element consists primarily of bones, though meat may also be included. (Technically, a stock made with both bones and meat is considered a bouillon.) The aromatics are divided into two further categories: *mirepoix*—celery, carrot, and onion; and *bouquet garni*—a collection of herbs and spices, the most common of these known as a *standard* bouquet garni: bay leaf, thyme, parsley sprigs, and peppercorns. The liquid element consists of water, sometimes augmented with wine, pan drippings, lemon juice (for fish stock), or tomato juice (for brown stock).

Both brown and white stocks can be created from any of the following types of bones: beef, veal, chicken, turkey, duck, lamb, or game. Fish bones are used for creating a white stock only. There are occasions when one may combine several different varieties of meat bones to create one all-purpose stock. When a single variety of nutritional ingredient (bones) is used, it is because a large quantity is required, or because a stock with a single flavor is needed, which will be used to create a particular stock reduction and subsequent sauce for use with a specific dish. If one is preparing a grilled venison steak, for example, roasted venison bones are used for the stock, which is then reduced to create an accompanying sauce that will have a dominant venison flavor to harmonize with the grilled venison dish. A roast leg of lamb may have a sauce made from a stock derived exclusively from lamb bones, and so on.

Regardless of the type of bones used, they should always be washed thoroughly with cold water before being subjected to heat. It is also important to begin a stock with cold water, which allows for maximum extraction of flavor from the ingredients. Beginning with hot water prematurely coagulates the albumen in the bones, inhibiting its interaction within the stock, and the subsequent extraction of gelatin, which gives the stock both flavor and nutrients. After washing, the bones will be placed directly into a stock pot for white stock, or roasted first, for brown stock.

Procedure

When making a brown stock, a thin coating of tomato paste is spread over the roasting bones midway through the roasting, to add character and color and aid in the clarification process. When the bones turn a golden brown color, they are transferred to a stock pot, and the mirepoix is placed in that roasting pan, stirred to coat it with any fat remaining from the previous roasting. The mirepoix is then roasted until it too turns a golden brown color. Once the bones reach a first simmer, the top is skimmed, and the roasted mirepoix is added to the stock pot. Any caramelized bits of meat or vegetables remaining in the roasting pan are removed by *deglazing*, a technique by which a liquid is poured into the pan and heated, stirred with a wooden spoon to remove caramelized residue, then added to the simmering stock. An all-purpose dry red wine is appropriate for deglazing because it adds color and flavor, and because its acidity aids in the clarifying process.

As a rule, for both white and brown stock, enough cold water must be added to rise above the highest bone by approximately four inches. The stock is then brought just to a simmer, when the first skimming (*dépouiller*—pronounced "day-poo-yay") is performed. This skimming removes the first round of impurities that have collected on the top of the simmering stock—fat, coagulated blood, and albumin. Skimming is repeated periodically throughout the cooking process, as fat and albumen collect at the top. The albumin, a water-soluble simple protein found in animal bones and tissue as well as in vegetables and egg whites, is an essential part of the natural clarifying process. As the stock simmers, heat convection causes the liquid to move rhythmically around in the pot, while the naturally occurring albumin slowly coagulates, trapping minuscule impurities as the stock moves through it. For this reason, simmering is *absolutely vital* to stock preparation. It is why the stock is first brought to a simmer, as opposed to a boil. The vigorous activity of a boiling liquid inhibits the slow, careful collection of impurities, resulting in a cloudy stock, while slow, gentle simmering promotes clarification, and a gentle release of flavor from the ingredients, producing a rich, clear liquid.

Once the first skimming is completed, the aromatic elements are added—mirepoix (raw for white stock, roasted for brown stock) and bouquet garni. The aromatics can also be augmented with the dark green tops of leeks, though they *must* be well washed to eliminate sand. At this point, other additions can also be included, depending on the ethnic nature of the menu, as well as the philosophy of the kitchen. If a menu reflects a Mediterranean flavor, then a clove or two of crushed garlic would be appropriate. If the menu has an Asian bent, then a sliver of ginger is acceptable. It should be pointed out, however, that a stock pot is not a receptacle for leftover vegetables or odds and ends of vegetable trimmings. The mirepoix ingredients (celery, carrots, and onions) need to be of the highest quality—onions and carrots peeled (peels discarded), celery trimmed and washed. The top end of a carrot should also be discarded. The dictum here is *garbage in, garbage out*. The final stock will only be as good as the ingredients from which it is created.

The average simmering time for a white stock is 4 to 6 hours (with the exception of fish stock, at 1–1½ hours), and for a brown stock, 10–12 hours. In large commercial kitchens, a brown stock begun in a 60-gallon stationary steam kettle may continue cooking uninterrupted for as long as three days to a week. Stock is drawn as needed from a built-in spigot near the bottom of the kettle, with water added at the top (in this case hot, since the stock is already hot) to replace what has been taken. When all the flavor of the stock elements has been extracted, the stock is drained, the elements removed and discarded, and the process begun all over again.

After a white or brown stock is simmered, a second stock is sometimes produced with the same ingredients. This step is referred to as *rémouiller* which produces a *rémouillage* (French for *rewet*, pronounced "ray-moo-yay, ray-moo-yazh"). The resulting stock is not as strong as the first, but can be used as the start-up liquid for the next stock, for blanching vegetables, or for dishes that do not require a highly flavored stock.

PREPARING FISH STOCK

Fish stock is different from all of the other stock preparations for a variety of reasons. Fish bones are thinner and more delicate than other bones, therefore requiring less simmering time. Also, there is some disagreement on the correct meaning of *fumet* (pronounced "foo-may"), a term that is often used when referring to fish stock. Technically, a fumet is a stock in which (1) the aromatics and nutritional elements are sweated in butter before the liquid is added; and (2) the liquid element is a stock or rémouillage (in place of water). Consequently then, a fumet can be made from veal, chicken, or game, provided that the bones and mirepoix are first sweated in butter, and the liquid element consists of a stock. And since it is made with a stock as the liquid element—and this is generally agreed upon, no matter what the technique used—a fumet is approximately twice as strong in flavor as an ordinary stock.

Ingredients

The bones used for making a fish stock should be from a low-fat white-fleshed fish, such as cod, flounder, haddock, halibut, or sole. Varieties with higher fat content—bluefish, mackerel, salmon, swordfish, or tuna—tend to produce a cloudy, strong-flavored stock. (There are exceptions to this, as in the case of a salmon prepared Chambord style—poached or stewed in red wine, then used in making a demi-glaze based sauce.) The bones must be very fresh and very thoroughly washed in cold water. Fish heads, gills, and skin should be eliminated.

Strict purists will employ a *white* mirepoix for fish stock, consisting of onion and celery only, claiming that the carrot adds unwanted color. White wine and a small amount of lemon juice included in the liquid element aid in the clarifying process, and counteract fishy aromas. The final stock should reflect a flavor and aroma of the sea, not of the fish.

Procedure

At the end of the cooking period, all stocks are strained—carefully, since the liquid is still very hot. If there is a large quantity of stock to be strained, a large-holed strainer (conical strainer, or "chinoise gros") or colander is used first, with the solids allowed to sit until all liquid has drained. The stock can then be strained a second time, through a fine screen strainer ("chinoise mousseline"). Sometimes several layers of muslin are placed inside the strainer for more refined straining.

The stock must be cooled to room temperature before refrigerating. The warm, dark, moist environment of the stock, particularly when it is within the range of 40–140°F, is the optimum breeding ground for bacteria. If dealing with a quantity of five gallons or more, it will take some time for the liquid to cool. Occasionally, a *hot spot* develops, wherein the exterior portions of the stock cool down, leaving the interior hot and within the danger zone. For this reason, the cooling is sometimes expedited by placing the container of strained stock into a sink of cold water and ice and stirring the stock periodically. When the stock has sufficiently cooled, it should be covered, labeled, and refrigerated.

Once it has fully chilled in the refrigerator, the stock may have a gelatinous (jellylike) consistency. This gelatin comes from the nutritional element—the bones, connective tissue, and cartilage. Its presence indicates that the stock is a flavorful one. Any fat still present in the stock will rise to the top and congeal under refrigeration. This can easily be lifted from the top and discarded.

- Use quality ingredients.
- Wash ingredients thoroughly in cold water.
- Begin a stock with cold water.
- Perform the initial skimming before adding aromatics.
- Add hot water only to a simmering stock.
- Skim regularly as needed.
- Always simmer, never boil. Simmering allows the *natural clarifying* process to manifest, producing a rich, clear stock.
- Simmer white stock a minimum of 4 hours; brown stock a minimum of 8 hours; fish stock, 1 hour.
- Strain, cool, and store properly.

$\mathcal{B}$ROWN VEAL OR BEEF STOCK
(Fond Brun de Veau/Boeuf)

6 pounds veal or beef shanks and knuckle bones, cut into 4-inch lengths
1 cup tomato paste
3 stalks celery, trimmed, rinsed, and roughly chopped
2 carrots, peeled, tops removed, and roughly cut
2 medium Spanish onions, peeled and roughly chopped
1 leek, green tops only, well rinsed, and roughly chopped
2 gallons (approximately) cold water
1 garlic clove, crushed
2 bay leaves
3 sprigs fresh thyme
1 bunch parsley stems, trimmed, rinsed, and tied together
1 teaspoon black peppercorns, cracked
1 quart dry red wine

- Preheat oven to 400°F.
- Wash the bones thoroughly in cold water. Place them into a roasting pan, and roast for 20 minutes. Remove from the oven, and spread a light coating of tomato paste over the bones, using a rubber spatula. Continue roasting another 15–20 minutes, or until golden brown.
- Remove the bones from the pan and place into a stock pot that has been wiped out with a clean towel. Fill with cold

water 4 inches above the highest bone, and place on a high flame. When it just begins to boil, turn down to a simmer. Skim impurities from the top (albumen, fat, coagulated blood), and discard.

- Place the mirepoix and leeks into the pan from which the bones came, and stir with any fat remaining in the pan. Roast for 40 minutes, stirring occasionally, until the vegetables are well caramelized.

- Add the mirepoix and the bouquet garni to the simmering stock. Place the roasting pan over a high flame on the stove, add the dry red wine, and deglaze. Add this to the simmering stock. Simmer 8–12 hours, skimming periodically as needed. Strain, cool, cover, label, and refrigerate.

———— • ————

Additional tomato can be added along with the aromatics, in the form of over-ripe (not rotten or spoiled) tomatoes, tomato ends from the pantry, or tomato juice.

————————————

White Veal Stock
(Fond Blanc de Veau)

5 pounds veal knuckle bones, cut into 3- or 4-inch pieces
5 pounds veal shank, cut into 3- or 4-inch pieces
2½ gallons (approximately) cold water
2 stalks celery, trimmed, rinsed, and roughly chopped
2 carrots, peeled, tops removed, and roughly chopped

1 large Spanish onion, peeled, and cut into eighths
2 bay leaves
3 sprigs fresh thyme
1 bunch parsley stems, trimmed, rinsed, and tied together
1 teaspoon white peppercorns, cracked

- Wash the bones thoroughly in cold water. Place them into a stock pot that has been wiped out with a clean towel. Add the cold water (should be roughly 4 inches above the highest bone), and set over a high flame. When it just begins to boil, turn down to a simmer. Skim impurities from the top (albumen, fat, coagulated blood), and discard.

- Add the mirepoix and the bouquet garni to the simmering stock. Simmer 4–8 hours, skimming periodically as needed. Strain, cool, cover, label, and refrigerate.

$\mathcal{B}$ROWN DUCK STOCK
(Fond Brun de Canard)

5 pounds of duck carcasses with giblets (excluding livers)
½ cup tomato paste
2 stalks celery, rinsed, and roughly chopped
1 large carrot, peeled and roughly chopped
1 large Spanish onion, peeled, and roughly chopped

1 leek, green tops only, well rinsed, and roughly chopped
1 pint dry red wine
1 bay leaf
2 sprigs fresh thyme
1 sprig fresh rosemary
1 bunch parsley stems, trimmed, rinsed, and tied together
½ teaspoon black peppercorns, cracked
2 gallons cold water

- Preheat oven to 400°F.
- Wash the bones thoroughly in cold water. Drain and dry. Place them into a roasting pan and roast for 25 minutes. Remove from the oven, and spread a light coating of tomato paste over the bones, using a rubber spatula. Continue roasting another 20–30 minutes, or until golden brown.
- Remove the bones from the pan and place into a stock pot that has been wiped out with a clean towel. Fill with cold water 4 inches above the highest bone, and place on a high flame. When it just begins to boil, turn down to a simmer. Skim impurities from the top (albumen, fat, coagulated blood), and discard.
- Pour off some of the excess fat from the pan, saving for another use. Place the mirepoix and leeks into the pan from which the bones came, and stir with any fat remaining in the pan. Roast for 40 minutes, stirring occasionally, until the vegetables are well caramelized.
- Skim the simmering stock (duck will yield a considerable amount of fat), then add the mirepoix and the bouquet garni. Place the roasting pan over a high flame on the stove, add the dry red wine, and deglaze. Add this to the simmering stock. Simmer 8 hours, skimming periodically as needed. Strain, cool, cover, label, and refrigerate.

In a commercial kitchen that has roast duck on the menu, carcasses will often be removed from the roasted birds, as well as an abundance of giblets and wings. All of these are used to create the stock from which a very fine duck sauce can then be created.

Excess duck fat is particularly good in roux, or for sautéing the vegetable in various soups, as well as potato and rice dishes.

White Chicken Stock

6 pounds fresh chicken bones, backs, necks, and wings
1 whole fresh chicken (optional)
2 gallons water
1 large Spanish onion, peeled and cut into eighths
1 large carrot, top removed, scrubbed, and roughly chopped
2 stalks celery, rinsed and roughly chopped
1 leek, green tops only, well rinsed, and roughly chopped
2 bay leaves
3 sprigs fresh thyme
1 bunch parsley stems
1 teaspoon white peppercorns, cracked

- Rinse the bones (and whole chicken, if used) thoroughly in cold water.
- Place the bones (and chicken) into a stock pot, and cover them with cold water (should be 3 to 4 inches above the highest bone). Heat over a high flame just until the stock comes to a boil. Turn down to a simmer.
- Skim the top, removing, then discarding, fat and impurities.
- Add the vegetables, herbs, and spices.
- Simmer 1 hour, then lift out the whole chicken (if used) and set it aside to cool. Separate the meat from the skin and bones, reserving the meat for another dish, and returning the skin and bones to the stock pot. Continue simmering, 6–8 hours, periodically skimming off and discarding impurities.
- Strain, cool, cover, and refrigerate.

The optional chicken is included for additional flavor. In commercial kitchen production, this step is appropriate if cold poached chicken is utilized in another dish.

The clear, savory broths found in the soups in Asian restaurants may be the result of the following technique. When the water first comes to a simmer, pour the contents of the pot into a colander, discarding the liquid. Rinse the bones again in cold water, then begin the stock all over again with fresh water. A stock made from bones rinsed in this manner will be clear and savory if it is carefully simmered throughout the remaining cooking time.

𝒢AME STOCK
(Fond Brun de Gibier)

5 pounds venison bones, cut into 3- or 4-inch pieces
1 pheasant, cut into 3- or 4-inch pieces
½ cup melted butter
½ cup dried bacon
½ cup tomato paste
2 stalks celery, rinsed, and roughly chopped
2 carrots, peeled, tops removed, and roughly chopped
1 large Spanish onion, peeled, and roughly chopped

1 leek, green tops only, well rinsed, and roughly chopped
1 quart dry red wine
1 bay leaf
2 sprigs fresh thyme
2 sprigs fresh sage
1 bunch parsley stems, trimmed, rinsed, and tied together
½ teaspoon black peppercorns, cracked
2 whole cloves
10 juniper berries
1½ gallons cold water

- Preheat oven to 400°F.

- Wash the bones and pheasant thoroughly in cold water. Drain and dry. Place them into a roasting pan, and brush with the melted butter. Roast, along with the bacon, for 20 minutes. Remove from the oven and spread a light coating of tomato paste over the bones, using a rubber spatula. Continue roasting another 20–30 minutes, or until golden brown.

- Remove the bones from the pan and place into a stock pot that has been wiped out with a clean towel. Fill with cold water 4 inches above the highest bone, and place on a high flame. When it just begins to boil, turn down to a simmer. Skim impurities from the top (albumen, fat, coagulated blood), and discard.

- Place the mirepoix and leeks into the pan from which the bones came, and stir with any fat remaining in the pan. Roast for 40 minutes, stirring occasionally, until the vegetables are well caramelized.
- Skim the simmering stock, then add the mirepoix and the bouquet garni. Place the roasting pan over a high flame on the stove, add the dry red wine, and deglaze. Add this to the simmering stock. Simmer 8–12 hours, skimming periodically as needed. Strain, cool, cover, label, and refrigerate.

The pheasant may be an extravagant addition to this stock, but it makes for an exceptional flavor. The bones and carcasses from rabbit, partridge, or quail, if available, can also be used.

FISH STOCK

3 tablespoons butter
1 Spanish onion, peeled and
   cut into eighths
1 stalk celery, roughly cut
1 leek, green top only, well
   rinsed, and roughly cut
3 or 4 mushrooms, rinsed
   and roughly cut
10 pounds fresh white fish
   bones, cut into 3-inch
   lengths

1 cup dry white wine
2 gallons cold water
juice of 1 lemon
1 bay leaf
1 sprig fresh thyme
1 sprig fresh dill, rinsed, and
   roughly chopped
1 bunch parsley stems,
   trimmed and rinsed
½ teaspoon white
   peppercorns, crushed

- Wash and soak the bones in cold water for 1 hour. Drain and rinse.
- Place the onions, celery, leeks, and mushrooms in a stock pot with the butter. Cover and sauté for 10 minutes over a medium flame, stirring occasionally. Add the bones and sauté another 5 minutes.
- Add the wine, water, and lemon juice (the liquid should rise about 4 inches above the highest bone). Bring to a boil, then turn down to a simmer. Skim and discard the impurities from the top.
- Add the herbs and spices, and continue simmering for 1–1½ hours, skimming periodically. Strain, cool, cover, label, and refrigerate.

Escoffier calls his fish stock "fumet blanc de poisson," and it is made by buttering the bottom of a saucepan, layering it with blanched onions, then the fish bones, followed by parsley stems and the juice of a lemon. This is covered and simmered gently, in order to ". . . allow the fish to exude its essence. . . ." White wine is the liquid element, and the stock is simmered for 20 minutes. This may be the origin of applying the term *fumet* to fish stock. It is also interesting to note how few aromatics are included here, as well as the use of wine only for liquid.

*L*OBSTER STOCK

3 tablespoons butter
2 shallots, roughly chopped
1 small Spanish onion, peeled and roughly chopped
1 stalk celery, rinsed, trimmed, and roughly cut
1 leek, white part only, roughly cut, and well rinsed
5 pounds lobster bodies and shells, broken up

1 cup dry white wine
1½ gallons cold water
juice of 1 lemon
1 bay leaf
1 sprig fresh thyme
1 small piece of fennel root, rinsed, and roughly chopped
1 bunch parsley stems, trimmed and rinsed
½ teaspoon white peppercorns, crushed

- Wash the lobster shells well in cold water.
- Place the shallot, onion, celery, and leek in a stock pot with the butter. Cover and sauté for 10 minutes over a medium flame, stirring occasionally. Add the shells and sauté another 5 minutes.
- Add the wine, water, and lemon juice (the liquid should rise about 4 inches above the shells). Bring to a boil, then turn down to a simmer. Skim and discard the impurities from the top.
- Add the herbs and spices and continue simmering for 1½ hours, skimming periodically. Strain, cool, cover, and refrigerate.

This stock is used for any soup or sauce based on lobster. Shrimp or crayfish shells can be substituted.

ESSENCES

An essence is made by simmering a liquid with the addition of an aromatic. Typical essences are created using celery, garlic, mushrooms, tarragon, and truffle. The liquid medium used to create an essence can be either a combination of white wine and white vinegar, or lightly flavored white chicken or veal stock, or any combination of the three. Truffle essence should be made using only the peelings of the truffle as a way of utilizing the peels, which ordinarily would not be used in a finished dish.

After simmering the aromatic in the liquid, it can be strained and further reduced 50–75% to concentrate the flavor. Essences are not commonly used in commercial production, but on a smaller scale, they are a good way to utilize a part of an aromatic vegetable or herb that might otherwise be discarded. A concentrated celery essence, for example, can be a powerful flavor enhancer for a cream of celery soup, or a mushroom essence made with the washed stems and trimmings of wild mushrooms can add just the right accent of mushroom flavor to a Forestière sauce. The same axiom that applies to stock—"garbage in, garbage out"—applies to essences. Keep the ingredients clean.

MEAT GLAZE (GLACE DE VIANDE)

A glaze is a 90% (or more) reduction of a stock. Any stock can be reduced to create a glaze, either brown or white, including fish stock. (The only exception in the case of fish is that to produce a proper glaze, the fish stock should be clarified first. This is discussed a little further on.) A stock made from several different nutritional components can also be reduced into a glaze. Glazes are one of the most important tools in a saucier's repertoire.

On a small scale, such as in a home kitchen, where large quantities of stocks are not continuously simmering on the stove, a small quantity of stock can be creating using several different varieties of bones.

The word *glace* in French also means "mirror," possibly a linguistic connection to its reflecting qualities, which are amazingly effective, in spite of the fact that it turns dark brown and syrupy as the reduction nears completion.

The commercial counterpart to glaze is referred to as *base*, and is available in beef, chicken, clam, and lobster varieties. These too have a concentrated flavor of the food from which they are made, but they consist primarily of salt and a high percentage of monosodium glutamate (MSG), as well as numerous other chemical additives. In the consumer market, bouillon cubes are the home version of a concentrated stock base, and these too are made up of primarily salt and additives. Commercial bases are used primarily in hotels and other large production houses, where time and labor cost prohibit the creation of natural glazes; bouillon cubes are used at home as a convenience food. Once consumers and those who pursue cooking as an avocation learn the ease with which a good, flavorful stock can be made, they rarely return to the use of the "convenient" cube.

One of the most important first steps in making a glaze is to begin with a very clear stock. As it is reduced, the minute solid particles in the stock that make up the flavor of the stock become so concentrated that only a clear stock will yield a smooth and flavorful glaze, without it burning or turning bitter. A clear stock can be achieved in two ways: (1) by the slow and careful simmering of the stock; and (2) by clarifying the stock through a separate procedure undertaken after the first stock is made. The slow, careful simmering enables a *natural clarifying process* to take place, yielding a clear stock. (The second procedure is discussed in detail a little later on.)

Glazes are also naturally salty, an indication of the amount of salt that is found naturally in the meats, fish, and aromatics that are used to create a glaze. Therefore, stocks should not be salted.

To prepare a glaze, a stock is simply simmered until reduced by approximately half. It is then strained through a screen strainer (chinoise mousseline) or through several layers of muslin, into a smaller vessel, and reduced by half again. This second, smaller vessel should consist of a heavy-gauge metal. As the stock becomes thicker, the heat must be evenly dispersed to prevent it from burning. A pan that is at least ⅛-inch thick at its bottom is recommended. At this point, the stock begins to thicken noticeably, a result of the concentration of the gelatin content of the stock and the minute particles that give the stock its color and flavor. The reduction is continued, each time reducing by approximately half, then straining through a fine strainer into a smaller, heavy-gauge saucepan. Eventually, the glaze reaches a thick, dark, syrupy consistency, similar in appearance to molasses. It should then be stored in small individ-

Bouillon is the noun form of the French verb *bouillir*, meaning "to boil."

ual containers, preferably with securely fitting lids (cool first before sealing). They will keep for approximately one month under refrigeration. If any mold should form on the top surface, it can be scraped off and discarded. The underlying glaze is so dense that it will not be adversely affected by surface growths. The glazes can also be stored in the freezer, where they will keep for up to a year.

Brown stocks reduced to glazes will be darker and thicker than white stocks, but both produce viable glazes. Choosing which variety of stock to reduce will depend on its use. A student of mine, a navy messman, spent three months at a time submerged in a submarine. During the subsequent three months on shore, he took classes at the university where I taught. He thoroughly enjoyed my class on stock and sauce production, and several months after completing it, I received a note from him, sharing the following story.

At the naval base where he was stationed, several weeks before shipping out for a three-month tour, he had produced roughly ten gallons of assorted stocks, reduced it all to several quarts of glace de viande, and stored the half-dozen varieties in small sealed containers. On board, galley size prohibited him from making stocks. But he was able to create all manner of fine soups and sauces by using the glazes as a base. For this act of ingenuity, he received a commendation from his commanding officer.

Whether or not this enterprising student revolutionized food service practices aboard submerged navy vessels, I do not know. But the story illustrates at least one function of a meat glaze. In actual culinary practice (on land), glazes can be used to fortify the flavor of sauces, as well as soups and numerous

Type of Stock	Technical Name
beef	glace de boeuf
veal	glace de veau
lamb	glace d'agneau
chicken	glace de poulet
duck	glace de canard
turkey	glace de dinde
game	glace de gibier
fish*	glace de poisson

*white only

other dishes. I once served an appetizer consisting of cheese ravioli (cooked al dente), sautéed in butter, then finished with a little chicken glaze, chopped parsley, and grated cheese ("Ravioli au Fromage, à la façon du chef").

In a more serious dining situation, a glaze should be prepared with the ingredients that come directly from the dish being prepared. For example, I prepare a roast chicken dish in which the entire bird is boned out, then stuffed with a pork, veal, chicken, and vegetable farce (stuffing) bound with bread crumbs and cream. The remaining chicken bones and carcass are roasted, then simmered very gently overnight to create a stock. The following day, it is reduced to create a glaze that will later be used to create a sauce for the roast. I have also had the opportunity to work with fresh venison, using the bones to create the rich dark stock that later became a Chief Ranger sauce (Sauce Grand Veneur).

Clarifying Stocks

When a meat, poultry, game, or fish stock is simmered with a fresh round of nutritional and aromatic ingredients, the result is an ultraclear, highly flavored broth. When this broth is garnished, in any of nearly 400 ways, the result is consommé, a

---

Because they are labor- and cost-intensive, the preparation of consommés is something of a dying art, and they are rarely found in ordinary restaurant fare. The Culinary Institute of America, in Hyde Park, New York, helps keep this and other such classical dishes alive by retaining it in their second-year curriculum. Candidates for teaching positions at the Institute are also required to produce a consommé as part of the interviewing process.

There are in excess of 400 specific varieties of consommé, named for notable individuals (among them Sarah Bernhardt, Georges Bizet, Napoleon Bonaparte, Jean Anthelme Brillet-Savarin, Cleopatra, Johann Gutenberg, Mona Lisa, and Gioacchini Rossini), places (Alsace, Britain, Cincinnati, the Jockey Club, Palermo, Palestine, and Vienna), and ingredients (among them Bird's Nests, Chicken Wings, Lettuce, Love Apples, Pheasant, Ravioli, Spring Vegetables, Tapioca, and Vermicelli). Consommés are served both hot and cold. One of the best known of the cold varieties is *Consommé Madrilène* (Madrid Style), a chicken consommé highly flavored with and garnished with tomato.

---

simple, refined, richly flavored, and highly nutritious soup, often served as a first course at elegant dining affairs. To illustrate what a consommé is, consider the dark juices that drain from a roast, and later congeal under refrigeration. Underneath a layer of congealed fat, one often finds a layer of dark, gelatinous liquid. This is the natural equivalent of a consommé.

When a consommé is reduced by 25–35%, that reduction effectively increases its gelatin content and flavor. Combined with a wine, such as Madeira, port, or sherry, consommé moves into the realm of *aspic*. Aspics are used to coat individually served foods or larger dishes served on a classical buffet, or to embellish certain dishes such as goose liver pâté (pâté de foie gras), cold poached eggs, vegetables, fish, poultry, meat, and mousses. (In modern practice, unflavored gelatin is sometimes used to fortify the gelatin content of a stock or consommé, which is unnecessary if the aspic is properly prepared.) Aspics are an exquisite addition to many dishes, and a sublime epicurean experience, though it is definitely an acquired taste. In the United States, when we see a chilled jelly, we are most accustomed to the sweet commercial variety, and the savory version takes some getting used to.

In any case, when the consommé is further reduced, by 90% or more, the result is a clear, highly gelatinous, exquisite form of a glaze. The saucier need only decide if time and fiscal boundaries allow him or her to make the extra effort.

⨍ISH CONSOMMÉ
(For Producing Fish Glaze)

1 gallon fish stock (cold)
juice of 1 lemon
3 pounds white fish bones, thoroughly washed
2 pounds coarsely ground fish (such as cod, sole, or whiting)
6 egg whites, briefly beaten with the dry white wine
1 cup dry white wine
1 celery stalk, trimmed, rinsed, and finely chopped

1 Spanish onion, finely chopped
1 small leek, white part only, finely chopped, and well rinsed
1 small bunch parsley stems, trimmed, rinsed, and finely chopped
1 bay leaf
1 sprig thyme

- Combine all the ingredients in a heavy-gauge marmite and blend thoroughly. Place over a medium flame, and gently stir once every 5 minutes, until the mixture gets warm (about 100–110°F).
- When the brew just barely begins to simmer, turn the flame down low enough to maintain the barest simmer. Allow to simmer for 2 hours.
- Using a perforated skimmer, *very gently* cut and lift out a portion of the "raft" that has formed on top. Remove the clear broth underneath the raft using a ladle, and strain it through several layers of muslin.
- Return the consommé to the flame, and continue the process of reduction until it is reduced to a thick, slightly viscous liquid. Cool, cover, label, and store.

The "raft" that forms on the surface of the consommé as it is simmering is created by the albumin in the egg whites and ground fish. The frequent stirring at the beginning of the process is very important. The egg whites are denser than the liquid, and will drift to the bottom of the pot while the mix is still cold and quickly burn, spoiling the entire dish. Once the brew moves past 100°F, the egg whites begin to rise toward the top, slowly coagulating into what will become the raft. The slow coagulation of the raft, as the gently simmering stock moves through, is the same phenomenon that takes place when an ordinary stock is made. As the liquid moves rhythmically through the slowly coagulating albumin, the minute particles and impurities in the stock are trapped within the coagulating mass.

It is also of the utmost importance to cut into the raft *very gently* in order to remove the broth for straining. If it is shaken up, particles that have been collected within the raft may dislodge and return to the liquid.

Because the flavors of fish stock are very delicate, all fish stocks require clarification before turning into a glaze.

*M*EAT CONSOMMÉ
(For Preparing Meat Glaze)

1 gallon brown beef or veal stock
1 cup dry tomato purée
2 pounds ground lean beef
6 egg whites, briefly beaten with the dry red wine

½ cup dry red wine
1 celery stalk, trimmed, rinsed, and finely chopped
1 carrot, peeled, top removed, and finely chopped

Stocks derived from chicken, game, duck, lamb, etc., can all be clarified by substituting the variety of stock in this recipe.

1 Spanish onion, finely chopped
1 small leek, white part only, finely chopped, and well rinsed
1 garlic clove, crushed
1 bunch parsley stems, trimmed, rinsed, and finely chopped
1 bay leaf
1 sprig thyme
1 tablespoon black peppercorns, cracked

- Prepare this consommé by following the instructions for fish consommé.

CHAPTER 4

THICKENING AGENTS

thicken: v. To make more intense, intricate, or complex.[1]

liaison: n. An instance or means of communication between bodies, groups, and units; a close relationship (from Old French *lier,* "to bind").[2]

*I*n the French language, an agent (food) that causes liquid foods to increase in viscosity is, at least molecularly speaking, considered a form of close communication. *Liaison* is the word that qualifies such relationships.

We divide *thickening agents* into two subheadings: *starch thickeners* and *final liaisons*. While gelatin is the primary element that gives a reduced stock its viscosity, since it is an intrinsic part of a well-prepared stock, we don't address it as a separate thickening agent. And in its most concentrated form—a glaze—it is added primarily as a flavor enhancer. (A description of meat glazes can be found at the end of the section on stocks.) Purées are also a form of thickening agent (as in coulis, tomato sauces, and certain vinaigrettes and dessert sauces); these too are an integral part of the flavor and character of a given dish, and are not included separately as a thickener.

ROUX The primary thickening agent for three of the mother sauces is a roux, a combination of equal parts by weight of fat and flour. Traditionally, the fat used has been clarified butter. Whole butter does not work properly, since whole butter includes roughly 20 percent liquid (water and milk solids), which conflicts with the kinetic function of a roux (explained later in this section). Animal fats can also be used, when their flavors are appropriate to the sauce. These include chicken, duck, ham, lamb, veal, and pork fat. Olive and other vegetable oils can also be used, again, if their flavor (or lack of flavor in the case of many vegetable oils) is an appropriate addition to the finished sauce.

The three mother sauces traditionally thickened with a butter roux are Espagnole, velouté, and béchamel.

The degree to which a roux is cooked *before* applied to a liquid will affect the color and flavor of the roux, and ultimately the liquid it thickens. There are three varieties of roux: dark brown (roux brun), light brown (pale, or roux blonde), and white (roux blanc).

[1] *The American Heritage Dictionary.* New York: American Heritage Publishing Co., Inc., 1975.
[2] Ibid.

It is important to point out that Espagnole is the traditional first step in creating a brown sauce. It is combined with an equal volume of brown stock, simmered by half, and finished with dry sherry, resulting in *demi-glaze*, a darker and richer foundation sauce from which the compound derivatives are then created. In actual culinary practice, however, this separate step of creating an Espagnole is rarely used. Instead, a richly flavored and colored brown stock is thickened with a very dark brown roux, then simmered and reduced sufficiently, to create a demi-glaze.

Escoffier's tomato sauce was also thickened with a roux, but we have discarded that approach, and instead subscribe to the use of puréed vegetables, herbs, ground meat, and/or reduction as the best means of creating a thick tomato sauce. Hollandaise is a cooked egg emulsion, and beurre blanc is a butter emulsion, both discussed in detail under Butter Sauces.

A roux is precooked, primarily to increase its thickening power, and secondly to diminish the taste of flour (not desired in a sauce) and add color. Equal quantities of flour and fat are blended in a saucepan, then stirred continuously over medium heat until each attains the appropriate color. A white roux requires no browning, since it is used to thicken milk into a cream sauce. This roux will however emit a distinctive toasted-nut-like aroma, the signal that the first stage of cooking is completed. A light brown roux is cooked long enough to lightly caramelize, which later adds a light brown color to a chicken, fish, or veal velouté. And finally, the dark brown roux should be

Liquid	Roux	Aromatics	Sauce (common term)
brown stock +	brown roux +	aromatics =	Espagnole (brown sauce)
white stock +	light brown roux +	aromatics =	Velouté (blond sauce)
milk +	white roux +	aromatics =	Béchamel (white or cream sauce)

cooked to as dark a color as possible, without burning, in order to later incorporate as much color into a brown sauce as possible.

———————————— • ————————————

Toasting flour before blending it with fat, then using it to create both a light brown and dark brown roux, produces an excellent product, and can save considerable time. Place a quantity of flour into a pan, and bake at 375°F, until it turns a dark, tannish color. It should be stirred every 15–20 minutes, since it will clump up in parts and overbrown at the edges. The flour will require 2–4 hours to properly caramelize, at which point it should be sifted through a drum sifter or other screen strainer. It can be stored indefinitely and simply blended with the appropriate fat to create a light brown or dark brown roux.

There is a fourth roux, a "black roux," originating from the Cajun cooking styles of Louisiana, and generally restricted to specific dishes from that region.

At some point the question will arise as to why flour is combined with fat, and not some other liquid, to create the roux. The answer to this question can be found in the bakery. The fat (butter, lard, and oil) used in baking is referred to as *shortening*. It is called shortening because it inhibits the development of gluten (a protein element in flour), specifically "shortening" the gluten strands, and rendering that baked product light and flaky. We desire this quality in biscuits, pie dough, shortbread, scones, and so on. When flour is combined with water, a completely different type of baked item is created—hard crusted bread and rolls. The application of water to flour, plus kinetic action (kneading), develops the gluten strands, developing a chewy character in numerous varieties of bread.

The use of roux evolved with a similar function—we want the thickening power but not the elasticity that comes with gluten development; hence the use of fat (usually clarified butter). Flour mixed with water or stock and used to thicken a soup or sauce—"whitewash" or "slurry," as it is commonly called—will give that dish a sticky, gluey character. (Consider the paper maché we made in elementary school—a flour and water paste that functioned as an adhesive when applied to strips of newspaper.) It is for this reason that a roux is the most effective and professional way to thicken a sauce—it gives body (thickness) without the gumminess.

CORNSTARCH AND ARROWROOT

Cornstarch and arrowroot are very similar—they are both highly purified and finely ground powders that when liquefied with a cold liquid and briefly simmered, create an instantly thickened sauce. The difference between them is that cornstarch is extracted from a seed (corn), while arrowroot is extracted from a West Indian plant. Arrowroot also possesses a slightly greater thickening power, compared to an equal amount of cornstarch.

Cornstarch and arrowroot are appropriate as a thickening agent for certain dessert sauces, particularly certain fruit poaching mediums, that when thickened with a small amount of starch, become sauce accompaniments for the poached fruit. Some recipes for crème pâtisserie (classical pastry cream) and crème Anglaise utilize cornstarch as thickeners, giving these dishes a creamy, smooth quality. Cornstarch is also a common binder for many dishes of Asian, particularly Chinese, origin.

JUS LIÉ

It is important to point out that Escoffier included a curious sauce in his *Guide Culinaire*, called a *jus lié* (literally, "thickened juice"). "Boil one pint of poultry or veal stock (according to the nature of the dish the gravy is intended for). Thicken this sauce by means of . . . cornstarch, diluted with a little cold water or gravy." Escoffier understood the physics of flour, that it was made up of mostly extraneous components (protein) which had little function in the thickening of a sauce, and were a large part of the *depouillage*, the foamy substance that arose to the top of the sauce during its simmering, and was skimmed and discarded. Furthermore, he believed that, "It is therefore infinitely probable that before long starch or arrowroot obtained in a state of absolute purity will replace flour in the roux." This clearly presents a considerable enigma.

———————— • ————————

In contemporary culinary vernacular, *gravy* is generally accepted as a colloquial term for a sauce created in a pan in which meat or poultry is roasted. The traditional Thanksgiving roast turkey is a typical example. (For additional information on use of the term "gravy," see "A Brief History of Sauces," pages 7–8.)

A recipe for *Pinot Noir Sauce* in the section on brown sauces (page 94) is a good example of a jus lié.

The science of cooking is no less filled with odd and quirky decrees than any other creative pursuit. During my early years in the profession, I found some of these precepts inconsistent with basic common sense. The use of cornstarch as a thickening agent for primary sauces was considered a positive approach among some of the chefs I worked under, not just for the ease with which it thickened, but for the *sheen* it added to a sauce. While the visual appearance of food (and sauces) *is* important, the ability of food to reflect light excessively seemed absurd. In addition to this, the use of quick-acting refined starches effectively threw out the entire concept and reason for using a roux. In spite of the fact that Escoffier himself considered sauces the "partie capitale [principle part] of the cuisine," his jus lié was inconsistent with the fundamental core of his mother sauce matrix—specifically the first three roux-thickened leading sauces.

Escoffier's conviction that cornstarch and arrowroot were superior thickening agents compared to flour (i.e., roux), and that their use would someday be a common practice, seems to be a clear contradiction of the organic function of roux in the three mother sauces. Furthermore, teaching the use of cornstarch as a thickening agent to a student of the sauce craft, before he/she fully understands roux, final liaisons, and natural reductions, might tempt that student to employ cornstarch in place of roux, preventing that saucier from attaining a level of excellence. Cornstarch and arrowroot definitely have a place in the saucier's repertoire, but it should be limited to the few applications where it properly belongs.

FINAL LIAISONS

Beurre Manié

Beurre manié (roughly translated to "manipulated," or "kneaded butter," from *manier:* "to handle, to touch"; and from *le main,* meaning "hand") consists of equal parts by weight of raw butter and flour. It is different from roux for several reasons: (1) it is uncooked; (2) whole butter retains its liquid and milk solids, giving it a different quality than roux; and (3) it is added at the end of a sauce's preparation, instead of the beginning.

Beurre manié is prepared by mashing together whole, unsalted, softened butter with an equal part (by weight) of flour. It is used to augment the thickness of a sauce, soup, or stew at the end of its cooking time. It is generally whipped into the hot liquid in small, walnut-sized portions, and simmered for about 15 minutes to allow it to cook out and expand.

Butter Montée

The terms *montée* and *mount* are fairly interchangeable. (The first, the past participle of *monter:* "to mount, ascend, raise, lift"; the latter a colloquial American equivalent.) While it is clear that a montée does not literally "lift" a sauce, it is a sort of poetic allegory referring to the improvement in the *taste* of a sauce when whole butter is emulsified into it, as in "I lift the taste with butter." And although a butter montée is considered a liaison, when it is applied to a sauce, its actual thickening power is negligible. (When used in a beurre blanc, however, its thickening function is more significant. See the following section on Butter Sauces.)

Any sauce can be mounted with butter to improve and round out the flavor. Some of the recipes for finished sauces that follow specifically call for the addition of butter—among them Burgundy, Geneva, Hunter, Supreme, and Wine Merchant sauces. Others call for a montée of a specific compound butter, such as lobster butter in Diplomat, herb butter in Mirabeau, and crayfish butter in Orléans (all derived from velouté); and anchovy butter in Garibaldi (derived from demi-glaze). And even the sauces that specifically call for the addition of butter can still be made without it, if the dietary restrictions of dining guests warrant a restriction of the use of fat.

Egg Yolks and Cream

Egg yolks, when used as a final liaison, are most commonly combined with heavy cream. This liaison is then *tempered* into a sauce as follows: beat the yolks and cream in a clean bowl. While beating, pour in a small amount of the sauce it is to be applied to, adding the sauce in a slow, steady stream. When the temperature (hence the term *tempering*) is close to that of the simmering sauce, the liaison is poured into the sauce, and beaten as it is brought up to a simmer. It should be simmered briefly (1 minute will suffice) while continually stirring, in order to utilize its thickening power, then served promptly. And it is important *not* to bring the sauce to a vigorous boil after the liaison is added (this can curdle the eggs). Among the sauces that specifically designate an egg yolk and cream liaison are Diplomat, Housewife, Normandy, and Village sauces (all derived from velouté). Sauces that call solely for egg yolks are Berchoux and German sauces (derived from velouté); Holstein (derived from béchamel); and Champagne (derived from demi-glaze, béchamel, and Dutch sauces).

Cream can also be added as a final liaison, though in its original state it will add more flavor (fat), richness, and lightening, than thickening. In some cases, the cream can be simmered for a short period, reducing it until it is thickened, then added to the sauce. Among the sauces that specifically designate a cream liaison are Chief Ranger sauce (derived from demi-glaze); Marly and Supreme sauces (derived from velouté); Newburgh (derived from velouté or béchamel); and Princess sauce (derived from béchamel).

Cream in its kinetically thickened (aerated) form can also be added to a sauce, that is, whipped cream, folded in at the last moment, just before it is served. Examples of this are Ambassadress (derived from velouté); Virgin sauce (derived from béchamel); Divine, Dunant, Mousseline, and Royal Glaze (derived from Dutch sauce).

Sour Cream, Crème Fraîche, and Yogurt

Sour cream is an integral ingredient in numerous sauces, among them: Esterhazy, Lavallière, Livonian, and Paprika sauces (derived from demi-glaze); Russian and Hungarian sauces (derived from velouté); Smitane sauce (derived from béchamel), as well as Dijon Cream (accompanying Sea Scallops). Sour cream is also an important ingredient in our innovation of crème fraîche, a cultured cream unique to France, and similar to our sour cream. By combining sour cream with cream, yogurt, and buttermilk, and allowing it to ferment, we can create a facsimile of crème fraîche, which has more complexity than plain sour cream. Crème fraîche can be found in Vodka Cream (with Salmon Tortellini) and Vergé sauce (an accompaniment for asparagus), both in the béchamel section (page 144).

Since both sour cream and crème fraîche are made from heavy cream, they both have significant levels of fat. For this reason, they will hold up well when blended into a sauce. Yogurt, on the other hand, is a bit more delicate, particularly when a low-fat or nonfat variety is used. Yogurt figures in numerous chutneys, but among classical sauces (and the advocates of classical sauces), yogurt is an outsider, perhaps because it is more familiar in Middle Eastern and Mediterranean cuisines. Still, it has a pleasantly acidic quality that can be used innovatively in finishing sauces. And in its low-fat and nonfat versions, it is a healthy alternative to its high-fat relatives. When using yogurt, remember to handle it gently—temper it into a sauce at the end, bring it just up to a simmer, then serve.

CRÈME FRAÎCHE

2 cups heavy cream   ½ cup sour cream or yogurt
½ cup buttermilk   ¼ teaspoon salt

- Combine all the ingredients in a clean saucepan and bring to a temperature of 100°F.
- Place into a clean stainless steel bowl, cover, and set into an oven heated by only a pilot light (12 hours).
- Refrigerate for 24 hours. Carefully remove thickened top part (this is the crème fraîche) and discard any liquid left at the bottom. Cover and refrigerate until ready to use.

Goat Cheese (Liaison au Chèvre)

Thanks to innovative entrepreneurs like Laura Chenel, who lived in France in the early 1970s to learn the generations-old methods of cheese making, goat cheese has become quite popular in the United States. Easier to digest than cheeses made from cow's milk, goat cheese boasts considerably less fat, yet significant amounts of protein, carbohydrates, vitamins, and minerals. It is excellent as a liaison, and can be found in "Grilled Chicken Breast with Black Beans and Goat Cheese Sauce," under Béchamel (page 158).

———————————— • ————————————

For information on goat cheese and where to purchase it, contact Laura Chenel's Chèvre, 1550 Ridley Avenue, Santa Rosa, California 95401; (707) 575-8888.

LIVER AND BLOOD

Though not common techniques in the United States, sauces thickened with a liaison of foie gras (fattened goose and duck liver) and giblets is fairly traditional in game sauces and stews. The liver and/or giblets are puréed with cream or butter and then tempered into a game sauce in the same manner as a cream and egg yolk liaison. For an example of this technique, see "Creamed Chicken Sauce," an innovation created by Wolfgang Puck (served at the International Economic Summit held in Virginia in 1983).

The use of blood is even less common in the United States than the use of liver, and is actually outlawed in many states because of its perishability and high bacteria content. It may also be considered vulgar by American standards. A sauce that typically employs this type of liaison is Chief Ranger sauce (Sauce Grand Veneur), a derivative of Pepper sauce (a demi-glaze small sauce). In areas where the blood from freshly slaughtered game and poultry is legally available, it should be obtained directly from the producer, and placed in a jar with a tablespoon each of brandy and red wine vinegar (to prevent coagulation). When incorporated into a sauce, it is combined with heavy cream and tempered into the sauce. Like all final liaisons, it must be handled carefully, the sauce brought just to a simmer after tempering, then served.

CORAL AND TOMALLEY

The ovary and liver (respectively) of a lobster can be used as a final liaison for any lobster or shellfish sauce. The coral is located just inside the shell at the top of the tail, adjacent to the carapace (the body of the lobster). The tomalley is located on the upper inside of the body, just below the head. They must be removed from a freshly killed lobster, pressed through a fine sieve, then blended with whole butter or cream. The same careful steps that apply to the other final liaisons apply here. Any shellfish dish or sauce will be improved with this liaison (see American Sauce, under Velouté, page 104).

CHAPTER 5

THE EVOLUTION OF FOUNDATION SAUCES

*W*hen Charles Rector sent his son to Paris on a covert mission to uncover the ingredients and method of preparation for *Sauce Marguery*, at the request of Diamond Jim Brady, young George probably had little idea of the enormity of the assignment. With no culinary experience, he was denied a position in the kitchens of Restaurant Marguery. Instead, he worked as a commis (the bottom spot in kitchen hierarchy) at *Café de Paris* for a full year, after which he secured a position at Marguery. It was another two years, however, before he managed to witness one of their seven chefs actually complete the dish. At that point, he promptly returned to New York to prepare the dish for his father, Brady, and a handful of other distinguished New Yorkers (see note following Sauce Marguery, under Velouté, page 181).

This story illustrates a theme common among culinary practitioners, particularly the "old timers," that they would never reveal the *real* secrets of the dishes in their repertoire and thus give away their valuable trade secrets. Historically, there was some sense to this, given the highly competitive and cutthroat environment that has been known to exist in commercial kitchens. But we like to think that we are now a little more enlightened, and know that in the giving there is also the receiving. Some of my contemporaries and I, who have had the opportunity to work with the "old timers," long ago vowed not to become like them, but to promote fellowship and esprit de corps, instead of selfishly hoarding our prized recipes. Furthermore, we learned early on that recipes are very stagnant representations of the real thing, and no recipe can include every subtle nuance, every extemporaneous little step or impromptu addition, that may become the crowning step in the creation of a dish.

———————————— • ————————————

M. F. K. Fisher's comment on creating an omelette underscores the metaphysical side of cooking: "By now I know, fatalistically, that if I am using a pan I know, and if I have properly rolled the precise amount of sweet butter around in the pan, and if the stars, winds, and general emotional climates are in both conjunction and harmony, I can make a perfect omelette without ever touching a spatula to it."

As an artist, I know that I can never prepare a dish exactly the same way twice, even if I so intend. Each time I approach the range and begin creating a meal, the weather, my frame of mind, availability of ingredients, personalities of my guests, and even the position of the stars, will have an influence on the final results. For the artist in the kitchen, that's just the way it is.

The recipes that follow here too, are stagnant representations of the real thing. Though nothing has been left out, intentionally or otherwise, these recipes must be considered as guides to each sauce. Salt and pepper, for example, if included, are in the quantity of "a pinch," or "to taste." Some ingredients, such as shallots, and other aromatics, are listed in unspecified amounts, such as "1 shallot," "1 medium carrot," and so on. Reductions are indicated as "simmer until reduced by two-thirds" or "three-fourths," and sauces are reduced "until desired thickness is achieved." Obviously, most chefs do not actually measure to discern if one cup of white wine has been reduced to exactly one-quarter cup. Nor do many use a viscometer to determine the degree to which a fluid resists flow under an applied force—that is, to measure how thick it is. Since the exact amount of these ingredients is not scientifically critical, we expect the readers (sauciers) will use these ingredients in quantities to suit their own style, and they will use their palate to determine if a sauce if ready to be served.

We are talking about a "second sense," a *feel* of the rhythm in a kitchen, that a seasoned saucier develops over a period of many years which tells him or her that production is moving along as anticipated, that the creative process is unfolding as it should. And the final test will be perhaps a quarter of a tasting spoon worth of the sauce, just to confirm what is already sensed.

What we look for in sauces is a harmonious balance of qualities based on six criteria (given in the respective order of their perception): color, luster, aroma, taste, texture, and viscosity. These criteria are primarily used as a teaching guide, to break down a sauce for a student, giving him or her a structure within which to consider the intrinsic and subtle characteristics of that sauce. In actual practice, as a sauce is completed, little can be done to correct the color, aroma, or texture of that sauce, and luster is simply a visual quality that is or isn't there. All of these are a record, a tally so to speak, of all the little steps a saucier has taken to produce a sauce with the color, luster, aroma, taste, texture, and thickness he or she has intended to manifest.

The taste and thickness of a sauce, however, *can* be adjusted toward the completion, and this is part of the process of completing that sauce. If all the other elements of a sauce are present in desired proportion, the balance of flavors—sweet, sour, and salt—can be heightened with the addition of salt, or pepper, or citrus juice, wine, brandies and liqueurs, and so on.

The addition of a squeeze of fresh lemon or lime juice, at the very end of preparing a sauce, even if a particular sauce recipe does not call for either, sometimes adds just the right amount of acidity to "bring a sauce up."

The saucier may augment the sauce with the addition of cream (if the recipe includes cream), or a reduction of cream, or butter, an important finishing step well within the bounds of flexible ingenuity. The addition of butter (*monter au beurre*, literally "to lift [the taste] with butter"), helps to round out the flavor of the sauce in an almost magical way. This lifting is the polar opposite of flat, an absence of acidic ingredients necessary for our palates to taste all of the other flavors of the dish.

Meat glaze (glace de viande), a 90 percent or more reduction of a stock, is also one of the most important tools in a saucier's repertoire. It must be used with discretion, however, since it is highly concentrated.

The viscosity (thickness) of a sauce can also be adjusted—thinned by adding an appropriate liquid, or thickened by additional simmering, or in some cases, with the addition of beurre manié, a paste made of equal parts of raw flour and butter. All of these steps will be decided on and employed by the saucier as he or she deems necessary.

CHANGES IN AMERICAN COOKING

American cooking styles have changed considerably in recent years, all part of a renewed appreciation of our own "melting pot" culinary identity. Sauce making has been affected in two primary ways: (1) diminished use of roux (flour plus fat), replaced with more frequent use of *natural reductions;* and (2) the use of innovative accompaniments to replace traditional sauces (chutneys, compotes, relishes, salsas, etc.). Based on these trends, we can now identify the following modifications to the mother sauce matrix:

The Mother Sauce Matrix

As formulated by Auguste Escoffier in his *Guide Culinaire* (1902):	As it is now practiced in present-day cookery:		
	French	*English*	*Common Term*
ESPAGNOLE VELOUTÉ	Sauce demi-glace	Demi-glaze sauce	Brown sauce
BÉCHAMEL HOLLANDAISE	Sauce velouté	Velouté sauce	Blond sauce
TOMATE	Sauce béchamel	Béchamel sauce	White or cream sauce
	Sauces aux beurre	Butter sauces	
	Sauce Hollandaise	Hollandaise sauce	Dutch sauce
	Beurre blanc	Butter sauce	Beurre blanc
	Sauce tomate	Tomato sauce	Red sauce

With regard to roux-thickened sauces, there has been a trend to eliminate roux altogether in the preparation of brown, blond, and white sauces. They have been replaced by 100 percent reductions, finished with a variety of final liaisons—cream, butter (as in beurre blanc), and delicate cheeses (goat cheese, yogurt, and crème fraîche), and more recently, a new generation of vegetable and herb purées, which take into consideration a dining public's awareness of the health hazards in a diet of excessive animal fats.

The problem with such carefully attended to creations is that they are time- and labor-intensive. Someone must pay for these expenditures, and these costs are reflected in menu prices. A restaurant that is wholeheartedly dedicated to the pursuit of gastronomic excellence and culinary innovation limits the size of the market to which it can cater, and it also limits the number of patrons that can be served in any given evening.

THE SAUCIER'S APPROACH

In light of the state of the culinary craft in the late twentieth century, in our attempt to explain the essentials of the sauce craft, we have taken a middle road. We've presented the fundamentals and explained why they are the way they are. It is up to the saucier to develop his or her own style, using this work as a base for dedicated study of the art of sauce making. As this pertains to the making of three roux-thickened sauces, it means that a roux is used, but a bit less than in the past, substituting part of that thickener with a slow, careful reduction of the liquid involved. The result: a nominally starch-thickened sauce with a deep, rich flavor as the result of reduction. And while completely starch-free versions are included in recipe form, the ultimate decisions on style and approach will be made by the saucier. In a given food service establishment, these decisions will be reflected in the menu offerings and the quality of those offerings. This then reveals the degree of the chef-saucier's dedication to his or her craft.

The challenge is to find the proper balance so that the final work reflects decisions based on the personal philosophies of the individual, as well as those of the establishment in which the saucier works. To illustrate this further, consider a saucier charged with the production of a Madeira sauce sufficient to serve 500 guests. The saucier would need to prepare approximately 10 gallons of sauce (10 gallons × 128 ounces ÷ 500 = 2.56 ounces per portion). If this brown sauce were to be made using the natural reduction method, it would require roughly 100 gallons of brown stock. Even in a commercial kitchen with the equipment capacity to produce this volume of stock, the time required to produce it might interfere with other production duties. The natural reduction would be out of the question. But, if one created a demi-glaze with a carefully prepared brown roux, 10 gallons of sauce could be produced from approximately 20 gallons of rich brown stock—obviously a more logical approach. On the other hand, a dinner for a dozen members of a gastronomic society would demand the time and extra effort to develop sauces employing natural reductions. Therefore, the dynamics of the service application (number of guests and their focus) both come into play when deciding on the appropriate approach. And through it all, the saucier must maintain an emotional and artistic balance, demonstrating both a wide repertoire of techniques and the creative flexibility to adapt to a given situation.

CHAPTER 6

BROWN SAUCES

Demi-Glaze
and Its Derivatives

*A*s explained earlier, the separate step of creating Espagnole has been eliminated, replaced with the creation of demi-glaze directly from brown stock. This is probably a reflection of expedience (we are always looking for ways to be more time efficient). So we have shortened a three-step process (brown stock → Espagnole → demi-glaze) to a two-step process (brown stock → demi-glaze). Using a rich, well-colored brown stock, combined with a dark brown roux, and reducing sufficiently to increase natural viscosity, we move more quickly to our basic brown sauce, demi-glaze.

*B*ROWN SAUCE
(Demi-Glaze)

¼ pound unsalted butter (1 stick)
2 shallots, roughly cut
1 stalk celery, rinsed, trimmed, and roughly cut
1 carrot, peeled, top removed, and sliced
1 medium Spanish onion, peeled and roughly cut
1 small leek, well rinsed and roughly cut
1 clove garlic, crushed
1 cup dry red wine

1½ gallons rich brown beef, veal, or chicken stock, hot
1 bunch parsley stems
4 sprigs of thyme, trimmed, rinsed, and tied together with string
2 bay leaves
1 teaspoon black peppercorns, crushed
1 cup tomato purée
1 cup toasted flour
½ cup clarified butter

- In a 2-gallon heavy-gauge saucepan, sauté the vegetables in the vegetable oil over a medium flame for about 20 minutes, stirring frequently. When the vegetables have caramelized lightly, add the red wine, then brown stock, and bring to a simmer.

- In a large stainless steel bowl, blend the toasted flour and clarified butter until smooth. Ladle in the simmering stock, and with a piano wire whip, work in about 2 quarts of the simmering stock and the tomato purée into the roux until it is smooth. Return this mixture to the simmering stock (be sure to remove all of it by scraping the bowl with a rubber spatula), blending thoroughly. Add the aromatics, and simmer for 2 hours, or until reduced by one-third. Skim the surface of the sauce periodically, removing impurities as they collect.

- Strain, cool, cover, label, and refrigerate.

Sauce Matrix I
Demi-Glaze and Its Derivatives

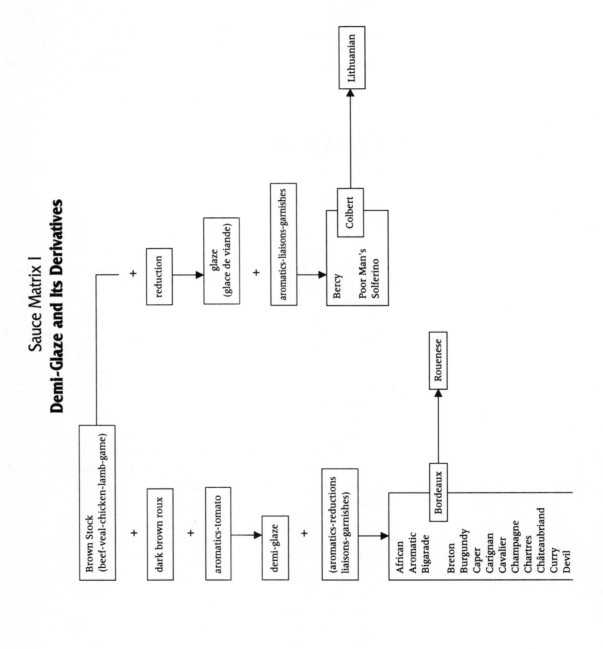

Brown Stock
(beef-veal-chicken-lamb-game)

+ dark brown roux

+ aromatics-tomato

→ demi-glaze

+ (aromatics-reductions
liaisons-garnishes)

→ African
Aromatic
Bigarade
Breton
Burgundy
Caper
Carignan
Cavalier
Champagne
Chartres
Châteaubriand
Curry
Devil

Bordeaux → Rouenese

+ reduction

→ glaze
(glace de viande)

+ aromatics-liaisons-garnishes

→ Bercy
Poor Man's
Solferino

Colbert → Lithuanian

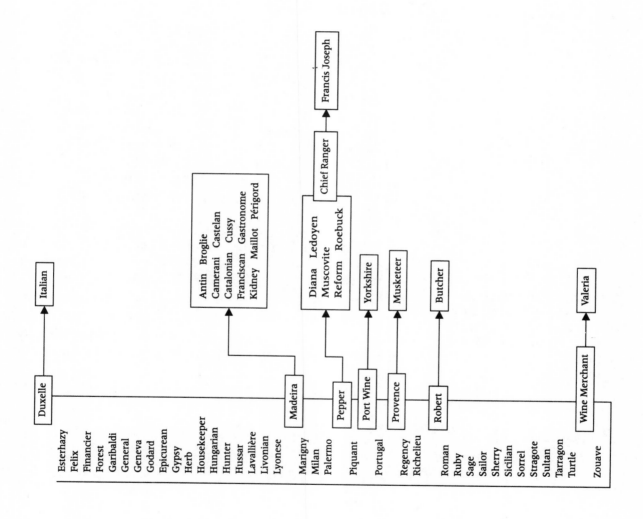

Duxelle

Italian

Esterhazy
Felix
Financier
Forest
Garibaldi
General
Geneva
Godard
Epicurean
Gypsy
Herb

Madeira

Antin   Broglie
Camerani   Castelan
Catalonian   Cussy
Franciscan   Gastronome
Kidney   Maillot   Périgord

Housekeeper
Hungarian
Hunter
Hussar
Lavallière
Livonian
Lyonese

Marigny
Milan
Palermo

Pepper

Diana   Ledoyen
Muscovite
Reform   Roebuck

Chief Ranger

Francis Joseph

Port Wine

Yorkshire

Piquant

Portugal

Provence

Musketeer

Regency
Richelieu

Robert

Butcher

Roman
Ruby
Sage
Sailor
Sherry
Sicilian
Sorrel
Stragote
Sultan
Tarragon
Turtle

Wine Merchant

Valeria

Zouave

Shallots are an important ingredient in the saucier's repertoire in every first-class kitchen. Shallots are unique among aromatic vegetables, and are a separate variety of onion species. They have been described as having a better-bred (subtler) flavor than other onions, with a hint of garlic.

$\mathcal{B}$ROWN SAUCE II
(A Flourless Demi-Glaze)

2 shallots, roughly cut
1 stalk celery, roughly cut
1 carrot, peeled, top removed, and roughly cut
1 medium Spanish onion, peeled and roughly cut
1 small leek, well rinsed and roughly cut
1 garlic clove, crushed
¼ cup vegetable oil

1 gallon brown beef, veal, or chicken stock, hot
1 cup tomato purée
1 bunch parsley stems, trimmed and rinsed
4 sprigs fresh thyme
2 bay leaves
1 teaspoon black peppercorns, crushed

- Sauté the vegetables in the oil in a 2-gallon stock pot until they are *well caramelized*. Add the stock and remaining ingredients. Simmer until reduced by half (1 to 2 hours).
- Strain the stock into a small saucepan, discarding the aromatics. Simmer, and reduce once again by half.
- Strain again into a smaller pan. Continue reducing until the demi-glaze is thick and rich. Strain, cool, cover, label, and refrigerate.

This recipe was innovated by Alan R. Gibson, formerly chef de cuisine at The Pillar House, Newton Falls, Massachusetts.

TRADITIONAL DERIVATIVES OF DEMI-GLAZE

$\mathcal{A}$FRICAN SAUCE
(Sauce Africaine)

1 tablespoon unsalted butter
1 shallot, minced
¼ cup Madeira wine

¼ teaspoon cayenne pepper
2 tablespoons tomato purée
1¼ cups demi-glaze

- Sauté the shallot in the butter for 5 minutes. Add the wine and simmer until reduced by three-fourths. Add the cayenne, tomato, and demi-glaze, and simmer another 5 minutes, or until suitable thickness is achieved. Strain, and adjust seasoning.

•

The term *africaine* generally refers more to a specific accompaniment to large roasts, often mutton, than to an actual sauce. The garnish commonly consists of olive-shaped ("turned") potatoes roasted in butter, and steamed or sautéed cucumbers, zucchini (sliced or "turned"), and/or eggplant.

Aromatic Sauce (Sauce Aromate)

Aromatic sauce is typically served with large roasted or braised joints of meat.

A demi-glaze flavored with a reduction of white wine, shallot, white pepper, nutmeg, basil, chives, marjoram, sage, tarragon, and thyme, garnished with chopped tarragon and chervil.

*B*ERCY SAUCE
(Sauce Bercy)

This version of Bercy sauce is typically served with grilled meat (see Bercy Sauce under Velouté).

1 shallot, minced
½ teaspoon white peppercorns, cracked
1½ cups dry white wine
¼ cup meat glaze

4 tablespoons unsalted butter, cut into ¼-inch cubes
2 tablespoons parsley, chopped

- Simmer the shallot, peppercorns, and wine until reduced by half. Strain, and return to the saucepan.
- Add the meat glaze and mount with butter. Add the chopped parsley, and adjust seasoning.

*B*IGARADE SAUCE

1 tablespoon unsalted butter
1 teaspoon shallot, minced
1 tablespoon brown sugar

juice and zest of 1 orange
juice of 1 lemon
1¼ cups demi-glaze

2 tablespoons Grand Marnier
(or other orange liqueur)
2 tablespoons Cognac

1 orange, peeled and cut
into membrane-free
segments

- Blanch the orange zest in boiling water for 5 minutes. Strain and set aside.
- Sauté the shallot in the butter for 5 minutes. Add the brown sugar, and melt. Add the orange and lemon juice, and simmer until reduced by three-fourths.
- Add the demi-glaze, and simmer for about 5 minutes, or until suitable thickness is achieved. Strain.
- Add the orange liqueur, Cognac, orange zest, and orange segments, and season to taste.

——— • ———

Bigarade sauce is typically served with roasted or grilled duck, but can be served with any variety of winged game.

Bigarade is a word for a bitter orange, also called a Seville orange, cultivated in temperate growing areas, including the south of France. It is so bitter that some believe it should be utilized only for its oil—used as a flavoring agent in cosmetics and liqueurs—or candied peel, a specialty of Nice.

Duck à l'Orange is one of the most commonly corrupted dishes, rarely resembling the fine dish it can be when properly prepared. A true bigarade sauce should be made utilizing a bitter bigarade orange, and is developed from pan juices retained from the roasted bird, simmered down with sugar, vinegar, and orange juice. In true practice, it can be made from any variety of orange. The ideal approach is to create an orange-flavored demi-glaze, with a balance of sweet, sour, fruit, and meat (duck) flavors.

*B*ORDEAUX SAUCE
(Sauce Bordelaise)

1 teaspoon shallot, minced
1 cup dry red wine
1 sprig fresh thyme
1 bay leaf

1¼ cups demi-glaze
¼ cup beef marrow, medium diced, blanched in boiling salted water

- Simmer the shallot, wine, and herbs until reduced by three-fourths. Add the demi-glaze, and simmer briefly. Season to taste with salt and pepper. Strain, add the diced marrow, and serve with grilled steak.

---●---

Bordelaise, literally "Bordeaux style," reflects the fact that Bordeaux is an important red wine producing region in France. There are so many variations to this well-known sauce, however, that the primary identifying constant is not a red wine reduction, but the garnish of bone marrow. For example, Bonnefoy sauce, one variation, is named after a Parisian restaurant of the same name, circa 1850. In this sauce, the red wine reduction is substituted with a white wine reduction, combined with demi-glaze, and served with fish.

Bordeaux sauce is typically served with sautéed or grilled meat.

Rouenese Sauce
(Sauce Rouennaise)

Bordeaux sauce seasoned with a little lemon juice and very finely puréed duck livers, and served with any wild or domestic duck dish.

---●---

Any dish classified as *à la Rouennaise* (in the style of Rouen) is likely to be some kind of duck. Rouen, located approximately 75 miles northwest of Paris, is well known for the exceptional duck raised in that area. Pressed duck, for example, was created by Méchenet, a restaurateur from Rouen, in the early nineteenth century. La Tour d'Argent, Paris's oldest restaurant (1582), adopted the dish around 1890 when Frédéric, a well-known maître d'hôtel, took over operation of the restaurant. The dish is prepared in front of the seated guests, employing one of two antique presses. Frédéric initiated a practice of assigning a number to each duck served, and began recording the service of each duck. Number 328 was served to Edward VII, the Prince of Wales, in 1890; No. 33,642 was served to Theodore Roosevelt; and No. 253,652 was served to Charlie Chaplin. By 1982, the service of 613,000 pressed Rouenese ducks had been recorded.

Rouenese sauce is also typically served with soft-boiled or poached eggs.

BRETON SAUCE

(Sauce Bretonne)

2 tablespoons unsalted butter
1 shallot, minced
1 medium onion, sliced
2 garlic cloves, crushed
½ cup dry white wine
½ cup brown beef or veal
  stock

¼ cup tomato purée
1¼ cup demi-glaze
3 tablespoons unsalted
  butter, cut into ¼-inch
  cubes
2 tablespoons parsley,
  chopped

This version of Breton sauce is typically served with light meats, and braised, pan-fried, or deep-fried offal (see Breton Sauce under Velouté).

- Sauté the shallot and onion in the butter until well caramelized. Add the garlic, wine, and stock, and simmer until reduced by three-fourths. Add the tomato purée and demi-glaze, and simmer until desired thickness is achieved. Strain, mount with the butter, season to taste, and finish with the chopped parsley.

BURGUNDY SAUCE

(Sauce Bourguignonne)

1 thick slice bacon, small
  diced
2 large shallots, minced
1 small onion, thinly sliced
3 parsley stems

1 sprig thyme
1 bay leaf
1 cup dry (Burgundy) red
  wine
1¼ cup demi-glaze

- Render the bacon in a heavy-gauge saucepan, over medium heat, until lightly browned. Add the shallots and onion, and sauté 5 minutes. Add the herbs and wine and reduce by three-fourths. Add the demi-glaze, simmer until suitable thickness is achieved, and strain.

Although Burgundy sauce can be made as a separate sauce and served with grilled or roasted meat or poultry, it is commonly known as part of a dish of braised beef. The same ingredients pertain, with the addition of cubed beef seared in rendered bacon fat, then lightly dusted with flour. The herbs should also be tied together so that they can be pulled from the stew before service.

Burgundy sauce is typically served with soft-boiled or poached eggs; braised or baked fish; sautéed poultry; and sautéed, fried, or grilled meat.

Caper Sauce (Sauce aux Câpres)

Demi-glaze garnished with capers (see Velouté).

Carignan Sauce

A tomato-flavored demi-glaze (sometimes simmered with roasted duck bones and truffle peelings), finished with Málaga or Port wine.

Carignan sauce is typically served with sirloin steak and lamb medallions, and is served on a base of Anna potatoes (the classical version).

Cavalier Sauce (Sauce Cavalière)

A tomato-flavored demi-glaze, seasoned with mustard and tarragon vinegar, garnished with capers and diced sour gherkins.

Chambord Sauce

Chambord sauce is created by stewing a whole salmon, carp, flounder, sole, or other large fish that has been stuffed with a fish forcemeat. The fish is baked with mirepoix, bouquet garni, red wine, and fish fumet. The remaining liquid is reduced, added to a demi-glaze, and mounted with anchovy butter.

*C*HAMPAGNE SAUCE
(Sauce au Champagne)

1 shallot, minced
1 sprig fresh thyme
1 bay leaf
1 cup champagne wine (or sparkling chardonnay)

1¼ cup demi-glaze
2 tablespoons unsalted butter, cut into ¼-inch cubes
¼ cup Cognac

- Simmer the shallot, herbs, and wine until reduced by three-fourths. Add the demi-glaze, and simmer until suitable thickness is achieved. Mount with butter, strain, and finish with the Cognac.

A Champagne sauce can also be found under Béchamel and Dutch Sauce.

Chartres

Any dish or sauce flavored strongly with tarragon.

Chaud-Froid Sauce

Chaud-froid (pronounced "show-fwa," literally "hot-cold sauce") refers to a brown, green (herb-colored), red, or white-colored sauce that is prepared hot and served cold. It is typically used as a base coating for pieces of meat, poultry, fish, or game, which are then decorated in elaborate fashion, coated with aspic, then served on a buffet table with other cold food items.

Philéas Gilbert (1857–1942), a notable chef, writer, and gastronomic scholar of the twentieth century (he collaborated with Escoffier on his *Guide Culinaire*), contended that chaud-froid was created in 1759 at the Château de Montmorency. "One evening, the Marshall of Luxembourg had invited a large number of illustrious guests to his château. Occupying a place of honor on the menu was a fricassée of chicken in white sauce. When it was time to sit down at table, a messenger arrived; the Marshall was summoned without delay to the King's Council. The Marshall gave orders that his absence should not delay the serving of the food. Returning late, and desiring only one dish, he was served with the cold chicken fricassée, congealed in the ivory-colored sauce. He found this food succulent, and a few days later expressed a wish to have it served again. Presented under the name of *refroidi*, this term displeased the marshal, who insisted on the name of *chaud-froid*."

CHÂTEAUBRIAND SAUCE

1 shallot, minced
1 large mushroom, roughly chopped
1 sprig fresh thyme
1 bay leaf
1 cup dry white wine
1¼ cup demi-glaze

2 tablespoons unsalted butter, cut into ¼-inch cubes
1 tablespoon parsley, minced
1 tablespoon tarragon, minced
1 tablespoon lemon juice
pinch of cayenne pepper

- Simmer the shallot, mushroom, herbs, and white wine until reduced by three-fourths. Add the demi-glaze, and simmer until suitable thickness is achieved. Mount with butter, strain, and finish with the chopped herbs, lemon juice, and cayenne pepper.

Châteaubriand, a thick steak cut from a beef tenderloin, then grilled or roasted, was named in honor of the Vicomte de Châteaubriand (1768–1848), by Montmireil, his chef. This is the traditional sauce that was served with the dish, though in modern times it is almost exclusively served with B Sauce.

Châteaubriand sauce is typically served with any grilled or roasted meat.

Colbert Sauce

Colbert sauce was probably named after Jean-Baptiste Colbert (1619–1683), French statesman and economic adviser to Louis XIV. It is typically served with grilled or roasted meat.

A meat, poultry, or fish glaze (depending on its use), moistened with an appropriate stock (2 parts glaze to 1 part stock and 1 part Madeira wine), mounted with unsalted butter, seasoned with lemon juice, a pinch of cayenne and nutmeg, minced parsley, and sometimes a little Madeira.

Lithuanian Sauce
(Sauce Lithuanienne)

Colbert sauce, garnished with fresh bread crumbs sautéed in butter, and minced herbs.

*C*URRY SAUCE
(Sauce à l'Indienne)

1 tablespoon unsalted butter
¼ cup mirepoix, finely
 chopped
2 cloves garlic, crushed
½ banana, roughly chopped
½ Granny Smith apple,
 cored, and roughly
 chopped
zest of ½ orange, roughly
 chopped

1 tablespoon ginger root,
 grated
1 sprig thyme
1 dried hot red chile pepper
2 tablespoons imported
 curry powder
1 cup brown stock
½ cup tomato purée
1¼ cups demi-glaze

- Sauté the mirepoix and garlic in the butter until well caramelized. Add the fruit, ginger, thyme, chile, and curry powder, and sauté another 3 minutes. Add the stock, blend well, and simmer until reduced by two-thirds. Add the tomato purée and demi-glaze, and simmer, stirring frequently, until desired thickness is achieved.

- Pass the sauce through a food mill (or pound in a large china cap until dry). Strain again, through a fine strainer, and adjust seasoning.

Curry is a blend of as few as 10 to as many as 30 different herbs and spices, among them anise, cardamon, chile pepper, cinnamon, clove, coriander (seed and leaf), cumin, fennel (seed and root), fenugreek, garlic, ginger, lemon grass, mace, mustard, nutmeg, onion, saffron, tamarind, and turmeric.

Curry can be applied to various dishes in a number of ways, using either brown or blond sauce as their base (see Curry Sauce under Velouté). A curry can be a stew, in which a tough cut of meat (beef, lamb, mutton, etc.) is seared, seasoned, then simmered slowly, until tender; the prepared sauce (as given here) can be used to create an à la carte dish made with a tender cut of fish, shellfish, chicken, veal, beef, lamb, etc.; and the sauce can dress a dish of poached or sautéed poultry, or rice.

𝒟EVIL SAUCE
(Sauce Diable)

1 shallot, minced	1¼ cup demi-glaze
1 cup dry white wine	½ teaspoon black
¼ cup white wine vinegar	peppercorns, cracked
1 sprig fresh thyme	¼ teaspoon cayenne pepper
1 bay leaf	1 tablespoon parsley, minced
¼ teaspoon dry mustard	1 tablespoon lemon juice
2 tablespoons tomato purée	

Devil sauce is typically served with grilled or roasted poultry; pig's feet; and boiled beef.

- Simmer the shallot, white wine, vinegar, herbs, and mustard, until reduced by three-fourths. Add the tomato, demi-glaze, and two peppers, and simmer until suitable thickness is achieved. Strain, then add the chopped parsley. Season to taste with salt and pepper.

ᗞUXELLE SAUCE

1 tablespoon unsalted butter
1 shallot, minced
2 tablespoons Spanish
   onion, minced
5 large mushrooms, well
   rinsed
½ cup dry white wine

½ cup tomato purée
¾ cup demi-glaze
2 tablespoons unsalted
   butter, cut into ¼-inch
   cubes
2 tablespoons parsley,
   minced

- Sauté the shallot, onion, and mushrooms in the butter for 5 minutes. Remove to a food processor, and purée. Return to the sauté pan, add the white wine, and simmer until almost dry.
- Add the tomato purée and demi-glaze, and simmer until suitable thickness is achieved. Mount with butter and add the parsley.

Italian Sauce (Sauce Italienne)

Duxelle sauce, garnished with diced ham sautéed in butter, and chopped parsley.

ℰSTERHAZY SAUCE

1 tablespoon unsalted butter
1 small onion, peeled and
   minced
½ cup dry white wine
1 teaspoon paprika
1¼ cup demi-glaze
¼ cup sour cream

2 tablespoons carrot, and 2
   tablespoons celery root,
   cut into julienne, and
   simmered in 1 tablespoon
   unsalted butter until
   tender, but firm

- Sauté the onion in the butter for 5 minutes. Add the white wine and paprika, and reduce by three-fourths. Add the demi-glaze, and simmer until suitable thickness is achieved. Stir in the sour cream, bring to a boil, and add the carrot and celery root julienne.

Felix Sauce

Demi-glaze mounted with lobster butter, finished with lemon juice.

Duxelle sauce is typically served with hard-boiled eggs (served hot); gratins; pasta; risotto; braised or sautéed poultry; and sautéed or fried meat.

Italian sauce is typically served with braised or sautéed vegetables; grilled, braised, or baked fish; light meats; and boiled, sautéed, or fried beef.

Financier Sauce (Sauce Financière)

Demi-glaze reduced with chicken stock, truffle essence, and Sauternes or Madeira, garnished with truffle and mushrooms.

Financier sauce is typically served with croustades; pasta; veal sweetbreads; braised poultry; and sautéed or fried beef.

*F*OREST SAUCE
(Sauce Forestière)

1 tablespoon unsalted butter
1 shallot, minced
1 cup dry red wine
1¼ cup demi-glaze
½ cup julienned shiitake, chanterelle, and oyster mushrooms, cut into julienne, and sautéed in unsalted butter, rinsed with lemon juice, and drained

- Sauté the shallot in the butter for 5 minutes. Add the red wine, and reduce by three-fourths. Add the demi-glaze, simmer until suitable thickness is achieved, and add the mushrooms.

In culinary terms, *forestiére*, from *fôret* (forest), refers to any dish with wild mushrooms. Any variety of wild mushroom, or combination of wild varieties, can be included in this sauce, such as black fungus, yellow boletus (cèpe), chanterelle, morel, shiitake, oyster, straw, etc. If only the standard white variety (also called "field mushroom") is employed, the sauce becomes a Mushroom sauce (Sauce Champignon).

Garibaldi Sauce

Demi-glaze seasoned with mustard, cayenne pepper, and garlic, and mounted with anchovy butter.

General Sauce (Sauce Général)

Demi-glaze seasoned with lemon juice, tarragon vinegar, and garlic, garnished with orange zest, and finished with dry sherry.

Geneva Sauce (Sauce Génevoise)

Traditionally, *à la genevoise* (in the style of Geneva) referred to a number of fish dishes served with a brown sauce flavored with salmon and/or fish fumet and other fish derived flavoring elements. It is nearly identical to Chambord sauce, though usually applied to salmon. It is created with a reduction of red wine, salmon bones and trimmings, mirepoix, and herbs, then added to a demi-glaze and mounted with anchovy butter.

GODARD SAUCE

¼ cup ham, finely chopped
¼ cup mirepoix, finely
   chopped

1 cup champagne wine (or
   sparkling chardonnay)
1¼ cups demi-glaze
¼ cup mushroom essence

- Simmer the ham, mirepoix, and wine, until reduced by three-fourths. Add the demi-glaze and mushroom essence, simmer until desired thickness is achieved, and strain.

———————— • ————————

The Godard garnish consists of veal and chicken quenelles (small oval-shaped ground meat dumplings), sliced lamb sweetbreads, fluted mushrooms, truffles, ox tongue, cockscombs, and Godard sauce. Named for Godard d'Aucour (1716–1795), it is typically served with sweetbreads; braised poultry; and large roasted or braised joints of meat.

———————————————

Gourmet Sauce

Demi-glaze flavored with a reduction of red wine and fish stock, mounted with lobster butter, and garnished with diced lobster and chopped truffles.

Gypsy sauce is typically served with sautéed poultry; light meats; and sautéed or fried meat.

Gypsy Sauce (Sauce Zingara)

A strongly tomato-flavored demi-glaze, seasoned with paprika, and garnished with a julienne of pickled tongue, ham, mushroom, and truffle.

Herb Sauce
(Sauce aux Fines Herbes)

Herb sauce is typically served with sautéed or fried meat, and poached poultry (see Herb Sauce under Velouté).

Demi-glaze garnished with chopped fresh fine herbs (typically chervil, chives, parsley, and tarragon), and a little lemon juice.

Housekeeper Sauce
(Sauce Ménagère)

Demi-glaze flavored with onions, garnished with chopped anchovies and parsley, and finished with lemon juice.

Housekeeper style refers to dishes that use domestic (home-style) cooking methods, in which simple and relatively inexpensive ingredients are used, and is similar to peasant style (Paysanne), housewife style (Bonne Femme), and citizen style (Bourgeoise). Technically, this sauce is created as part of a dish qualified with the name housekeeper (ménagère), such as Entrecôte à la ménagère, Omelette à la ménagère, Sole à la ménagère, and so on.

Hungarian sauce is typically served with soft-boiled or poached eggs; braised, pan-fried, or deep-fried offal; baked or braised fish; sautéed poultry; light meats; and sautéed or fried meat.

Hungarian Sauce (Sauce Hongroise)

Demi-glaze flavored with sliced onions sweated in salt pork, seasoned with paprika, and finished with sour cream.

Hunter Sauce (Sauce Chasseur)

Hunter sauce can be fashioned as a separate sauce, but is often created as part of a dish of braised game or poultry (Chicken Cacciatore is the same dish, Italian style).

*B*RAISED CHICKEN, HUNTER STYLE
(Poulet à la Chasseur)

1 fresh chicken, cut into 12 pieces	salt and black pepper as needed
¼ cup olive oil	2 large shallots, minced

1 cup sliced mushrooms
1 cup dry white wine
2 sprigs fresh tarragon and 6
   parsley stems, tied
   together

½ cup tomato purée
2 cups demi-glaze
¼ cup parsley and tarragon
   leaves, minced

- Sprinkle the chicken lightly with salt and pepper, and sauté in the olive oil on all sides, until lightly browned. Place the pan into a preheated oven for 20 minutes. Remove the chicken to a platter and set aside.

- Sauté the shallot and mushroom in the same pan for 5 minutes. Add the white wine and deglaze. Add the bouquet garni and simmer until reduced by one-third. Add the tomato purée and demi-glaze, and blend thoroughly. Return the chicken to the sauce, and simmer for another 20 minutes. Remove the bouquet garni, season to taste with salt and pepper, and serve topped with the minced herbs.

Hunter sauce is also typically served with soft-boiled or poached eggs; omelettes; rice; sautéed poultry; and sautéed or fried meat.

ℋussar Sauce

(Sauce Hussarde)

1 tablespoon unsalted butter
2 tablespoons chopped ham
1 shallot, minced
1 small Spanish onion,
   peeled and minced
1 garlic clove, crushed
1 cup dry white wine
1 sprig each thyme,
   rosemary, and tarragon

6 parsley stems
¼ cup tomato purée
1¼ cup demi-glaze
1 tablespoon prepared
   horseradish, squeezed dry
2 tablespoons ham, finely
   diced
1 tablespoon parsley,
   chopped

A *hussar* (Fr. *hussarde*) refers to a horseman of the Hungarian light cavalry, which originated in the fifteenth century. Hussar sauce is typically served with sautéed or fried meat.

- Sauté the ham, shallot, onion, and garlic in the butter for 5 minutes. Add the white wine and herbs, and reduce by three-fourths. Add the tomato and demi-glaze, and simmer until suitable thickness is achieved. Strain, and add the ham, horseradish, and parsley.

Lavallière Sauce

Demi-glaze flavored with game essence, garnished with julienne of truffle and minced tarragon, and finished with sour cream.

Lavallière sauce is believed to have been named in honor of Louise de la Vallière, Louis XIV's mistress.

Livonian Sauce (Sauce Livonienne)

Demi-glaze garnished with chopped fennel root sautéed, mounted with butter, and finished with sour cream.

LYONESE SAUCE
(Sauce Lyonnaise)

1 tablespoon butter	½ cup dry white wine
1 medium onion, medium	½ cup white wine vinegar
diced	1¼ cup demi-glaze

- Lightly brown the onions in the butter. Add the wine and vinegar, and simmer until reduced by three-fourths. Add the demi-glaze and simmer until suitable thickness is achieved.

———————————— • ————————————

The town of Lyon is considered the preeminent gastronomic center of France. Though it is well known for dozens of specialties, any dish qualified *à la Lyonnaise* will be identified by the use of chopped onions. These are typically glazed in butter until lightly caramelized, flavored with pan juices deglazed with vinegar, and sprinkled with chopped parsley. Lyonese Sauce can also be found under Velouté and Cream Sauce.

MADEIRA SAUCE
(Sauce Madère)

1 tablespoon unsalted butter	2 tablespoons unsalted
1 shallot, minced	butter, cut into ¼-inch
1 cup Madeira wine	cubes
1½ cups demi-glaze	

- Sauté the shallot in the butter for 3 or 4 minutes. Add the Madeira, and simmer until reduced by three-fourths. Add the demi-glaze, and simmer until suitable thickness is achieved. Mount with butter.

Madeira is a fortified wine originating on the island of the same name, off the coast of Portugal. It is produced by a process known as *estufa*, in which the wine in the cask is gradually heated, then allowed to cool down. Madeiras are named after the grapes from which they are produced: Sercial is the driest, Verdelho is nutty and mellow, Boal and Malmsey are sweet and full-bodied. In exceptional vintage years, there are Madeiras produced that can last a century or more in the bottle.

Madeira sauce is frequently used, either as is or as a base for numerous other sauces. It is typically served with omelettes; ham; sautéed or fried meat; grilled or sautéed kidney; and large roasted or braised joints of meat. The following are compound sauces made from Madeira sauce as their base.

Antin Sauce

Madeira sauce, flavored with a reduction of dry white wine, garnished with mushrooms, truffles, and fine herbs.

Broglie Sauce

Madeira sauce, flavored with mushroom, and garnished with diced ham.

Camerani Sauce

Madeira sauce garnished with minced black truffle.

André Camerani (1735–1816) was an Italian comedian and gourmand who left his mark on haute cuisine. A vegetable dish, chicken liver dish, and pasta soup were created in his name, as well as a garnish for a dish of poached chicken and sweetbreads—a tartlette filled with goose liver pâté, topped with sliced truffle, ox tongue cut to look like cockscombs, and small pasta, all bound in Suprême sauce.

Castelan Sauce (Sauce Castellane)

Madeira sauce, flavored with tomato, garnished with diced bell peppers and ham, served with lamb or beef medallions (tournedos), garnished with diced tomatoes cooked in olive oil, potato croquettes, and fried onion rings.

Catalonian Sauce (Sauce Catalane)

Madeira sauce, seasoned with garlic, mustard, tomato, and cayenne. It is served with sautéed beef medallions, served on a base of sliced, sautéed eggplant, garnished with large mushroom caps stuffed with risotto or rice pilaf.

Cussy Sauce

Madeira sauce finished with poultry glaze.

———————————— • ————————————

Cussy sauce was named after Louis, the Marquis de Cussy (1766–1837), known as one of the wittiest gastronomes of the nineteenth century. He held the post of Prefect of the Palace under Napoleon I, and according to his friend Grimod de La Reyniére, invented 366 different ways of preparing chicken (hence the poultry glaze in his sauce namesake).

Franciscan Sauce (Sauce Cordelier)

Madeira sauce finished with goose liver purée, and garnished with sliced black truffle.

Gastronomer's Sauce (Sauce Gastronome)

Madeira sauce seasoned with cayenne pepper and meat glaze, and finished with a reduction of champagne.

Kidney Sauce (Sauce aux Rognons)

Madeira sauce garnished with small diced veal kidneys sautéed in butter.

In practical application, a kidney sauce is more accurately created around kidneys as a main course. A typical example of this is Veal (or Lamb) Kidneys Armagnac Style (Rognons de Veau [d'Agneau] à l'Armagnac). The kidneys are sautéed in butter with minced shallots, deglazed with Armagnac, reduced, Madeira sauce added and simmered briefly, mounted with butter, then served, sometimes tableside.

Maillot Sauce

Madeira sauce seasoned with a reduction of shallot and white wine, and garnished with diced hard-cooked egg whites.

Périgord Sauce (Sauce Périgueux)

Madeira sauce simmered with truffle peelings (or truffle essence), and garnished with minced black truffle.

The town of Périgord, in southwestern France, is known for many gastronomic specialties, among them wild mushrooms, duck and goose confit, and truffles, hence the inclusion of truffles in this sauce. (Sauces Périgueux and Périgordine are on occasion referred to as Sauce Rossini.) The difference between Périgueux and Périgourdine is based on two elements: (1) the size of the truffle garnish—minced in the former, and sliced or diced in the latter; and (2) Périgourdine includes a final liaison of mashed goose liver (foie gras).

Gioacchini Antonio Rossini (1792–1868), the prolific opera composer and gastronome, is credited with creating a dish which included a Périgord sauce at Café Anglais in Paris. Rossini had become bored with the usual menu, and gave his waiter instructions for a dish he innovated on the spot. "Never would I dare to offer a thing as . . . as unpresentable." "Well! Then arrange not to let it be seen." ("Tourne le dos," "turn the [your] back"). Thus was created *Tournedos Rossini*, a medallion of beef filet, sautéed, topped with a slice of goose liver, and served with Périgord sauce.

Périgord sauce (both versions) is typically served with croustades; soft-boiled or poached eggs; poached or shallow-fried poultry; sautéed or fried beef; game; and veal sweetbreads.

Richelieu Sauce

Madeira sauce flavored with a reduction of white wine, fish stock, and truffle essence.

Marengo Sauce

Chicken Marengo (Poulet à la Marengo) is one of the most denigrated dishes in culinary history. Since it is a dish of considerable historical significance, an unspoken mandate requires that it be fashioned as a complete dish, in its original form, and not as a separate sauce.

Chicken Marengo was reputedly created by Dunand, Napoleon Bonaparte's chef, after Bonaparte's defeat of the Austrian army at the Battle of Marengo, on June 14, 1800. It was fashioned out of the only ingredients Dunand could gather—3 eggs, 4 tomatoes, 6 crayfish, a small hen, a little garlic, some oil, a saucepan, a little brandy from the general's flask, and some stale bread. Served on a tin plate, the braised chicken was surrounded by the fried eggs, the crayfish, and the sauce, after which Bonaparte rejoined to Dunand, "You must feed me like this after every battle."

Marigny sauce is believed to be named in honor of the brother of the Marquise (Madame) de Pompadour (1721–1764), mistress of Louis XV.

Marigny Sauce

A strongly tomato-flavored demi-glaze, flavored with mushroom essence, garnished with sliced mushrooms and pitted black olives.

Middle-Class Sauce
(Sauce Bourgeoise)

A style of braising beef, veal, lamb, or poultry, typical of family meals made without a set recipe. The sauce is part of the dish, in this case a white wine flavored demi-glaze, with a garnish of browned diced bacon, olive-shaped carrots, and browned pearl onions.

Milanese Sauce (Sauce Milanaise)

A strongly tomato- and garlic-flavored demi-glaze, garnished with julienned mushrooms sautéed in butter.

Palermo Sauce (Sauce Palermitaine)

Demi-glaze, flavored with a reduction of shallots and a hearty Italian red wine, finished with shallot butter, and garnished with orange zest.

Paprika Sauce (Sauce Paprikás)

A Hungarian-style stew, made with veal or chicken. A large amount of sliced onions are sautéed in butter, the meat is added, generously sprinkled with paprika and a little flour, simmered in stock until tender, then finished with sour cream.

𝒫EPPER SAUCE
(Sauce Poivrade)

1 tablespoon vegetable oil
1 tablespoon bacon, small dice
1 small carrot, peeled and finely chopped
1 small onion, peeled and finely chopped
1 garlic clove, crushed

4 parsley stems, chopped
1 sprig fresh thyme
1 bay leaf
¼ cup white wine vinegar
½ cup dry white wine
1 teaspoon black peppercorns, crushed
1¼ cup demi-glaze

- Sauté the bacon, carrot, and onion in the oil, stirring frequently, until the vegetables are lightly caramelized. Add the garlic and herbs, and sauté another 5 minutes. Add the vinegar and wine, and simmer until reduced by three-fourths. Add the pepper and demi-glaze, and simmer until suitable thickness is achieved. Mount with butter, and strain.

———————— • ————————

Pepper sauce is often served with game, particularly venison. In such a case, the demi-glaze should ideally be made from a brown stock created from the roasted venison bones. Also, since venison is usually marinated for several days before preparing, a portion of the marinade is often reduced with the white wine, or added to the finished sauce for additional flavor.

Pepper sauce is also served with large roasted or braised joints of meat. The following sauces are derivatives of Pepper sauce.

Chief Ranger Sauce (Grand Veneur)

Pepper sauce either simmered with game or venison bones and trimmings, or fortified with a game or venison glaze, then finished with red currant or gooseberry jelly, and heavy cream.

This sauce should technically include a final liaison of the cream, blended with a portion of the animal's blood, which is then tempered into the sauce just before service. This technique is not a very common practice today, however, since it is somewhat vulgar by modern standards, as well as difficult to obtain. The blood must be *very* fresh, and most health statutes forbid its use (it is outlawed in many states) because of its perishability.

This sauce is believed to have been named in honor of Franz Josef, Austrian Emperor (1848–1916) and King of Hungary (1867–1916).

Francis Joseph Sauce (Sauce François Joseph)

Chief Ranger sauce finished with a reduction of champagne.

Diana Sauce (Sauce Diane)

Pepper sauce to which game glaze is added, finished with heavy cream, and garnished with diced hard-cooked egg whites and black truffle.

Ledoyen Sauce

Pepper sauce simmered with the roasted bones and trimmings of game birds, seasoned with orange marmalade, dry mustard, and lemon juice, mounted with butter, and finished with dry sherry.

Muscovite Sauce (Sauce Moscovite)

Pepper sauce to which juniper berries (or an infusion of juniper berries) are added and later strained, garnished with sultanas (golden raisins) and pine nuts, and finished with Marsala or Málaga wine.

Reform Sauce (Sauce Réforme)

Pepper sauce garnished with a julienne of hard-cooked egg whites, mushrooms, ox tongue, and gherkins, and served with lamb or venison cutlets.

Dishes prepared Muscovite style (à la Moscovite) reflect the cooking styles developed by French and European chefs who worked in Russia in the nineteenth century. Muscovite sauce is typically served with all forms of game.

Reform sauce was created by Alexis Soyer (1809–1858) while chef at the Reform Club in London in the 1830s. Soyer was one of the most eccentric and scholarly culinary personalities of his time, and the author of five major books in gastronomic literature, including *The Gastronomic Regenerator* and *The Poor Man's Regenerator*. He served with the British army in the Crimean War; during this time he designed a portable camp kitchen for the army. He also invented a "magic oven," a precursor to the table hotplate (chafing dish). When his wife died, he devoted himself to charitable causes, opening soup kitchens for the underprivileged in Dublin and London. He once entered a competition in the town of Slough, to create "the most novel dish which is as light as possible." The other competitors included two chefs from the Royal Household and the chef to Baroness Rothchild.

When his entry was brought in ("La Croustade Sylphe en Surprise à la Cerito"), and the lid to the croustade was removed, a carrier pigeon flew out, exited through an open window, and headed for London. Where the pigeon had sat was the entire meal—Grouse Salad Bohemian Style, Veal Chop with Mushrooms, and Peaches in Cream. The pigeon arrived in London 24 minutes later. There a group of friends, with whom Soyer had wagered that he could send part of his dish to London nearly as fast as a telegraph, pulled out the message from under the bird's wing, which read: "Please pay the chef de cuisine of the Reform Club the sum of 50 pounds, for my apartment in his new dish."

Reform sauce is typically served with omelettes, game, and lamb.

Roebuck Sauce (Sauce Chevreuil)

A pepper sauce, to which ham trimmings are added with the mirepoix and herbs, flavored with a pinch of cayenne pepper, and finished with Port wine and red currant jelly.

———————————— • ————————————

Roebuck (also roe deer) is a small white-tailed deer, found in Eurasian forests, and considered the most flavorful form of venison. While certain cuts of venison require marinating and braising to make them tender enough for consumption, most cuts of roebuck are tender enough to roast. Roebuck sauce is typically served with game.

————————————————

$\mathcal{P}$IQUANT SAUCE
(Sauce Piquant)

——— • ———

Piquant sauce is typically served with pork; ox tongue; and leftover grilled, roasted, or boiled beef.

————————

1 shallot, minced
½ cup dry white wine
½ cup white wine vinegar
1¼ cup demi-glaze
1 tablespoon parsley, minced

1 tablespoon tarragon, minced
2 tablespoons sour gherkins, finely diced

- Simmer the shallot with the wine and vinegar, until reduced by three-fourths. Add the demi-glaze, and simmer until suitable thickness is achieved. Add the herbs and gherkins.

$\mathcal{P}$OOR MAN'S SAUCE
(Sauce Pauvre Homme)

1 tablespoon butter or vegetable oil
¼ cup bread crumbs from stale bread
¼ cup red wine vinegar

1 shallot, minced
1 cup brown stock
1 teaspoon meat glaze
1 tablespoon parsley, minced
1 tablespoon chives, minced

- Brown the bread crumbs lightly in the butter. Add the vinegar and shallot, and simmer until reduced by half. Add the stock and glaze, and simmer until suitable thickness is achieved. Add the chopped herbs.

————————————— • —————————————

Any dish done in "poor man's style" is an improvised mixture of leftovers, illustrated in this sauce by the use of stale bread as a thickening agent. Poor Man's sauce is typically served with boiled beef or heavy game (boar, roebuck, venison, etc.).

_____

𝒫ORT WINE SAUCE
(Sauce au Porto)

——— • ———

Port is a fortified wine made from grapes grown in the Alto Douro, a mountainous region in northern Portugal. Port wine sauce is typically served with game birds.

1 shallot, minced
1 sprig thyme
1 bay leaf
¾ cup Port wine

juice and zest of 1 lemon
    and 1 orange
1¼ cups demi-glaze

• Simmer the shallot, thyme, bay leaf, Port, zest, and juice until reduced by three-fourths. Add the demi-glaze, and simmer until suitable thickness is achieved. Strain, and serve with wild duck.

Yorkshire Sauce

Port wine sauce flavored with currant jelly and garnished with orange julienne.

𝒫ORTUGAL SAUCE
(Sauce Portuguese)

2 tablespoons olive oil
1 small onion, finely diced
2 garlic cloves, pressed
½ cup tomato purée

1 cup demi-glaze
2 tablespoons parsley,
    chopped

• Sauté the onions in the olive oil for 5 minutes. Add the garlic and sauté another minute or two. Add the tomato and demi-glaze, and simmer until suitable thickness is achieved. Garnish with the chopped parsley.

This sauce is nearly identical to Provençale sauce, though a dish "Provence style" is more common than a separate sauce by the same name. All culinary dishes from regions bordering the Mediterranean tend to include ingredients indigenous to that region. Thus the foods of Portugal, southern Spain and France, Italy, Greece, and Turkey, as well as the countries of Northern Africa, will include tomato, olives and olive oil, garlic, Mediterranean fish, and so on.

Portugal sauce is typically served with baked or braised fish; soft-boiled or poached eggs; sautéed meat; grilled or fried kidneys; and sautéed poultry.

Provence Sauce (Sauce Provençale)

A strongly tomato- and garlic-flavored demi-glaze, garnished with diced tomatoes.

Musketeer Sauce (Sauce Mousquetaire)

Provence sauce garnished with chopped tarragon and parsley.

Regency Sauce (Sauce Régence)

Demi-glaze flavored with a reduction of Rhine wine, mirepoix, and truffle peelings, then strained.

Richelieu Sauce

Demi-glaze flavored with a white wine, chicken stock, and truffle essence reduction, finished with Madeira wine.

Provence sauce is typically served with soft-boiled or poached eggs; braised poultry; and sautéed or fried meat.

This version of Regency sauce can be served with sweetbreads, and large roasted or braised joints of meat (see Regency Sauce under Velouté).

Richelieu sauce is typically served with rice, and large roasted or braised joints of meat (see Richelieu Sauce under Tomato Sauces).

𝓡OBERT SAUCE

1 tablespoon unsalted butter	½ cup white wine vinegar
1 small onion, finely chopped	1¼ cups demi-glaze
½ cup dry white wine	2 tablespoon Dijon-style mustard

- Sauté the onions in the butter. Add the white wine and vinegar, and simmer until reduced by three-fourths. Add the

Robert sauce is typically served with boiled beef, pork, and grilled meat.

demi-glaze, and simmer until suitable thickness is achieved. Finish with mustard, and serve with any pork dish.

Butcher Sauce (Sauce Charcutière)

Robert sauce garnished with julienned sour gherkins.

....

ℛOMAN SAUCE
(Sauce Romaine)

2 tablespoons sugar
1 tablespoon water
¼ cup white wine vinegar
½ cup venison or game stock
1¼ cups demi-glaze

1 tablespoon sultanas
  (golden raisins)
1 tablespoon dried currants
1 tablespoon pine nuts,
  toasted

- Simmer the sugar and water, stirring continuously, until the sugar turns light brown. Add the vinegar and stock, and simmer until reduced by three-fourths. Add the demi-glaze, and simmer until suitable thickness is achieved. Add the sultanas, currants, and pine nuts, and serve with venison.

Ruby Sauce (Sauce Rubis)

Demi-glaze fortified with game glaze, flavored with a reduction of Port wine and the juice of blood orange, and served with feathered game.

Sage Sauce (Sauce à la Sauge)

Demi-glaze flavored with a reduction of sage and white wine, garnished with minced sage leaves.

Sailor Sauce (Sauce Matelote)

Demi-glaze flavored with a reduction of red or white wine, fish stock or fish trimmings, and cayenne pepper, and mounted with butter.

———————— • ————————

Matelote is a loose term referring to a fish stew, technically made with any variety of freshwater fish—often eel,

Roman sauce is typically served with ox tongue, light meats, and game.

———— • ————

A blood orange is a small, sweet variety of orange, with a slightly rough-textured skin and a bright red flesh and juice.

———— • ————

Sage sauce is typically served with pork and goose.

but also of barbel, carp, small pike, shad, trout, etc. The Normandy style matelote is made with sea fish, often brill, conger eel, turbot, etc. The dish is usually garnished with pearl onions, mushrooms, bacon, and buttered croutons rubbed with garlic.

Salmis Sauce

A salmis is technically a game stew, made with virtually any variety of game leftover from a previous service. The word is an abbreviation of *salmagundi*, referring to a salad of chopped meat, vegetables, anchovies, eggs, and onions, arranged in rows on a bed of lettuce, served with oil and vinegar. It also refers to "type of ragoût made from various cooked meats, reheated in a sauce."

Sherry Sauce (Sauce au Xerès)

Demi-glaze flavored with dry or medium-dry sherry.

Sherry sauce is typically served with croustades; braised poultry; ham; sautéed or fried meat; and sautéed, pan-fried, or deep-fried offal.

Sicilian Sauce (Sauce Sicilienne)

Demi-glaze flavored with game glaze, or a reduction game stock, finished with Marsala wine, served with a garnish of fried onion rings.

Solferino Sauce

A light meat glaze, flavored with tomato purée, cayenne pepper, and lemon juice, and mounted with Montpelier (an herb and shallot) butter.

This sorrel sauce is typically served with a Veal Fricandeau (a type of veal roast).

Sorrel Sauce (Sauce à l'Oseille)

Demi-glaze garnished with a chiffonade of sorrel leaves sautéed in butter.

Stragotte Sauce

A game demi-glaze flavored with a reduction of mirepoix, herbs, tomato purée, game trimmings, red or white wine, mounted with butter, garnished with mushrooms, and finished with Madeira wine.

Sultan Sauce (Sauce Sultane)

Game demi-glaze, finished with Port wine, and garnished with sultanas (golden raisins).

Tarragon Sauce (Sauce à l'Estragon)

Demi-glaze flavored with a reduction of shallots and chopped tarragon, strained, and garnished with minced tarragon leaves.

Turtle Sauce (Sauce à la Tortue)

Demi-glaze flavored with a reduction of white wine with turtle herbs, flavored with truffle essence, cayenne pepper, and Madeira.

———— • ————

Tarragon sauce is typically served with soft-boiled or poached eggs; veal sweetbreads; and sautéed or fried meat.

Turtle herbs are the aromatic herbs—basil, chervil, fennel, marjoram, and savory—traditionally used to season turtle soup and mock turtle soup (made with a calf's head instead of a turtle). Turtle sauce is also served with poached and braised calf's head.

Wine Merchant Sauce (Sauce Marchand de Vin)

Demi-glaze flavored with a shallot and red wine reduction, mounted with butter.

———— • ————

Wine Merchant sauce is typically served with grilled and roasted meat.

Valeria Sauce

A Wine Merchant sauce flavored with mustard, and garnished with grated horseradish and chopped chervil.

Zouave Sauce

A strongly tomato-flavored demi-glaze flavored with mustard and garlic, and garnished with chopped tarragon.

———— • ————

Zouave comes from the Algerian tribal name *zwawa*, and refers to a French infantry unit, originally composed of Algerian recruits.

CONTEMPORARY INNOVATIONS

⨍OUR PEPPERCORN SAUCE

2 tablespoons unsalted butter
1 tablespoon green
   peppercorns, mashed
1 tablespoon each black,
   white, and pink
   peppercorns, crushed

2 shallots, minced
1 cup demi-glaze
1½ cups heavy cream
salt to taste

- Sauté the peppercorns and shallot in the butter for 3 or 4 minutes. Add the demi-glaze and cream, and simmer until reduced by half, or until suitable thickness is achieved. Season to taste with salt.

This sauce accompanies "Filet Mignon," as seen in *The Pillar House Cookbook.*

Different varieties of pepper are all variations of the same berry, produced on a climbing vine native to India and Indonesia. Black pepper is picked green, then "fermented" in the sun, drying the berries, which develops a more pungent flavor. The blackening is caused by a fungus, present even in healthy berries. White pepper is produced by allowing the berries to mature to their red stage, soaking them in salt water, then rubbing off the outer skin.

ℐINOT NOIR SAUCE

1 small shallot, minced
½ tablespoon unsalted butter
1 tablespoon fresh tarragon
   leaves, minced
2 tablespoons Pernod

½ cup Pinot Noir
1 cup beef stock
1 small bay leaf
1 teaspoon cornstarch
2 teaspoons cold water

- Sauté the shallot in the butter for 4 or 5 minutes. Add the tarragon, Pernod, and wine. Simmer until reduced by one-third. Add the stock and bay leaf, and reduce by half.
- Dissolve the cornstarch in the water. Add it to the sauce, and simmer briefly until the sauce has thickened. Strain and set aside, keeping warm until ready to serve.

This sauce accompanies "Rack of Lamb," as seen in *A Taste For All Seasons.*

RASPBERRY-GINGER SAUCE

1 shallot, minced
2 tablespoons unsalted butter
2 tablespoons brown sugar
½ pint raspberries
2 tablespoons raspberry
   vinegar
¼ cup brandy

2 tablespoons chambord
1½ cups rich duck stock
1 bay leaf
1 sprig thyme, chopped
6 parsley stems, chopped
1 teaspoon ginger root,
   grated

———— • ————

This sauce accompanies
"Roast Breast of Nantucket
Duckling," as seen in *The
Pillar House Cookbook*.

- Sauté the shallot in the butter, over low heat, covered, for 5 minutes. Add the sugar and lightly caramelize. Add the raspberries and mash with a fork. Add the remaining ingredients and simmer, until reduced by half, or until the sauce reaches the suitable viscosity. Strain, and set aside, keeping warm until ready to serve.

BREAST OF DUCK
WITH RASPBERRY-TANGERINE SAUCE

1 tablespoon cracked black
   pepper
½ teaspoon salt
4 boneless duck breasts, skin
   on
3 cups dry vermouth
1 tablespoon butter
2 large shallots, minced
3¼ cups fresh raspberries (or
   frozen dry-pack)

juice of 2 tangerines
1 cup demi-glaze
2 tablespoons unsalted
   butter, cut into ¼-inch
   cubes
salt and black pepper to taste
3 tangerines, peeled, seeded,
   and trimmed of pith and
   membranes
1 bunch watercress

- Rub the salt and cracked pepper into the duck breasts. Place in a bowl along with the vermouth. Cover and refrigerate for 24 hours.

- Preheat oven to the lowest possible setting.

- Place a cast-iron skillet or sauté pan over a medium flame, and allow it to become very hot. Remove the breasts from the vermouth, reserve the marinade, and pat them dry. Carefully place them into the skillet, skin side down, and cook over medium heat for 5 minutes, or until the skin is very dark brown. Turn them over, and cook for 1 minute more. Remove to a serving platter, and place into the oven to stay warm.

- Pour off and discard the excess fat from the skillet. Add the butter, and sauté the shallots for 3 minutes. Add 2 cups of the raspberries, and mash them with a fork. Add the tangerine juice and ¼ cup of the vermouth marinade, and stir to loosen any caramelized particles in the pan. Simmer until reduced by two-thirds.

- Add the demi-glaze, and simmer for several minutes. Mount with butter, and season to taste with salt and pepper.

- Strain the sauce through a sieve. Set aside 12 raspberries and 8 trimmed tangerine segments, and add the remaining berries and segments to the sauce.

- Cut the breasts into thin slices, on a slight angle across their widths. Arrange the slices on 4 serving plates. Top each serving with 2 ounces of sauce, and garnish with 3 raspberries, 2 tangerine segments, and fresh watercress.

——— • ———

This recipe is borrowed with permission from A Taste For All Seasons.

———————

ℛOASTED PORK LOIN, TEQUILA SAUCE

¼ cup fresh sage leaves, minced	2 garlic cloves, pressed
¼ cup fresh basil leaves, minced	¼ cup tequila, warm
2 tablespoons fresh oregano leaves, minced	2 tablespoons honey
	1 teaspoon salt
	½ teaspoon black pepper
2 tablespoons fresh thyme leaves, minced	1 boneless pork loin, tied
1 tablespoon chili powder	½ cup olive oil
1 teaspoon ground cumin	1 shallot, minced
½ teaspoon ground cloves	½ cup mirepoix, finely chopped
¼ teaspoon freshly ground nutmeg	1 cup tequila
	1½ cup demi-glaze
	2 tablespoons tomato purée

- Preheat oven to 325°F.
- Combine the herbs, spices, garlic, tequila, honey, and salt in a bowl, and blend thoroughly into a paste. Rub this paste vigorously into the exterior of the pork loin.

- Heat the oil in a sauté pan until it begins to smoke. Sauté the loin, until golden brown on all sides. Remove and set aside. Add the shallot and mirepoix, and sauté several minutes.
- Spread the shallot and mirepoix on a roasting pan and place the pork loin on top. Roast for 45 minutes, turning the roast every 10 minutes.
- Set the pork loin aside. Deglaze the roasting pan with the tequila, then transfer this mixture to a saucepan. Simmer until reduced by two-thirds. Add the demi-glaze and tomato purée, and continue simmering until desired thickness is achieved. Adjust seasoning with salt and pepper, strain, and serve with the sliced pork loin.

———————————— • ————————————

This recipe is a creation of James Daw, a former student of the author's, at Los Medanos College, Pittsburg, California. Mr. Daw suggests that if only dried herbs are available, they should be toasted in a hot sauté pan, covered, for 5 minutes, before being made into a paste.

$\mathcal{Z}$INFANDEL-MOREL SAUCE

2 tablespoons unsalted butter
¼ cup each minced onion, celery, carrot, and leek
1 shallot, minced
1 garlic clove, pressed
1 sprig fresh thyme, chopped
3 sprigs fresh oregano, chopped
1 bay leaf

½ cup zinfandel wine
1½ cups demi-glaze
1 cup morel mushrooms
1 teaspoon unsalted butter
3 tablespoons unsalted butter, cut into ¼-inch cubes
salt and black pepper to taste

- Sauté the mirepoix, leek, and shallot in the butter, until the vegetables begin to caramelize (lightly brown). Add the garlic and herbs, and sauté another minute.
- Add the zinfandel, and reduce until nearly dry.
- Add the demi-glaze, and simmer 10 minutes. Strain, season with salt and pepper, and return to the fire.
- Sauté the morels in one teaspoon of butter, then add them to the sauce. Mount with the remaining butter, and serve.

——— • ———

This sauce accompanies "Filet Mignon," as seen in *The Pillar House Cookbook*.

If fresh morels are unavailable, we suggest substituting another variety of wild mushroom (shiitake, chanterelle, oyster, etc.). Fresh mushrooms are always superior to dried or canned.

Zinfandel is a robust dry red wine unique to California. It is believed to be a hybrid developed by Italian immigrants to the Pacific coast, in the mid-nineteenth century.

CHAPTER 7

BLOND SAUCES

Sauce Velouté

*V*elouté (literally "velvet") is a very light tan-tinted sauce, fashioned from a chicken, fish, or veal stock, thickened with a white or light brown roux. Carême's original béchamel was actually a velouté finished with heavy cream, which is why velouté, as well as béchamel, are both occasionally referred to as *white sauce*. In Escoffier's later modification of the sauce system, béchamel and velouté each represented a separate classification.

Blond sauce derives its color, and hence its common name, from both the stock and the light brown roux. Velouté can, however, be thickened with a white roux, taking its color from chicken, fish, or veal stock, which naturally have some color to them. Using a light brown roux simply adds more color.

Certain veloutés are specifically designed to accompany certain dishes, and their recipes indicate a specific stock, such as Sauces American (fish stock, for lobster), Bontemps (chicken stock, for grilled meat), Joinville (fish stock, and for fish), and Mariner's (fish stock, for mussels). In other velouté sauce derivatives, the stock is generic, meaning that that sauce can be made with chicken, fish, or veal stock, depending on its application. Examples of this are Aurore, Cucumber, German, and Suprême sauces.

———————————— • ————————————

Velouté is also a traditional classification of soup (potage velouté), though there are some distinct differences between the sauce and the soup. The base of velouté is generally the same for both, but when used to create a velvet soup: (1) it includes a purée of the primary ingredient (poultry, game, fish, or vegetable), and (2) it is finished with an egg yolk and cream liaison. Velouté soups can also be thickened with dried beans, potatoes, rice, tapioca, and the like.

As for the difference in viscosity between the soup and the sauce, a velouté soup will be slightly thicker than a velouté sauce, though such decisions are strictly a matter of personal style. Typical velvet soups are Potage Velouté Excelsior (asparagus), Potage Velouté d'Artichaut (artichoke), Potage Velouté de Victoria (fish), Potage Velouté de Cherville (rabbit), and Potage Velouté à la Bretonne (lobster).

Sauce Matrix II
Velouté and Its Derivatives

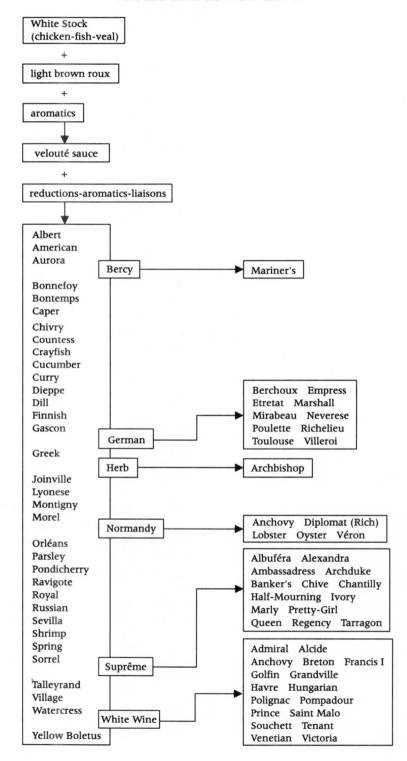

White Stock
(chicken-fish-veal)

+

light brown roux

+

aromatics

velouté sauce

+

reductions-aromatics-liaisons

Albert
American
Aurora

Bonnefoy
Bontemps
Caper

Chivry
Countess
Crayfish
Cucumber
Curry
Dieppe
Dill
Finnish
Gascon

Greek

Joinville
Lyonese
Montigny
Morel

Orléans
Parsley
Pondicherry
Ravigote
Royal
Russian
Sevilla
Shrimp
Spring
Sorrel

Talleyrand
Village
Watercress

Yellow Boletus

Bercy → Mariner's

German →
Berchoux Empress
Etretat Marshall
Mirabeau Neverese
Poulette Richelieu
Toulouse Villeroi

Herb → Archbishop

Normandy →
Anchovy Diplomat (Rich)
Lobster Oyster Véron

Suprême →
Albuféra Alexandra
Ambassadress Archduke
Banker's Chive Chantilly
Half-Mourning Ivory
Marly Pretty-Girl
Queen Regency Tarragon

White Wine →
Admiral Alcide
Anchovy Breton Francis I
Golfin Grandville
Havre Hungarian
Polignac Pompadour
Prince Saint Malo
Souchett Tenant
Venetian Victoria

Basic Velouté Sauce

1 gallon rich white chicken,
    fish, or veal stock (hot)
½ cup unsalted butter,
    clarified
1 cup all-purpose flour
½ cup mirepoix, finely
    chopped

6 parsley stems, finely
    chopped
2 sprigs thyme
1 bay leaf
salt and white pepper to taste

- Sauté the mirepoix in the butter, in a six-quart heavy-gauge saucepan, for about 5 minutes. Add the flour, and blend thoroughly. Continue cooking over medium heat, stirring continuously, until the roux turns light brown.

- Remove this mixture to a large bowl. Add about half of the hot stock, and blend in thoroughly. Return this mixture to the saucepan, and add the remaining stock, blending thoroughly. Add parsley stems, thyme, and bay leaf, and simmer for 1 hour, skimming impurities regularly. Season to taste with salt and pepper. Strain, cool, cover, label, and refrigerate.

Velouté can also be prepared as a flourless sauce. The mirepoix should be sautéed in a small amount of butter, then combined with the stock and other aromatics. It is then simmered and strained repeatedly, similar to the way that a flourless demi-glaze is prepared. Since many velouté small sauces are finished with cream reductions, cream and egg yolk liaisons, butter montées, etc., this adds sufficient body to create a final sauce.

TRADITIONAL DERIVATIVES OF VELOUTÉ SAUCE

Albert Sauce

1 cup white veal or chicken
    stock
2 tablespoons lemon juice

1 tablespoon Dijon-style
    prepared mustard
½ cup fresh white bread
    crumbs

½ cup heavy cream
2 egg yolks
2 tablespoons unsalted butter,
　cut into ¼-inch cubes

2 tablespoons prepared
　horseradish, squeezed dry
salt and white pepper to taste

- Simmer the stock, lemon juice, mustard, and bread crumbs for 15 minutes. Whip the cream and yolks in a small bowl, and slowly pour in the hot liquid, while whipping continuously. Return to the heat, and bring to a simmer, still stirring continuously. Mount with the butter, add the horseradish, and season to taste with salt and pepper.

Technically speaking, Albert sauce is a variation of English butter sauce, also called bastard sauce (sauce bâtarde). It is a rather tasteless concoction, consisting of water thickened with white roux or bread crumbs, beaten with butter, and finished with a cream and egg yolk liaison. (Is this sauce not a reflection of French disdain for the bland and unsophisticated nature of English cuisine?) When made with a stock, however, it is considerably more flavorful, and the mustard, lemon, and horseradish add to its depth. It is typically served with roast beef, or other larger roasted cuts of meat.

American Sauce
(Sauce Américaine)

American sauce can be served as a separate sauce, but it is best known as an integral part of a lobster dish of the same name.

*L*OBSTER AMERICAN
(Homard à l'Américaine)

2 1¼- to 1½-pound lobsters
3 tablespoons olive oil
1 shallot, minced
1 garlic clove, minced
¼ cup onion, finely chopped
¼ cup carrot, peeled and
　finely chopped

¼ cup Cognac
¼ cup dry vermouth
2 cups fish stock
¼ cup tomato purée
2 sprigs thyme
1 sprig tarragon
1 bay leaf

1. *Tearing the lobster tail from the body.*

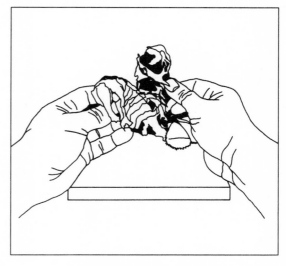

2. *Pulling the tail shell away,
and sliding out the meat.*

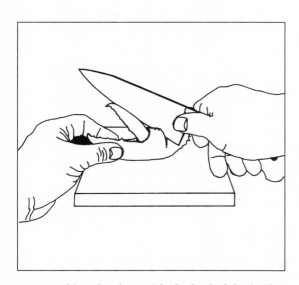

3. *Cracking the claw with the heel of the knife.*

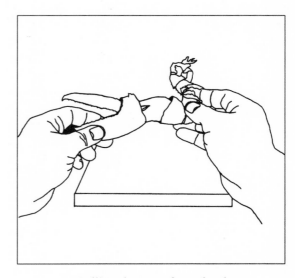

4. *Pulling the meat from the claw.*

6 parsley stems, chopped
4 tablespoons beurre manié
   (2 tablespoons unsalted
   softened butter, kneaded
   with 2 heaping
tablespoons all-purpose
   flour)
½ cup cream
salt and white pepper to taste

- Place the lobster on a cutting board atop a pan to collect any juices. With the point of a cook's knife, make an incision into the center of the back of the head, at a point about an inch below the eyes. (This stuns the lobster, to spare the creature—and the cook's conscience—excessive discomfort.) Tear the tail from the main body and cut it lengthwise in two. Carefully remove the tomalley (the crustacean's liver, identified by its dark green color) from the main body, and the coral (also green) from inside the tail, just under the shell, at the end where it was separated from the body. Press these through a fine sieve, blend with the heavy cream, and refrigerate.

  Cut the body up into 6 to 8 pieces. Remove the claws and arms, and gently crack them with the heel of a knife. Reserve any juice collected in the pan.

- Heat the oil in a large saucepan, sprinkle the lobster pieces with salt and pepper, and sauté for several minutes on all sides, until they turn dark red. Remove the lobster pieces and carefully pull out the meat from the claws, arms, and tail. Cut the meat into ½-inch pieces, place onto a serving platter, cover, and set aside. Crack the remaining shells into smaller pieces and return to the pan along with the shallot, garlic, onion, and carrot. Sauté for 5 minutes, stirring continuously. Add the Cognac, and ignite. Extinguish with the vermouth, then add the fish stock, tomato purée, and herbs. Simmer until reduced by half.

- Pour some of the remaining liquid into a bowl, and blend in the beurre manié until smooth. Return to the pan, blend well, and simmer for 15 minutes. Strain through a large-holed sieve or china cap, pounding the solid ingredients to extract as much liquid as possible. Strain again through a fine sieve, then return to the fire.

- Temper in the tomalley, coral, and cream mixture by placing it into a small bowl and slowly pouring in about half of the sauce, while stirring continuously. Return this mixture to the pan, add the lobster meat, bring to a simmer, and adjust seasoning.

It has been suggested that Lobster à l'Américaine is a misnamed Lobster à l'Armoricaine, originating in Brittany, and so named for the Armorican massif, a mountain mass in the northwesternmost region of France. Brittany is well known for many lobster dishes, given its proximity to the North Atlantic. A conflict arises, however, since Brittany is not known for tomatoes, and until the nineteenth century, tomatoes were scarcely known outside of the Mediterranean region. All versions of this dish, however, do include tomatoes, garlic, and olive oil, giving credence to Jules Gouffé's name for this dish—Lobster à la Provençale—as seen in his *Le Livre de Cuisine*, published in 1867. Provence, a region of France located on the Mediterranean coast, and a region of considerable gastronomic esteem, is known for an abundant use of tomato, garlic, and olive oil.

In 1854, Pierre Fraisse opened a restaurant in Paris, after having lived in the United States for a period. Originally named Peter's, and later renamed Noël Peter's after Fraise took on a partner, Noël Peter's was quite a celebrated dining establishment, frequented by many notable writers and journalists. Fraise introduced dishes from the United States that were unknown in France then, such as turtle soup and roast beef sliced at the table to the customer's specifications. (He also pioneered the marketing concept of offering a *plat du jour,* a daily special for each day of the week.) About 1860, M. Reculet, the chef at Noël Peter's, supposedly created a dish entitled Homard à l'Americaine (Lobster American) for a distinguished American diner at that establishment.

August Escoffier, however, contended that an unnamed cook created Langouste de la Mediterranée at Le Restaurant Français in Nice, then exported the Provence-style dish to the United States when he opened a restaurant there by the same name. It was then re-imported to France with the new name, Lobster à l'Americaine.

American sauce is typically served with soft-boiled or poached eggs; braised or baked fish; and shellfish.

Aurora Sauce (Sauce Aurore)

Chicken, fish, or veal velouté, flavored with tomato purée, and mounted with butter.

Aurore is a French word meaning daybreak or morning. The bright red color of aurora sauce is an imitation of the color of a bright red sky often seen at sunrise.

Aurora sauce is typically served with hard-boiled eggs (served hot); soft-boiled or poached eggs; quenelles; poached or sautéed poultry and light meats.

BERCY SAUCE

Bercy is a district in Paris that once boasted the largest wine market in Europe. Dishes qualified with the name Bercy generally include a wine and shallot reduction, and the addition of beef marrow.

1 shallot, minced	2 tablespoons unsalted
½ cup dry white wine	butter, cut into ½-inch
½ cup fish stock	cubes
1 cup fish velouté	2 tablespoons parsley,
	minced

- Simmer the shallot, white wine, and stock until reduced by three-fourths. Add the velouté, and simmer until suitable thickness is achieved. Mount with butter and add the parsley. Serve with poached fish.

Mariner's Sauce (Sauce Marinière)

Mariner's sauce is typically served with croustades or mussels.

Bercy sauce made with the addition of mussel stock to the reduction of fish stock and wine, garnished with poached mussels.

BONNEFOY SAUCE

This version of Bonnefoy sauce is a variation of a brown sauce of the same name, also made with a white wine reduction.

1 shallot, minced	1 cup fish velouté
1 cup dry white wine	2 tablespoons unsalted
1 sprig thyme	butter, cut into ¼-inch
1 bay leaf	cubes
¼ teaspoon white	1 tablespoon tarragon
peppercorns, crushed	leaves, minced

- Simmer the shallot, wine, thyme, bay leaf, and peppercorns until reduced by three-fourths. Add the velouté, and simmer until desired thickness is achieved. Mount with the butter, and adjust the seasoning with salt and pepper. Strain, then add the tarragon.

$\mathcal{B}$ONTEMPS SAUCE

1 tablespoon unsalted butter
2 tablespoons Spanish
   onion, minced
⅛ teaspoon paprika
1 tablespoon Dijon-style
   mustard
¾ cup apple cider

1 cup chicken velouté
3 tablespoons unsalted
   butter, cut into ¼-inch
   cubes
salt and white pepper to
   taste

- Sauté the onion in the butter for several minutes. Add the paprika, mustard, and cider. Simmer until reduced by three-fourths.
- Add the velouté and continue simmering until suitable thickness is achieved. Add the butter, and stir until thoroughly emulsified. Strain, season to taste, and serve with grilled meat or poultry.

Bontemps sauce is typically served with grilled poultry or meat.

Caper Sauce (Sauce aux Câpres)

Velouté garnished with capers.

$\mathcal{C}$HIVRY SAUCE

1 shallot, minced
1 cup dry white wine
1 tablespoon tarragon
   leaves, minced
1 tablespoon chervil (or
   parsley), minced

1 cup chicken velouté
3 tablespoons chivry butter
salt and white pepper to
   taste

- Simmer the shallot, wine, and herbs until reduced by three-fourths. Add the velouté and simmer until desired thickness is achieved. Mount with the chivry butter, adjust seasoning, and strain.

Chivry sauce is typically served with soft-boiled or poached eggs and poached or sautéed poultry.

Countess Sauce (Sauce Comtesse)

Fish velouté flavored with lemon juice, mounted with anchovy butter.

CRAYFISH SAUCE
(Sauce aux Écrevisses)

10–12 crayfish
1 shallot, minced
1 sprig thyme, 1 sprig
 tarragon, 6 parsley stems,
 and 1 bay leaf, tied
 together in a bundle

1½ cups champagne
1 cup fish velouté
1 teaspoon fish glaze
2 tablespoons crayfish
 butter, cut into ¼-inch
 cubes

- Simmer the crayfish, shallot, bouquet garni, and champagne, covered, for about 5 minutes. Remove the crayfish with a slotted spoon and set aside.

- Remove the meat from the crayfish tails and set aside. Chop up the remaining shells and carcasses and return to the liquid. Continue simmering the liquid until reduced by three-fourths. Strain, discarding the solids. Return this liquid to the saucepan, along with the velouté and glaze, and simmer until suitable thickness is achieved. Mount the sauce with the butter, and adjust seasoning. Add the crayfish tails.

Crayfish are a freshwater crustacean found throughout the United States, Scandinavia, Europe, Australia, and New Zealand. The Mississippi Delta variety, the most celebrated North American variety in modern times, is also one of the smallest varieties, averaging 3 inches in length. A Tasmanian variety has been recorded at 16 inches in length, weighing 8 pounds, though the average length is 3 to 6 inches. In the United States, they are also variously dubbed crawfish, crawdads, bay crabs, freshwater lobsters—and in Louisiana, creekcrabs, yabbies, and mudbugs. Sadly, water pollution as well as overconsumption has seriously depleted what was once an abundant source of seafood. The town of Breaux Bridge, Louisiana (population 5,000) was designated "The Crawfish Capital of the World" by the state legislature, though most classic crayfish dishes are qualified by "Nantua," the French town most identified with the crustacean (see Nantua Sauce under Béchamel).

Crayfish sauce is typically served with braised or poached fish.

Cucumber Sauce
(Sauce aux Concombres)

Velouté flavored with aniseed, garnished with julienned or sliced, fresh or pickled cucumbers and parsley.

———————————— • ————————————

Doria is a classical style of preparing fish and chicken, a throwback to the Doria's of Genoa, regular patrons at Paris's celebrated Café Anglais in the nineteenth century. The Doria garnish generally includes the colors green (cucumber, often as small turned ovals), white (white truffle or mushroom), and red (cockscombs or pimento), reflecting the colors of the Italian flag.

CURRY SAUCE
(Sauce à l'Indienne)

1 tablespoon unsalted butter
¼ cup mirepoix, finely chopped
1 clove garlic, crushed
½ banana, roughly chopped
½ Granny Smith apple, cored, and roughly chopped
1 tablespoon ginger root, grated
1 sprig thyme
1 dried hot red chile pepper
2 tablespoons imported curry powder
2 cups chicken or fish velouté (depending on its use)

- Sauté the mirepoix and garlic in the butter for 5 minutes. Add the fruit, ginger, thyme, chile, and curry powder, and sauté another 3 minutes. Add the velouté and simmer for 30 minutes, skimming frequently.
- Remove the sauce to a blender or food processor and purée. Strain through a fine sieve. Adjust the seasoning with salt, pepper, and glaze.

Curry is a blend of as few as 10 to as many as 30 different herbs and spices, whose origin is intimately connected with the history of the Mediterranean and Middle East. The merchants from ancient nations who traveled across oceans and deserts to access the Indian spice trade effectively transplanted spices indigenous to their homes to the foreign spice market. Among these were fenugreek, cumin, and mustard from Arabia; saffron from the Mediterranean coasts, successfully transplanted to Kashmir; and chile pepper from Portugal, via the Caribbean.

Within India (a nation of 15 major languages and 1,600 dialects) curry blends vary as much as tomato sauces among the families of Sicily, or barbecue marinades in the regions of southeastern United States. Among the herbs and spices used in curry blends are: anise, cardamon, chile pepper, cinnamon, clove, coriander (seed and leaf), cumin, fennel (seed and root), fenugreek, garlic, ginger, lemon grass, mace, mustard, nutmeg, onion, saffron, tamarind, and turmeric.

The recipe here is not a typical curry sauce, but one developed from many variations seen in many kitchens. It is designed to be used as a basic sauce, from which a dish of curry is then made. This velouté derivative works well when creating a curry dish with foods such as shrimp, lobster, chicken, or vegetable. When preparing curries using heavier foods, such as beef, lamb, or mutton, this recipe can be used, substituting demi-glaze for the velouté, and adding tomato purée and a higher level of spice.

Curry sauce can be served with virtually any food, including poached eggs, omelettes, offal, seafood, poultry, beef, pork, lamb, vegetables, and starches.

*L*ES CREVETTES SAUTÉ À L'INDIENNE, D'AUTEUR
(Shrimp Curry, in the Style of the Author)

1 tablespoon butter
6 U-10 shrimp, peeled and deveined
¼ cup dry vermouth

½ cup basic curry sauce (made with fish stock)
¼ cup heavy cream
1 tablespoon curry butter

- Sauté the shrimp in the butter for 2 minutes. Remove the shrimp, and deglaze the pan with the vermouth. Simmer until reduced by half, then add the velouté and cream. Simmer until reduced to desired thickness, and mount with curry butter.

- Return the shrimp to the sauce, and simmer another minute. Serve with plain boiled Basmati, Texmati, or Thai rice, pressed into a decorative mold, then inverted onto a large platter. Surround the rice with the curried shrimp. Serve a number of condiments, in individual ramekins: chopped toasted cashews, cilantro chutney, mango chutney, diced, peeled, and seeded cucumber, tzakiki, dried currants, sultanas, plain yogurt, chopped hard-boiled egg whites and egg yolks, pickled red cabbage, keem chee, etc. (see Accompaniments).

Dieppe Sauce (Sauce Dieppoise)

Fish velouté mounted with shrimp butter.

Dishes prepared in the style of Dieppe (à la Dieppoise), reflect the excellent sole found in the waters around the port town of Dieppe, in northwestern France. The sauce is made with a reduction of the wine in which the fish (sole, whiting, or brill are commonly used) is cooked, garnished with mussels, shrimp, and mushrooms.

Dill Sauce (Sauce à l'Aneth)

Fish velouté (usually, since it is often served with fish), seasoned with lemon juice, garnished with chopped dill.

Finnish Sauce (Sauce Finnoise)

Chicken velouté seasoned with paprika, garnished with julienne of green peppers and chopped herbs.

Gascon Sauce (Sauce Gascogne)

Velouté flavored with a reduction of white wine and herbs, mounted with a small amount of anchovy butter.

. . . . # *G*ERMAN SAUCE
(Sauce Allemande)

1 shallot, minced	⅛ teaspoon freshly grated
3 mushrooms, finely	nutmeg
chopped	1 egg yolk
½ cup chicken (or fish) stock	½ cup heavy cream
1 tablespoon lemon juice	salt and white pepper to taste
1 cup chicken (or fish)	
velouté	

- Simmer the shallot, mushrooms, stock, and lemon juice until reduced by three-fourths. Add the velouté and nutmeg, and simmer about 5 minutes. Strain.
- Whip the egg yolk with the cream in a bowl. Add the sauce slowly, while stirring continuously. Return to the pan, bring to a simmer, and season to taste.

———————————— • ————————————

According to Raymond Oliver, German sauce can be found as early as 1739, in a *Les Dons de Comus*, though the recipe in this work has little resemblance to the contemporary version. There is also a history of a trend to alter the name of this sauce, dating to the Franco-Prussian War of 1870, and continuing right through World War I. August Escoffier, perhaps by virtue of hostile feelings toward Germany, proposed changing the name of this sauce to Sauce Parisienne or simply Sauce Blonde. It is interesting to note that none of these terms—Allemande, German, or Parisienne—are listed in the index of the 1969 edition of *The Escoffier Cookbook* (the modern version of Escoffier's *Guide Culinaire*), though Allemande is included within the text, with the English equivalent of "Thickened Velouté."

German sauce is typically served with croustades; boiled vegetables; hard-boiled eggs (served hot); braised, pan-fried, or deep-fried offal; poached or pan-fried poultry. The following compound sauces employ German sauce as their base.

———————————————————————————

Berchoux Sauce

German sauce mounted with herb butter.

Empress Sauce (Sauce Impératrice)

German sauce flavored with truffle essence and chicken glaze, finished with unsweetened whipped cream.

Etretat Sauce

German sauce made with fish stock, flavored with tomato purée, and garnished with oysters and mushrooms.

Marshall Sauce (Sauce Maréchale)

German sauce garnished with diced mushrooms.

Mirabeau Sauce

German sauce flavored with garlic, mounted with herb butter.

Neverese Sauce (Sauce Nivernaise)

German sauce garnished with very small carrot and turnip balls simmered in butter. (They are cut with a "pois," or pea scoop, similar to a Parisienne scoop—melon baller—but smaller.)

Poulette Sauce

Poulette sauce is typically served with sautéed or braised mushrooms; pasta; poached fish; frogs; and mussels or snails. It can also be based on béchamel sauce (see Béchamel section).

German sauce flavored with mushroom essence, a little extra lemon juice, and garnished with chopped parsley.

Richelieu Sauce

German sauce flavored with a reduction of onions reduced with chicken stock, finished with chicken glaze, mounted with butter, and garnished with chervil.

Toulouse Sauce (Sauce Toulousaine)

Toulouse sauce is typically served with croustades, and poached or pan-fried poultry.

German sauce flavored with mushroom and truffle essence.

Villeroi Sauce

German sauce made with ham and truffle peelings (or ham and truffle essence) added to the initial reduction.

This sauce is dedicated to Marshal de Villeroi, mentor to Louis XV. Dishes prepared *à la Villeroi* refer to an unusual technique in which cooled-down Villeroi sauce—sometimes with the addition of onion purée, chopped truffles, and/or tomato purée—is used to coat offal, seafood, sweetbreads, poultry, or mutton, then coated in bread crumbs, and pan- or deep-fried.

GREEK SAUCE
(Sauce à la Grecque)

2 tablespoons olive oil
¼ cup celery heart, finely
   chopped
1 small onion, finely
   chopped
1 cup fish velouté
1 sprig fennel
1 sprig oregano

1 bay leaf
½ teaspoon coriander seeds
pinch of salt
pinch of pepper
½ cup heavy cream
3 tablespoons unsalted
   butter, cut into ¼-inch
   cubes

Greek sauce is typically served with braised or poached fish.

• Sweat the celery and onion in the olive oil for 10 minutes. Add the velouté, herbs, coriander, salt, and pepper. Simmer until reduced by one-third. Add the cream and simmer until desired thickness is achieved. Mount with the butter, adjust seasoning, and strain.

HERB SAUCE
(Sauce aux Fines Herbes)

1 shallot, minced
1 cup dry white wine
¼ cup tarragon, chervil,
   chives, and parsley,
   roughly chopped

1 cup velouté
2 tablespoons herb butter

• Simmer the shallot, wine, and herbs until reduced by three-fourths. Strain, return to the saucepan, and mount with the herb butter.

Herb sauce can be both a velouté or a demi-glaze fortified with herbs. The variety of herbs used should be determined by their availability in the market. Chervil, chives, parsley, and tarragon, called *fines herbes*, is a traditional congregation of herbs often used in classical cuisine. But above all, it is preferable to always use fresh ingredients. This also applies to herb butter—use what is available fresh. (A garnish of chopped fresh herbs and a mount of plain unsalted butter can also be substituted for the herb butter.)

Herb sauce is typically served with poached and pan-fried poultry, and sautéed or fried meat.

Archbishop Sauce
(Sauce Archevêque)

Herb sauce garnished with capers.

Housewife Sauce
(Sauce Bonne Femme)

Bonne femme style refers to the same rustic simplicity represented by ménagère (housekeeper style), bourgeoise (citizen style), and paysanne (peasant style). In keeping with the impromptu and economical spirit of such cooking styles, there really is no distinct sauce with this title attached to it. Each dish, be it chicken, lamb, eel, green beans, tomatoes, or apples, has such distinctly different recipes when prepared in the housewife style that spontaneity, frugality, and availability seem to be the overriding precepts.

Joinville Sauce

Joinville sauce is an integral part of Sole Fillets, Joinville, named after the Duke of Joinville. It can also refer to a Normandy sauce, mounted with shrimp butter, and the garnish in this dish is also used to make various small tartlettes (as a garnish), and as an omelette filling. It is typically served with any braised or poached fish.

SOLE FILLETS, JOINVILLE

8 sole fillets (with bones reserved)
8 U-12 shrimp (with head intact, if available)
4 U-12 shrimp, peeled and deveined (shells reserved)
2 tablespoons unsalted butter
6 large fresh mushrooms, cut into medium dice
1½ cups fish velouté
1 egg yolk
¼ cup heavy cream
1 tablespoon unsalted butter
2 tablespoons truffle, small dice
salt and pepper to taste

- Prepare about 1½ cups simple fish fumet with the sole bones and shrimp shells. Sauté the mushrooms in the butter, and set the mushrooms aside. (Use the remaining liquid from the mushrooms for the fumet.)

- Poach the sole and all the shrimp in the fumet. Set the fish aside, cover, and keep warm. Strain the fumet, and reduce to ¼ cup of liquid. Add the velouté and simmer for about 10 minutes.

- Beat the egg and cream together, and temper into the velouté. Adjust seasoning, strain, and keep warm.

- Dice the four peeled shrimp, combine with the truffle and mushrooms, and bind lightly with some of the sauce. Place the sole fillets on a serving platter and arrange the shrimp/truffle/mushroom mixture in the center. Top the fish with the sauce, and garnish with the 8 whole shrimp.

Lyonese Sauce (Sauce Lyonnaise)

Veal velouté flavored with a reduction of white wine with finely diced onions and garlic, garnished with chopped herbs.

———————————— • ————————————

The town of Lyon is considered the preeminent gastronomic center of France. Though it is well known for dozens of specialties, any dish qualified *à la Lyonnaise* will be identified by the use of chopped onions. These are typically glazed in butter until lightly caramelized, flavored with pan juices deglazed with vinegar, and sprinkled with chopped parsley.

Lyonese sauce can also be found under Demi-glaze and Cream Sauce.

Montigny Sauce

Veal velouté flavored with tomato purée and meat glaze, garnished with chopped herbs.

$\mathscr{M}$OREL SAUCE
(Sauce aux Morilles)

1 tablespoon unsalted butter
1 shallot, minced
½ sprig rosemary, roughly chopped
2 sprigs thyme
1 sage leaf, roughly chopped
3 basil leaves, roughly chopped
1 bay leaf
1 clove
4 white peppercorns, crushed
pinch of nutmeg
1 cup velouté

5–10 fresh (or dried) select morels, well rinsed (or soaked in hot stock until reconstituted), dried, and cut into ¼-inch dice
1 tablespoon unsalted butter
salt and white pepper to taste
1 tablespoon lemon juice
¼ cup heavy cream
1 tablespoon chicken glaze
2 tablespoons unsalted butter, cut into ½-inch cubes

- Sauté the shallot in the butter for 5 minutes. Add the herbs and spices and cook another 2 minutes. Add the velouté and simmer until suitable thickness is achieved. Strain.

- Sauté the morels in the butter for several minutes. Add the lemon juice and reduce until nearly dry. Add the cream and reduce by half. Add this to the finished velouté, mount with butter, and season with salt and white pepper.

Morels, along with truffles, are saprophytic, which means that they live on the decaying remains of other organisms. As unappetizing as this sounds, wild mushrooms are among the most prized gastronomic edibles. Morels are identified by a conical cap covered with honeycomb furrows. Because of these furrows, it is important to clean both the dried and fresh varieties several times, to remove sand, soil, etc.

Morel sauce is typically served with grilled meat. Morels can also be served as a dish by themselves (gratin style), or used as a garnish for omelettes, sweetbreads, poultry, and so on.

$\mathcal{N}$EWBURG SAUCE
(Sauce à la Newburg)

$\mathcal{H}$OMARD À LA NEWBURG
(Lobster Newburg)

2 1¼- to 1½-pound lobsters
3 tablespoons olive oil
salt, white pepper, and
    paprika as needed
1 shallot, minced
½ cup dry sherry
1 cup fish stock

¼ cup tomato purée
2 cups fish velouté
2 egg yolks
½ cup cream
2 tablespoons unsalted
    butter, cut into ¼-inch
    cubes

- Place the lobster on a cutting board atop a pan to collect any juices. With the point of a cook's knife, make an incision into the center of the back of the head, at a point about an inch below the eyes. (This stuns the lobster, so as to spare it excessive discomfort.) Tear the tail from the main body, and cut it lengthwise in two. Carefully removed the tomalley (the crustacean's liver, identified by its dark green color) from the main body, and set aside. Cut the body up into 6 to 8 pieces. Remove the claws and arms, and gently crack them with the heel of a knife. Reserve any juices collected in the pan.

- Heat the oil in a large saucepan, sprinkle the lobster pieces with salt, pepper, and paprika, and sauté them for several minutes on all sides, until they turn dark red. Remove the lobster pieces, and carefully pull out the meat from the claws, arms, and tail. Cut the meat into ½-inch pieces, and set aside. Crack the remaining shells into smaller pieces, return to the pan along with the shallot, and sauté for 5 minutes, stirring continuously. Add the sherry, stock, and tomato, and simmer until reduced by half. Add the velouté, and reduce again by half. Strain through a large-holed sieve or china cap, pounding the shells to extract as much liquid as possible. Strain again through a fine sieve.

- Beat the yolks, cream, tomalley, and reserved juice in a small bowl. Slowly pour in the sauce, stirring continuously. Return the sauce to the pan, continue stirring, and mount with the butter. Adjust seasoning. Pour the sauce over the lobster pieces, and serve.

———————— • ————————

The original Delmonico's was a wine and pastry shop opened in 1827 on the Battery in New York City by former sea captain John Delmonico. He was so successful that he called for his brother Peter to come over from Switzerland to assist in opening a second operation. The brothers hired a French chef in 1831 and converted the second operation to a full-fledged restaurant. The brothers' continued success led to the opening of 11 different restaurants over the next seventy years, employing numerous family members, including nephew Lorenzo and his three brothers—Siro, François, and Constant. Throughout its illustrious history, Delmonico's was the rendezvous of a great number of international personalities, including Chester A. Arthur (before he became president), Charles Dickens, Horace Greeley, Washington Irving, President Abraham Lincoln, Charles Napoléan (who was later crowned Napoléon III), William Thackerey, Mark Twain, Boss Bill Tweed (before he went to jail), and Oscar Wilde.

Several famous dishes were created there, among them Baked Alaska (commemorating the newly purchased Alaska territory), Chicken à la Keene (now called "à la King"), and Lobster Wenburg, in honor of Ben Wenburg, a shipping magnate who was a regular patron. Wenburg once described to Lorenzo Delmonico a dish he had enjoyed in South America. The next night, Lorenzo prepared the dish tableside—lobster dressed with a sauce of cream, sherry, egg yolks, and butter. Wenberg so enjoyed the dish that it was permanently added to the menu. Some weeks later, Wenberg, excessively inebriated, initiated a brawl and was subsequently barred from the restaurant. Since the dish had already become quite popular, the Delmonicos decided to keep it on the menu, but changed the name to remove the negative stigma of Wenberg's public disgrace. This was accomplished by simply inverting the first and third letters of Wenberg, and substituting a *U* for the *E*.

*N*ORMANDY SAUCE
(Sauce Normande)

1 shallot, minced
1 cup fish stock
¼ cup oyster liqueur
¼ cup mushrooms, finely
   chopped

1 cup fish velouté
1 egg yolk
¼ cup heavy cream
2 tablespoons unsalted butter,
   cut into ½-inch cubes

- Simmer the shallot, stock, oyster liqueur, and mushrooms, until reduced by three-fourths. Add the fish velouté and simmer until suitable thickness is achieved.
- Briefly beat the egg and cream in a small bowl. Slowly add the velouté while beating continuously. Return to the saucepan, and mount with the butter.

•

Dishes prepared Normandy style typically contain butter, cream, seafood, apples, apple cider, and Calvados, an apple-derived brandy. Sole à la Normande, one of the earliest precursors for a host of dishes braised in white wine, was actually created by Langlais, a Parisian native, in 1837, while chef at Rocher de Cancale, a celebrated restaurant in Paris which operated from 1795 until 1860.

Normandy sauce is typically served with croustades; omelettes; and braised or baked fish. It is also a base for the following sauces.

Anchovy Sauce
(Sauce aux Anchois)

Normandy sauce (or white wine sauce) mounted with anchovy butter, and garnished with additional diced anchovy if necessary.

Diplomat, or Rich Sauce
(Sauce Diplomate, Sauce Riche)

Normandy sauce mounted with lobster butter, garnished with diced lobster meat and diced truffle.

—————————— • ——————————

Diplomat sauce is typically served with braised or baked fish. There is also an elaborate omelette of the same name, though it employs two different sauces (a béchamel beaten with lobster butter, and a mornay sauce).

Dishes qualified *à la Riche* allude to Café Riche, a celebrated restaurant established in Paris in 1804. It began as a modest establishment, but attained notoriety under Louis Bignon (1816–1906). Bignon was the first restaurateur to become a member of the Legion of Honor, and was a founding member of the Agricultural Society of France. He took over management of the Café Riche in 1847, redecorating it with such elegance and grandeur that it became a frequent haunt of politicians, writers, and theater personalities. The two great specialties of the restaurant were "Sole à la Riche" (poached sole, garnished with crayfish tails and truffles, dressed with Riche sauce) and "Bécasses à la Riche" (roasted woodcock, served on a crouton spread with liver paste, accompanied by Riche sauce). Café Riche was adversely affected by the Franco-Prussian War of 1870 but survived, eventually closing its doors in 1916.

Lobster Sauce (Sauce Homard)

Normandy sauce (or plain fish velouté), mounted with lobster butter, garnished with diced lobster meat.

Oyster Sauce (Sauce aux Huîtres)

Normandy sauce flavored with lemon juice, garnished with poached oysters.

Véron Sauce

1 part Normandy sauce blended with 3 parts Tyrollian sauce, flavored with anchovy paste dissolved in veal glaze.

Louis Désiré Véron (1798–1867), was a medical doctor, and later in life a critic and editor of various literary reviews, administrator of the Opéra, and political journalist. Gastronomically, he had a reputation as a lavish host, whose guests included high-ranking politicos as well as celebrated writers, actors, and actresses.

Véron sauce is typically served with breaded and pan-fried, poached, braised, or grilled fish.

Orléans Sauce

Fish velouté flavored with a reduction of white wine and mushrooms, seasoned with cayenne pepper, and mounted with crayfish butter.

Parsley Sauce (Sauce Persil)

Velouté mounted with parsley butter, garnished with chopped parsley.

Though parsley is generally taken for granted as a ubiquitous garnish, it was well known in ancient western culture—chopped up and sprinkled on a piece of bread, it was a common breakfast in ancient Rome. Later, Charlemagne ordered it planted in his domain, and to this day, *fines herbes* always includes parsley. In medieval times, parsley was associated with the devil, and an old English proverb read, "Only the wicked can grow parsley." Good Friday was believed to be the only day of the year when it could be successfully sown, provided that the moon was rising. Historically, parsley has been used for it's medicinal properties, and no wonder, since it is rich in vitamins and minerals. As a tea or fresh juice, it has been used to treat asthma, conjunctivitis, coughs, hair loss, jaundice, and suppressed menstruation.

Parsley can be added to other sauce bases, such as beurre blanc and cream sauce, or puréed in a vinaigrette—it has an amazing emulsifying capability. It is typically served with poached fish, particularly mackerel and salmon; light meats; calf's head; and poached or pan-fried poultry.

Pondicherry Sauce

Veal velouté seasoned with curry, finished with tomato purée.

ℛAVIGOTE SAUCE

....

1 shallot, minced
½ cup dry white wine
½ cup tarragon vinegar
2 sprigs each tarragon,
  chervil, and chives,
  roughly chopped
1 cup velouté

2 tablespoons shallot butter,
  cut into ½-inch cubes
1 tablespoon fresh tarragon,
  minced
1 tablespoon fresh chervil,
  minced
1 tablespoon fresh chives,
  minced

- Simmer the shallot, wine, and vinegar until reduced by three-fourths. Add the velouté and roughly chopped herbs, and simmer until suitable thickness is achieved. Strain, then return to the heat and mount with the shallot butter. Garnish with the minced herbs.

————— • —————

There is another Ravigote sauce, a vinaigrette derivative. *Ravigoter* means "to revive, to refresh," possibly an etymological reference to the piquancy of both sauces, derived from the vinegar.

————————————

ℛOYAL SAUCE

....

(Sauce Royale)

1 cup chicken stock
2 cups chicken velouté
¼ cup heavy cream
3 tablespoons truffle, minced

3 tablespoons unsalted
  butter, cut into ¼-inch
  cubes
2 tablespoons dry sherry

- Simmer the stock and velouté until reduced by half. Add the cream and simmer a little longer. Strain, add the truffle, mount with the butter, and finish with dry sherry.

————————— • —————————

A *royale* (not to be confused with the sauce) is a savory custard, plain, or flavored with various vegetables, herbs, or poultry. It is cut into various shapes (small cubes, stars, crescents, diamonds, etc.), and used as a garnish for soups, primarily consommés.

A Royal sauce is typically served with poached poultry; it is also applied to a notable dish, Lièvre à la Royale (Hare, Royal Style).

Russian Sauce (Sauce Russe)

Velouté flavored with tarragon vinegar, garnished with grated horseradish, and finished with sour cream.

This version of Russian sauce can be served with large roasted or braised joints of meat (see Cold Sauces, Mayonnaise).

Sevilla Sauce (Sauce Sevillane)

Velouté flavored with tomato and red bell pepper purée.

Shrimp Sauce (Sauce aux Crevettes)

Fish velouté mounted with shrimp butter, garnished with diced shrimp. (Can also be made with a béchamel base.)

Spring Sauce (Sauce Printanière)

Velouté mounted with herb butter, garnished with spring vegetables cut into small dice (brunoise).

Printanière (same as the Italian *primavera*), literally "in the style of Spring," technically refers to any dish garnished with a bouquet of baby spring vegetables. It is one of the most delightful methods of cooking and presenting food, a way of celebrating the end of winter and the agriculturally bountiful seasons that follow. It is also rarely done in this manner, as attested by the ubiquitous Pasta Primavera or Consommé Printanière seen on restaurant menus all year round.

SORREL SAUCE
(Sauce à l'Oseille)

4 tablespoons unsalted butter
1 shallot, minced

1 cup sorrel leaves, washed, dried, and minced

3 tablespoons all-purpose
   flour
1 cup fish stock (hot)

1 cup heavy cream
salt and white pepper to taste

- Sauté the shallot in the butter for 3 minutes. Add the sorrel and sauté another 3 minutes.
- Place the cream in a small saucepan and simmer very gently, until reduced by half.
- Add the flour to the butter, shallots and sorrel, and blend thoroughly. Carefully add the fish stock, plus a pinch of salt and pepper, and blend well, using a wire whip. Simmer until reduced by about half, skimming the foam that rises to the top of the sauce.
- Remove both liquids to a blender, and purée. Strain through a sieve, return the sauce to the heat, and adjust seasoning.

SUPRÊME SAUCE
(Sauce Suprême)

1 small shallot, minced
½ cup finely chopped
   mushrooms
½ cup chicken stock
¾ cup heavy cream
¾ cup chicken velouté

2 tablespoons unsalted
   butter, cut into ¼-inch
   cubes
salt and white pepper to
   taste

- Simmer the shallot, mushrooms, and stock until reduced by three-fourths. Add the heavy cream and simmer several minutes. Add the velouté and simmer until suitable thickness is achieved. Strain, then return to the heat, mount with the butter, season to taste with salt and pepper.

———————— • ————————

Suprême sauce is typically served with croustades; sautéed or braised vegetables; soft-boiled or poached eggs; braised, pan-fried, or deep-fried offal; and poached, pan-fried, or roasted poultry.

The following compound sauces employ Suprême sauce as their base.

Albuféra Sauce

Suprême sauce flavored with meat glaze, mounted with pimento butter.

---•---

Albuféra sauce was named in honor of Marshall Suchet. Suchet was made the Duc d'Albuféra (a lake near Valencia, Spain) in 1812, after his military victories over the English at Oropeza, Murviendro, and Valencia.

Albuféra sauce is typically served with veal sweetbreads, and braised, poached, or pan-fried poultry.

Alexandra Sauce

Suprême sauce flavored with truffle essence.

Ambassadress Sauce (Sauce Ambassadrice)

Suprême sauce garnished with a purée of poached chicken breast, finished with whipped cream.

---•---

Dishes done in "ambassador" or ambassadress" style are typical of the old elaborate style of haute (classical) cuisine. The typical ambassador garnish consists of artichoke bottoms filled with mushroom duxelle, duchess potatoes, grated horseradish, and Supreme sauce; the ambassadress garnish consists of cockscombs and cock's kidneys, sautéed chicken livers and mushrooms, braised lettuce, and Parisienne potatoes moistened with Madeira sauce.

Archduke Sauce (Sauce Archiduc)

Suprême sauce finished with a reduction of champagne.

──────── • ────────

Archduke (Archiduc) is a name applied to dishes inspired by Austro-Hungarian cuisine at the time of La Belle Epoque, characterized by the generous use of paprika, cream, and Hungarian sauce (Sauce Hongroise).

Banker's sauce is typically served with croustades; soft-boiled or poached eggs; offal; and poached or sautéed poultry.

Banker's Sauce (Sauce Banquière)

Suprême sauce blended with tomato purée and veal glaze, finished with Madeira wine, mounted with butter, and garnished with chopped truffle.

Chantilly Sauce

Suprême sauce with whipped unsweetened heavy cream folded in.

This version of Chantilly sauce is typically served with poached chicken or veal sweetbreads (see also Dutch Sauce and Mayonnaise).

Chive Sauce (Sauce Civette)

Suprême sauce mounted with crayfish butter, garnished with chives.

Half-Mourning Sauce (Sauce Demi-Deuil)

Suprême sauce flavored with truffle essence, garnished with truffles.

──────── • ────────

Chicken, Half-Mourning Style (Poularde Demi-Deuil—*poularde* refers to a large castrated hen, i.e., a capon) is one of the most renowned dishes originating in Lyon, France.

The name of this dish is represented by the inclusion of black (truffle) and white (poached chicken, the light tinted sauce) ingredients.

CHICKEN, HALF-MOURNING STYLE
(Poularde Demi-Deuill)

1 large roasting chicken or capon, well rinsed, seasoned internally with salt and pepper, and trussed
1 quart chicken stock
bouquet garni, comprised of 1 sprig each, thyme, tarragon, and rosemary, and 1 bunch parsley stems

1 small calf's sweetbread
1 tablespoon unsalted butter
4 medium mushrooms
8 tartelette or barquette shells
1 large fresh (or canned) black truffle
2 cups Half-Mourning sauce

- Poach the chicken in the stock, covered, along with the bouquet garni, by simmering for approximately 1 hour. Remove from the fire, and set aside.

- Trim the sweetbread of excess membrane, and poach in a small amount of poaching liquid from the chicken, about 20 minutes. Remove and allow to cool. Break or cut the sweetbread up into ¼-inch pieces.

- Sauté the mushrooms in the butter. Drain, and set aside. Combine the sweetbreads with the mushrooms and bind lightly with the sauce. Fill the pastry shells with this mixture. Place on a pan and into a 200-degree oven.

- Remove the chicken from the poaching medium. Prepare the chicken for service by removing the string, the end wing joints, the knuckles from the end of the two drum sticks, and the skin. Place onto a serving platter, and nap with sufficient sauce to coat the chicken and cover the platter surface. Arrange the pastry shells around the periphery of the platter, and top each with a slice of truffle.

Ivory Sauce (Sauce Ivoire)

Suprême sauce flavored with a white veal or chicken glaze (sometimes called Wladimir sauce).

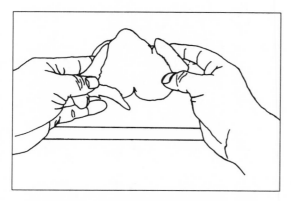

1. Hooking the wingtips under the wings.

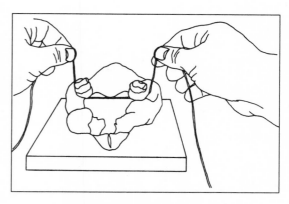

2. Placing cotton trussing cord under the chicken legs.

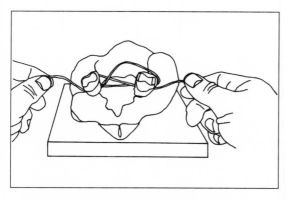

3. Crossing the two cords above the top, then bringing each one down, under each leg, and out.

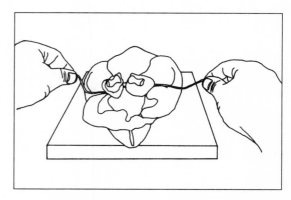

4. Pulling the cord taut and back along the sides, across the thighs, toward the top of the bird.

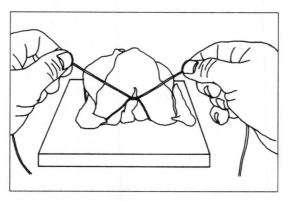

5. Pulling the cord taut across the top of the breast. Tie and knot.

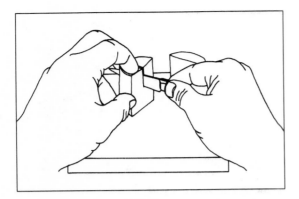

1. *Cutting 1¹/₂-inch-long pieces of cucumber
lengthwise, into quarters.*

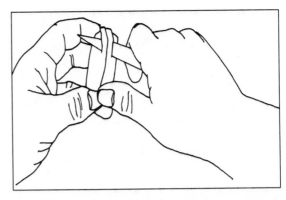

2. *"Turning" a paring knife around the exterior
of the cucumber quarters.*

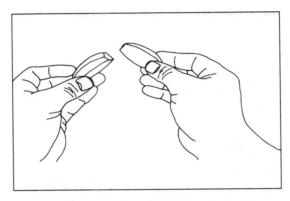

3. *The completed olive-shaped* tournés.

---•---

Chicken Ivory (Poulet à l'Ivoire) consists of poached
chicken, garnished with chicken quenelles, small mushroom
caps, small turned cucumber, and Ivory sauce.

Ivory sauce is typically served with soft-boiled or
poached eggs; offal; and poached and sautéed poultry.

Marly Sauce

Suprême sauce made with white veal stock, seasoned with
cayenne pepper, and garnished with diced mushrooms.

Pretty-Girl Sauce (Sauce Jolie-Fille)

Suprême sauce garnished with sieved hard-boiled egg yolks and chopped parsley.

Queen Sauce (Sauce à la Reine)

Suprême sauce blended with whipped cream, garnished with strips of poached chicken breast.

————————— • —————————

"À la Reine" refers to a number of elegant dishes characterized by chicken, originating from classic French cuisine. They often include sweetbreads, mushrooms, and truffles. One of the best known dishes is Cream of Chicken Soup, Queen Style ("Potage Crème de Volaille, à la Reine").

Regency Sauce (Sauce Régence)

Suprême sauce flavored with a reduction of mushrooms, truffle peelings, and Rhine wine, and served with poultry. (For fish, the same sauce is made with a base of Normandy sauce.)

————————— • —————————

This version of Regency sauce (see Demi-glaze for the other) is typically served with veal sweetbreads; and braised or poached poultry.

————— • —————

Tarragon sauce is typically served with poached or pan-fried poultry; veal sweetbreads; light meats; and sautéed and fried meat.

Tarragon Sauce (Sauce à l'Estragon)

Suprême sauce mounted with tarragon butter, garnished with chopped tarragon.

Talleyrand Sauce

Chicken velouté flavored with a reduction of white wine and shallot, finished with cream and Madeira wine, and garnished with a brunoise (fine dice) of celery, carrots, onions, truffle, and pickled tongue.

————————— • —————————

Charles-Maurice de Talleyrand-Périgord (1754–1838) preferred heavy dishes and light women at dinner ("Two things are essential in life: to give good dinners and to keep on fair terms with women"). He also liked to surprise guests by serving them rare and unusual food. During the winter of 1803, when there was no fish to be had in Paris, he served an enormous salmon, brought in on a silver platter. The butler carrying the fish stumbled and dropped it to the floor, much to the chagrin of the guests. At Talleyrand's request, another was promptly brought in. The catastrophe had been staged.

Talleyrand sauce is typically served with braised poultry; sautéed and fried meat; and large roasted or braised joints of meat.

Village Sauce (Sauce Villageoise)

——— • ———

Village sauce is typically served with braised poultry, and light meat.

Velouté blended with a white onion purée sweated in butter, flavored with mushroom essence, bound with an egg yolk and cream liaison, and mounted with butter.

Watercress Sauce (Sauce au Cresson)

Velouté garnished with capers and chopped watercress (or mounted with watercress butter).

𝒲HITE WINE SAUCE
(Sauce au Vin Blanc)

1 shallot, minced
1 cup dry white wine
1 sprig thyme
1 bay leaf
1 cup velouté

2 tablespoons unsalted butter, cut into ½-inch cubes
salt and white pepper to taste

- Simmer the shallot, wine, and herbs until reduced by three-fourths. Add the velouté and simmer until suitable thickness is achieved. Add the butter and stir continuously until emulsified. Season to taste with salt and white pepper, and strain.

Admiral Sauce (Sauce Amiral)

White wine sauce garnished with lemon zest and capers, mounted with anchovy butter.

Alcide Sauce

White wine sauce garnished with chopped sweated shallots and grated horseradish.

Anchovy Sauce (Sauce aux Anchois)

White wine sauce (or Normandy sauce) beaten with anchovy butter, garnished with diced anchovy fillets.

Breton Sauce (Sauce Bretonne)

White wine sauce finished with cream, garnished with a julienne of celery, leeks, mushrooms, and onions, sweated in butter.

Francis I Sauce (Sauce François I)

White wine sauce mounted with butter, garnished with diced tomatoes and mushrooms.

Golfin Sauce

White wine sauce garnished with julienne of gherkins and pickled tongue.

Grandville Sauce

White wine sauce garnished with diced truffles, mushrooms, and shrimp.

The following compound sauces employ White Wine sauce as their base.

Anchovy sauce is typically served with grilled or poached fish.

This version of Breton sauce is served with soft-boiled or poached eggs and braised or baked fish. (See Breton Sauce under Demi-glaze.)

Havre Sauce

White wine sauce flavored with a reduction of mussel stock, garnished with mussels and shrimp.

———— • ————

Hungarian sauce is typically served with soft-boiled or poached eggs; braised or baked fish; light meats; offal; and sautéed poultry.

Hungarian Sauce (Sauce Hongroise)

White wine sauce flavored with veal glaze, seasoned with paprika, and finished with sour cream.

Polignac Sauce

White wine sauce finished with heavy cream, garnished with julienned mushrooms.

Pompadour Sauce

White wine sauce mounted with crayfish butter, garnished with julienned truffles, diced crayfish tails, chopped tarragon, and chervil.

———————— • ————————

Jeanne Antoine Poisson, Marquise de Pompadour (1721–1764), was the wife of Charles le Normant d'Étoilles, a farmer-general, and became Louis XV's mistress in 1745. She played an important part in the king's life and was a notable influence in the arts. Many dishes were created in her honor, both during her lifetime and later by Escoffier and Urban DuBois. She is also credited with creating several dishes of her own, all prepared with truffles.

Prince Sauce (Sauce Princière)

White wine sauce mounted with crayfish butter, garnished with diced crayfish tails and julienned truffle.

Saint Malo Sauce

White wine sauce flavored with mustard and anchovy paste.

Souchett Sauce

White wine sauce garnished with julienned carrots, leek, and celery, cooked in butter and fish stock.

Tenant Sauce (Sauce Fermière)

White wine sauce garnished with medium diced leek, and half-circle or half-moon shaped slices of carrot, celery root, turnips, carrots, leek, and celery, cooked in butter.

———————— • ————————

À la Fermière, literally "farmer's style," technically refers to a style of braising meat, fish, or poultry, and adding a garnish of mixed seasonal vegetables cooked in butter near the end of the braising. The adaptable style of the dish resides in the selection of vegetables—whatever is fresh and available, or even leftover from a previous day's meal. An omelette à la fermière (farmer's omelette), for example, does not contain a standard filling, but rather a collection of leftover meat, poultry, fish, and/or vegetables.

———————— • ————————

Venetian sauce is typically served with soft-boiled or poached eggs; poached fish (served hot); and poached or pan-fried poultry.

Venetian Sauce (Sauce Vénetienne)

White wine sauce flavored with a shallot, tarragon, chervil, and vinegar reduction, mounted with green butter, and garnished with chopped tarragon and chervil.

Victoria Sauce

White wine sauce, seasoned with cayenne pepper, mounted with lobster butter, and garnished with diced truffles.

———————— • ————————

There are many dishes dedicated to England's Queen Victoria, and all are characterized by rich ingredients and elaborate presentation, including lobster and truffles, in a salpicon, or some other form. These dishes include poached and soft-boiled eggs, braised and poached fish, shellfish, game, an omelette, a salad, a bombe, and a dessert sandwich.

Yellow Boletus Sauce (Sauce aux Cèpes)

Velouté finished with heavy cream, garnished with thin-sliced yellow boletus mushrooms cooked in butter.

Cèpes are a type of wild mushroom of which there are more than 20 edible varieties.

CONTEMPORARY INNOVATIONS

CRIMSON SAUCE

2 medium beets, scrubbed
1 shallot, minced
1 bay leaf
1 cup dry white wine
1 cup chicken stock
salt and pepper to taste

• Preheat oven to 375°F.
• Roast the beets for 40 minutes. Allow to cool, then grate (by hand or in a food processor). Set aside.
• Simmer the shallot, bay leaf, and white wine until reduced by three-fourths. Add the stock and grated beets, and simmer until reduced by half. Remove to a blender or food processor and purée.
• Strain, adjust thickness, and season to taste.

This magnificently colored sauce was created by Dan Callahan, sous-chef at the Olympic Club, San Francisco, California, and is served with "Ravioli aux Épinards, Forestière" (spinach ravioli stuffed with wild mushrooms duxelle).

BLACK BEAN SAUCE

2 tablespoons olive oil
1 shallot, minced
1 garlic clove, pressed
¼ cup orange juice
¼ cup grapefruit juice
2 tablespoons lime juice
2 tablespoons lemon juice
3 cups chicken stock
1 cup black beans, soaked overnight in cold water, drained, culled, and thoroughly rinsed
2 tablespoons cilantro, minced

• Saute the shallot and garlic in the olive oil for 3 minutes. Add the fruit juices and simmer until reduced by two-thirds. Add the stock, beans, and cilantro, and simmer covered, about 2 hours, or until the beans are very soft.
• Purée the sauce in a food processor, and season to taste with salt and pepper. Strain.

This sauce and Hollandaise accompany "Grilled Swordfish," as seen in *Art Culinaire* (Volume 10).

CHAMPAGNE TARRAGON SAUCE

1 tablespoon unsalted butter
1 shallot, minced
⅓ cup basmati rice,
    well-rinsed and drained
2 sprigs tarragon, roughly
    chopped

2 cups rich chicken stock
½ teaspoon lemon zest
1 tablespoon lemon juice
1 tablespoon tarragon
    leaves, minced
salt and white pepper to taste

- Sauté the shallot in the butter for 3 minutes. Add the rice, and coat with the butter. Add the tarragon, stock, and zest. Simmer for 40 minutes. Remove to a blender, purée, and strain. Blend in the lemon juice, and season with salt and pepper. Set aside, keeping warm until ready to serve.

———————————— • ————————————

This sauce represents the sole dish in this book that comes closest to a low-fat item. It is an innovation of mine, created one evening when I had very little ingredients to work with. Lacking even flour to create a roux, I utilized rice as a thickening agent. With a rich chicken stock, it was quite exceptional. This particular recipe goes well with any form of roast, or sautéed chicken, but can also be prepared with a fish stock and just about any variety of herb or herbs.

CREAMED CHICKEN SAUCE

2 tablespoons unsalted butter
⅓ cup chicken livers,
    trimmed of connecting
    membranes, well washed
    in cold water, and roughly
    chopped

1 large shallot, minced
¼ cup dry white wine
¾ cup chicken stock
1 cup heavy cream
salt and pepper to taste

This sauce accompanied "Roast Quail Stuffed with Wild Rice," a dish served by Wolfgang Puck at the International Economic Summit in Williamsburg, Virginia, May 1983.

- Sauté the liver and shallot in the butter for 3 minutes. Remove the livers with a slotted spoon, and set aside.
- Add the white wine and chicken stock, and simmer until reduced by two-thirds.
- Add the cream and chicken livers, and continue simmering until reduced by half again. Remove to a blender or food

processor, and purée. Strain. Return to the fire, bring to a boil, and season with salt and pepper. Set aside, keeping warm until ready to serve.

SWEET RED PEPPER SAUCE

4 medium red bell peppers
olive oil as needed
1 medium Spanish onion,
  roughly chopped
3 tablespoons unsalted butter

1 garlic clove, pressed
1 small red jalapeño pepper,
  split, seeded and minced
1½ cups chicken stock
salt and white pepper to taste

- Preheat oven to 400°F.
- Rub the peppers with olive oil, place on a baking sheet, and roast until the peppers begin to turn black.
- Remove from the oven, place in a bowl, and cover tightly with plastic wrap. After 10 minutes, remove the peppers from the bowl, and separate the flesh from the skin and seeds.
- Sauté the onion in the butter for 5 minutes. Add the garlic and jalapeño pepper, and sauté another couple of minutes. Add the chicken stock, and simmer until reduced by one-third.
- Purée the sautéed ingredients and the roasted peppers in a food processor. Return to the fire, and simmer until reduced to desired thickness. Season to taste with salt and pepper and set aside, keeping warm until ready to serve.

This sauce accompanies "Deviled Crab Sausages," as seen in *A Taste For All Seasons*.

CHAPTER 8

CREAM (WHITE) SAUCES

Sauce Béchamel

*L*ouis de Béchameil, the Marquis de Nointel (1630-1703), was a fascinating mix of connoisseur, bon vivant, and shrewd political operator. Former Farmer-general and steward to the house of the Duke of Orleans, former Lord Steward of the Royal Household to Louis XIV (in effect, Louis' "major domo"), gourmet, and knowledgeable art lover, de Béchameil had made a fortune during The Fronde, a political party that led a civil uprising against Louis XIV and his chief minister, Jules Mazarin, from 1648 to 1653. There is speculation that his financial coup was achieved by less than scrupulous, and perhaps even fraudulent, means. And as for his sauce namesake, the consensus is even clearer that it was *not invented* by him, but *named after him* by an unknown court chef who honored the Lord Steward by applying his name to a thick velouté to which liberal amounts of fresh cream were added. This sauce had been known for some time before, probably under another name. Upon learning of Béchameil being honored with a sauce, the elder Duke d'Escars is reported to have said, "That fellow Béchameil has all the luck. I was serving *breast of chicken à la crème* twenty years before he was born, yet, as you can see, I have never yet had the chance of giving my name to the most insignificant of sauces!"

Carême's recipe for béchamel sauce, the velouté finished with cream, included a final liaison of cream and egg yolks. Somewhere between Carême's departure (1833) and Escoffier's *Guide Culinaire*, béchamel evolved into the milk-thickened white sauce it is still known as in contemporary practice. That Escoffier's béchamel included diced lean veal is probably a throwback to the earlier velouté finished with cream.

As with the criteria regarding the use of other flourless sauces, the same applies here. Heavy cream reduced by about half, along with the aromatics and garnish appropriate to a specific sauce, represents the purist's approach. Yet one must take into consideration the extreme richness of a white sauce created by reducing cream. In the case of a demi-glaze or velouté, this degree of richness is not quite the same. So we again take an intermediate approach, creating a traditional béchamel with a small amount of roux, and enrich it with whatever other garnish or final liaison a sauce or dish calls for. In the rare case when a cream is reduced to create a béchamel, it should only be served in a limited amount.

ℬ **ÉCHAMEL SAUCE**

1 small Spanish onion, peeled	3 tablespoons unsalted butter,
1 small piece of nutmeg	clarified
6 whole cloves	3 tablespoons all-purpose flour
1 bay leaf	2 cups hot milk
	salt and white pepper to taste

- Make a cut into the onion, about 1 inch deep, and slide the bay leaf into this slit. Stick the cloves into the onion, and place it, along with the milk and nutmeg, into a heavy-gauge, noncorrosive saucepan. Place this over medium heat.

- In a separate pan, cook the butter and flour for about 5 minutes, stirring continuously, without browning, until it emits a nutty aroma. Remove from the fire.

- When the milk is fairly hot, pour some into the cooled down roux, stirring until the milk is thoroughly blended in. Return this to the remaining milk, and simmer for 15 minutes, stirring frequently. Season to taste with salt and white pepper, strain, and set aside until ready to use.

————————— • —————————

Béchamel has a tendency to form a skin on top, in part because of its exposure to the air. To prevent this, take a piece of butter, impaled on a fork, and dab it on top of the sauce. This will leave a thin coating of butter on the top of the sauce which prevents a skin from forming.

Béchamel is typically served with hard-boiled eggs (served hot); as a binder and vehicle for gratins; poached fish (served hot); and light meat.

TRADITIONAL DERIVATIVES OF BÉCHAMEL SAUCE

Aurora sauce is typically served with poached, soft-boiled, and hard-boiled eggs (served hot).

Aurora Sauce (Sauce Aurore)

Cream sauce blended with tomato purée.

Avignon Sauce (Sauce Avignonaise)

Cream sauce flavored with garlic, seasoned with grated Parmesan cheese, finished with an egg yolk liaison, and garnished with chopped parsley.

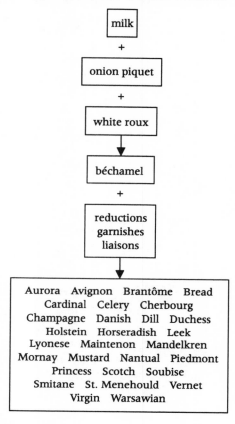

Sauce Matrix III
Béchamel and Its Derivatives

milk

+

onion piquet

+

white roux

↓

béchamel

+

reductions
garnishes
liaisons

↓

Aurora Avignon Brantôme Bread
Cardinal Celery Cherbourg
Champagne Danish Dill Duchess
Holstein Horseradish Leek
Lyonese Maintenon Mandelkren
Mornay Mustard Nantual Piedmont
Princess Scotch Soubise
Smitane St. Menehould Vernet
Virgin Warsawian

Brantôme Sauce

Cream sauce flavored with a reduction of shallot, white wine, and oyster liqueur, mounted with crayfish butter, seasoned with cayenne pepper, and garnished with grated truffle.

Bread sauce is typically served with boiled beef, game, roasted poultry, and large roasted or braised joints of meat.

Bread Sauce
(Sauce au Pain à l'Anglaise)

Milk heated with an onion cut in half, simmered with grated fresh bread crumbs, onion removed, seasoned with salt, cayenne, and nutmeg, finished with cream, and mounted with butter.

Cardinal Sauce (Sauce Cardinale)

Cream sauce flavored with fish stock and truffle essence, seasoned with cayenne pepper, and mounted with lobster butter.

Cardinal sauce is typically served with shellfish, though it can also be served with other braised or baked fish. The name is derived from the connection between the bright red robes of a church cardinal and the bright red color of crab, crayfish, lobster, and shrimp shells when cooked.

CELERY SAUCE
(Sauce au Céleri)

1 celery heart, roughly chopped and well rinsed
2 cups chicken or white veal stock

1 small onion, stuck with a clove
1 bay leaf
1 cup cream sauce
salt and white pepper to taste

- Simmer the celery in the stock, along with the onion and bay leaf, uncovered, for 30 minutes. Remove the onion and bay leaf, and discard. Continue simmering the celery until it is nearly dry. Pound the celery in a mortar and pestle (or mash thoroughly with a fork), and press through a sieve. Blend this purée into the cream sauce, and season to taste.

Cherbourg Sauce

Cream sauce mounted with crayfish butter, garnished with crayfish tails.

Champagne Sauce
(Sauce au Champagne)

A Champagne sauce can also be found under Demi-glaze and Dutch Sauce.

Cream sauce flavored with a reduction of minced shallots and champagne, mounted with butter.

Danish Sauce (Sauce Danoise)

Cream sauce blended with poached chicken purée pressed through a sieve, flavored with mushroom essence, and garnished with chopped herbs.

Dill Sauce (Sauce à l'Aneth)

Cream sauce flavored with lemon juice, garnished with chopped dill (or beaten with dill butter).

Duchess Sauce (Sauce Duchesse)

Cream sauce mounted with butter, garnished with julienned or diced pickled tongue and mushrooms.

Holstein Sauce

Cream sauce flavored with a reduction of white wine and fish glaze, seasoned with nutmeg, and bound with a liaison of egg yolks.

· · · · · · · · · · · · · · · · · ·

ℋORSERADISH SAUCE
(Sauce Raifort)

1 cup heavy cream
½ cup fresh white bread crumbs
¼ cup grated horseradish root, simmered in a little

vinegar and white beef stock
salt and cayenne pepper to taste

——— • ———

This is a very simple version of Horseradish sauce, though a variety of sauces can be used as a base.

———————

- Simmer the cream and bread crumbs for 10 minutes. Allow to sit for 10 minutes.
- Drain the horseradish, then blend into the sauce. Bring back to a simmer, and season to taste.

· · · · · · · · · · · · · · · · · ·

ℒEEK SAUCE
(Sauce aux Poireaux)

1 cup chopped leeks (white and light green part only), well rinsed
2 cups chicken or white veal stock
1 cup cream sauce

salt and white pepper to taste
⅓ cup julienned leek (white and light green part only), simmered in stock until tender

- Simmer the leek in the stock, uncovered, until it is nearly dry. Pound the celery in a mortar and pestle (or mash thoroughly with a fork), and press through a sieve. Blend this purée into the cream sauce, add the drained garnish, and season to taste.

Lyonese Sauce (Sauce Lyonnaise)

Cream sauce flavored with a reduction of white wine with finely diced onion and garlic, garnished with chopped herbs.

---•---

The town of Lyon is considered the preeminent gastronomic center of France. Though it is well known for dozens of specialties, any dish qualified *à la Lyonnaise* will be identified by the use of chopped onions. These are typically glazed in butter until lightly caramelized, flavored with pan juices deglazed with vinegar, and sprinkled with chopped parsley. Lyonese Sauce can also be found under Demi-glaze and Velouté.

Maintenon Sauce (Sauce Maintenon)

Cream sauce blended with (cooked) puréed white onions, flavored with a little garlic and grated Parmesan cheese, and seasoned with cayenne.

---•---

Maintenon refers to numerous dishes containing mushrooms, onion, and béchamel sauce, and sometimes truffles, tongue, and chicken breasts. It is believed to have been created by a chef in service to the Noailles, who owned the Château de Maintenon.

Mandelkren Sauce

Cream sauce flavored with almond milk (almonds pounded to a paste with water, then strained), garnished with grated horseradish (Austrian).

ℳORNAY SAUCE

(Sauce Mornay)

1 cup cream sauce
⅓ cup grated Gruyère (or other variety of Swiss) cheese

3 tablespoons grated Parmesan cheese
2 tablespoons unsalted butter, cut into ¼-inch cubes

- Blend the cheeses into the cream sauce, and mount with butter.

Mornay sauce is typically served with soft-boiled, poached, or hard-boiled eggs (served hot); gratins; steamed vegetables; and poached fish.

Mustard Sauce (Sauce Moutarde)

Cream sauce blended with Dijon-style prepared mustard.

Dishes prepared with mustard are often referred to as *Dijonaise* or *à la Dijon*, indicating the use of mustard, a specialty of the region around the city of Dijon. This sauce (or other mustard-flavored sauces) are typically served with grilled or boiled pig's feet or meat.

Nantua Sauce (Sauce Nantua)

Cream sauce mounted with crayfish butter, garnished with diced crayfish tails.

Nantua sauce is typically served with poached or soft-boiled eggs; veal sweetbreads; quenelles; and shellfish (see Crayfish Sauce under Velouté).

Newburg Sauce (Lobster Newburg)

Sliced lobster sautéed in butter, seasoned with salt, pepper, and paprika, lobster set aside, sherry and cream added and boiled down, thickened with egg yolks and cream, lobster then simmered briefly in the sauce.

A more involved recipe for Lobster Newburg can be found under Velouté Sauces. Whether this dish consists of primarily cream and sherry, or cream, sherry, and fish fumet, is one of those gastronomic issues eternally debated.

The original recipe was probably made with only cream, sherry, and seasonings, served at tableside. Today, as a plated dish, endless variations abound. Ideally, the dish should be prepared tableside, to adhere to the tradition of the dish (see Lobster Newburg under Velouté).

Oberskren Sauce

Cream sauce seasoned with paprika, salt, and a little sugar, and garnished with grated horseradish (Austrian).

PIEDMONT SAUCE
(Sauce à la Piémontaise)

2 tablespoons olive oil
1 small onion, finely
  chopped
4 garlic cloves, minced
1 cup cream sauce
¼ cup Piedmont (white)
  truffles, small dice

¼ cup pine nuts, lightly
  toasted
1 tablespoon chicken glaze
2 tablespoons lemon juice
2 tablespoons garlic butter
salt and white pepper to taste

- Sweat the onions and garlic in the olive oil for about 10 minutes. Add the cream sauce, and simmer another 10 minutes, or until desired thickness is achieved. Strain, and return to the fire.
- Add the truffles, pine nuts, glaze, and lemon juice. Mount with the garlic butter, and adjust seasoning.

The acclaimed white truffle of Piedmont is extremely rare, thus difficult to obtain. A North American variety (tuber gibbosum), found at the base of Douglas fir trees from California to British Columbia, is fairly common in Oregon. For information on how to obtain this, as well as other specialty food items from Oregon, contact the Oregon Department of Agriculture, 121 S.W. Salmon Street, Suite 240, Portland, Oregon 97204-2987, (503) 229-6734.

Princess Sauce (Sauce Princesse)

Cream sauce blended with chicken glaze and mushroom essence.

Royal Glaze (Glacé Royale)

Equal parts of cream sauce, Dutch sauce, and unsweetened whipped cream.

---•---

Though not commonly used in contemporary cookery, a royal glaze is made by gently folding together its three components, spreading it evenly over various dishes, then glazed under a broiler. Sole Marguery is a good example of a glazed dish (though it employs an egg yolk and cream enriched sauce instead). Glacé Royale should not be confused with royal icing (Glace Royale), a paste made from powdered sugar, egg whites, and lemon juice, that is used in confectionery work to create fine lattice-work and elaborate decorative work.

Scotch Sauce I (Sauce Écossaise I)

Light cream sauce blended with sieved hard-boiled egg yolks, garnished with julienned hard-boiled egg whites.

Scotch sauce is typically served with braised, pan-fried, or deep-fried offal; poached fish; and poached or pan-fried poultry.

Scotch Sauce II (Sauce Écossaise II)

Cream sauce garnished with finely diced (brunoise) carrots, turnips, celery root, onions, and green beans simmered in butter and white stock.

Soubise Sauce

Cream sauce simmered with onions sautéed in butter, seasoned with cayenne, then strained or puréed.

A soubise is the name applied to a thick rice, onion, and cream purée which is used as a base, coating, or stuffing in several classical dishes. A soubise sauce is a cream sauce flavored with an onion purée, though it can also be made with rice in place of roux as the thickening agent. These dishes are named after Charles de Rohan, Prince of Soubise, an eighteenth-century aristocrat.

Soubise sauce is typically served with croustades; sautéed or braised vegetables; hard-boiled eggs (served hot); soft-boiled or poached eggs; braised, shallow-fried, or deep-fried offal; braised poultry; quenelles; light meats; and mutton.

Smitane sauce is named after *smetana*, a soured cream product unique to Russia and eastern Europe. Smetana is typically served with borscht, stuffed cabbage, and Hungarian meat stews.

St. Menehould sauce is typically served with pig's feet, and grilled chicken, pork, or meat.

Sour Cream Sauce (Sauce Smitane)

Sliced onions sweated in butter, white wine added and reduced, finished with sour cream.

Saint Menehould Sauce

Cream sauce blended with meat glaze, garnished with parsley and diced mushrooms sautéed in butter.

Vernet Sauce

Cream sauce mounted with herb butter, garnished with diced truffle, sour gherkins, and hard-boiled egg whites.

Virgin Sauce (Sauce Vierge)

Cream sauce blended with artichoke purée, finished with whipped unsweetened cream.

Warsaw Sauce (Sauce Varsovienne)

Cream sauce flavored with orange juice, garnished with grated horseradish.

CONTEMPORARY INNOVATIONS

$\mathscr{A}$VOCADO SAUCE

. . . .

1 shallot, minced
1 mushroom, finely chopped
1½ cups fish stock
½ cup mussel (or bottled
    clam) juice
¼ cup dry white wine
¼ cup dry vermouth

1 cup heavy cream
¼ pound unsalted butter,
    cut into ½-inch cubes
salt and white pepper to taste
1 ripe Haas avocado, peeled
    and pitted

———— • ————

This sauce accompanies
"Beggars' Purses," as seen in
Art Culinaire (Volume 11).
(The recipe for the purses
can be found under Sauce
Arabesques.)

————————

- Simmer the shallot, mushroom, stock, and wine until reduced by half. Add the cream, and reduce by half again.
  Mount with the butter, and season with salt and pepper.
- Purée the sauce with the avocado in a blender. Strain, then
  return to the saucepan, and bring back to a simmer. Remove
  from the heat, cover, and keep warm until ready to serve.

$\mathscr{B}$EACH PLUM SAUCE

. . . .

1 large shallot, minced
1 tablespoon unsalted butter
½ cup Cognac
1 10-ounce jar beach plum
    (or plum) jelly

4 tablespoons Dijon-style
    mustard
1 cup heavy cream
salt and white pepper to taste

———— • ————

This sauce accompanies
"Roast Quail," as seen in *A
Taste For All Seasons.*

————————

- Sauté the shallot in the butter. Add the Cognac, and simmer
  until reduced to 2 tablespoons. Add the jelly, mustard, and
  heavy cream, and simmer until reduced by half. Season to
  taste with salt and pepper. Cover and keep warm until ready
  to serve.

———————— • ————————

The beach plum thrives in the very sandy soil found in
eastern and northeastern seashore communities in the
United States. The plant blossoms in May, and the berries
are ready to pick in early October. Ranging in diameter
from 1 to 2 inches, depending on the wetness of the sum-

mer, at harvest time the berries are pink on one side and red on the other. Round and smooth like plums—hence their name—the fruit is very juicy, with large pits. Because of their tartness, beach plums can only be used for jelly, jam, or wine, a Nantucket Island (off the coast of Massachusetts) specialty.

CHAMPAGNE SAUCE

This sauce is served with "Lobster and Scallops on Fettuccine," innovated by Alan R. Gibson, formerly chef of The Pillar House, as seen in *The Pillar House Cookbook* (the recipe follows).

1 large shallot, minced
2 tablespoons unsalted butter
1 cup dry champagne
1 fresh thyme sprig
¼ vanilla bean, split
1 pint heavy cream
salt and white pepper to taste

- Sauté the shallot in the butter, covered, for 1 minute.
- Add the champagne, thyme, and vanilla bean. Simmer until reduced to one-third. Add the cream, and continue simmering until reduced by half. Season with salt and pepper, strain, and set aside, keeping warm until ready to serve.

ROASTED LOBSTER IN WHISKEY, CHIVE SAUCE

¼ cup vegetable oil
4 lobsters, 1¼ pounds each
1 medium onion, roughly cut
1 carrot, roughly cut
1 rib celery, roughly cut
1 leek, well washed and roughly cut
2 garlic cloves, crushed
1 sprig fresh thyme
½ cup bourbon
½ cup dry white wine
1 shallot, minced
1 bay leaf
3 tablespoons chives, minced
1 cup heavy cream
4 tablespoons unsalted butter, cut into ¼-inch cubes
salt and white pepper to taste

- Preheat oven to 375°F.
- Stun each lobster by piercing the top center of the shell with the point of a cook's knife, about 1 inch below the eyes.

- Pour the oil into a roasting pan large enough to accommodate the four lobsters, and place the pan into the oven. Leave it there for 5 minutes.
- Carefully place the vegetables and thyme in the pan, then set the four lobsters upside down on top. Roast for 15 minutes.
- Pull the pan out of the oven and place it on top of the stove. Turn on the fire, and pour the bourbon over the lobsters and vegetables. Ignite *very carefully* with a lit match. Let flame a minute, then extinguish with the white wine.
- Remove the lobsters, and set aside. Place the remaining ingredients into a large saucepan, along with the shallot and bay leaf. Simmer until reduced by half. Add the cream, and continue simmering until reduced by half again. Strain the sauce, return it to the pan, and set aside.
- Place each lobster face down on a cutting board, its tail naturally curled underneath. Grasp the body of the lobster with one hand, and split the tail in half with a large cook's knife. Tear the two split portions from the body. Pull off the claws, and crack them with either the heel of the knife or with a lobster cracker (essentially the same as a nut cracker). Remove the meat from the tails and claws with a cocktail fork or nut pick.
- Bring the sauce to a simmer and add the butter, stirring continuously until fully incorporated. Adjust seasoning with salt and pepper.
- Arrange the lobster meat on appropriate serving plates. Top with the chive sauce, and serve.

*C*IDER SAUCE

1 large shallot, minced
2 tablespoons unsalted butter
½ cup apple cider
2 tablespoons sultana raisins

¼ cup dry white wine
1 tablespoon curry powder
1½ cups heavy cream
salt and white pepper to taste

This sauce accompanies "New York State Foie Gras and Wild Mushrooms," as seen in *A Taste For All Seasons*.

- Sauté the shallot in the butter over a medium flame for 5 minutes. Add the cider, raisins, wine, and curry powder. Simmer until reduced by two-thirds. Add the heavy cream, and reduce by one-third. Season to taste with salt and pepper, then set aside, keeping warm until ready to serve.

CILANTRO CREAM

1 cup shiitake mushrooms, stemmed and cut into julienne
1 cup oyster mushrooms, cut into julienne
4 cloves elephant garlic, cut into julienne

2 tablespoons unsalted butter
1 cup dry white wine
2 cups heavy cream
salt and white pepper to taste
½ cup cilantro, minced

This sauce accompanies "Grilled Shrimp Forestière," as seen in *A Taste For All Seasons*.

- Sauté the mushrooms and garlic in the butter for 3 or 4 minutes. Add the white wine. Simmer and reduce until 2 or 3 tablespoons remain.
- Add the cream, and simmer until reduced by half. Season to taste with salt and pepper. Add the chopped cilantro, then set aside, keeping warm until ready to serve.

SEA SCALLOPS, DIJON CREAM

For the crème fraîche
2 cups heavy cream
½ cup buttermilk

½ cup sour cream or yogurt
¼ teaspoon salt

- Combine all the ingredients in a clean saucepan, and bring to a temperature of 100°F.
- Place into a clean stainless steel bowl, cover, and set into an oven heated only by the pilot light (12 hours).
- Refrigerate for 24 hours. Carefully remove thickened top part (this is the crème fraîche), and discard any liquid left at the bottom. Cover and refrigerate until ready to use.

For the potatoes
½ teaspoon salt
1½ pounds all-purpose potatoes, peeled
4 tablespoons unsalted butter

⅓ cup half-and-half
3 egg yolks
salt and white pepper to taste
pinch of nutmeg

- Boil the potatoes in approximately 2 quarts of salted water until they are tender, but still firm. Drain them, and place on a pan in a 200° oven until completely dry.

- Purée the potatoes with a food mill, mashing tool, or hand-held electric mixer.
- Add the butter, half-and-half, yolks, and seasoning, and blend thoroughly.
- Place the potatoes into a pastry bag with a star tip, and pipe the potatoes out onto the edge of either a scallop shell or an oven-proof casserole.

For the scallops
1½ cups sea scallops
3 tablespoons unsalted butter
¼ cup dry white wine
1 cup crème fraîche
3 teaspoons Dijon-style mustard
pinch of fresh thyme
salt and white pepper to taste

- Preheat oven to 375°F.
- Sauté the scallops in the butter for 3 minutes. Remove them with a slotted spoon, and set aside. Place the shell or casserole into the oven, and bake for 8 to 10 minutes, or until golden brown. Set aside.
- In the meantime, add the white wine to the pan and reduce by half. Add the crème fraîche, mustard, thyme, salt and pepper. Return the scallops to this sauce, and bring to a boil.
- Ladle the scallop mixture into the shells or casseroles, and serve.

This dish was innovated by Alan R. Gibson, formerly chef of The Pillar House, as seen in *The Pillar House Cookbook.*

GINGER SAUCE

3 tablespoons grated ginger root
¼ cup dry white wine
1 shallot, minced
½ cup heavy cream
¼ pound unsalted butter, cut into ¼-inch cubes
salt and white pepper to taste

- Simmer the ginger, wine, and shallot until 1 tablespoon remains. Add the cream, and continue simmering until reduced by half.
- Add the butter and stir continuously, until fully incorporated. Remove from the fire, season to taste with salt and pepper, and strain. Cover and set aside, keeping warm until ready to serve.

This sauce accompanies "Grilled Swordfish, Ginger Sauce and Cranberry Compote, as seen in *A Taste For All Seasons.*

GRILLED CHICKEN BREAST WITH BLACK BEANS AND GOAT CHEESE SAUCE

For the beans
2 cups black beans, culled, and soaked overnight in cold water
2 cups chicken stock
1 small onion, quartered
1 small carrot, peeled and roughly chopped
1 stalk celery, roughly chopped
4 cloves
2 bay leaves
2 sprigs fresh thyme
pinch of salt

For the chicken
4 chicken breasts, skinless, boneless, and lightly pounded
salt and white pepper to taste

For the sauce
1½ cups dry white wine
6 shallots, minced
1 cup heavy cream
6 ounces goat cheese
2 tablespoons unsalted butter
pinch of white pepper

- Drain the beans. Place in a saucepan with the stock, vegetables, cloves, herbs, and salt. Bring to a boil, and skim foam and impurities from the top. Simmer 1½ hours, or until tender but not mushy. Drain, remove the vegetables, and set aside, keeping warm.

- Simmer the wine and shallots until reduced by half. Add the cream, and continue simmering until reduced by half again.

- Remove to a blender, along with the cheese, butter, and pepper, and purée. Strain through a sieve, cover, and keep warm until ready to serve.

- Season the chicken breasts with salt and pepper, and grill or broil 4 minutes on each side. Slice the breasts, and arrange on serving plates. Top with the sauce, accompanied by the beans to one side.

——— • ———

This recipe innovated by Thierry Rautureau, Chef/Proprietor of Rover's Restaurant, Seattle, Washington.

———

JALAPEÑO SAUCE

1 large Spanish onion, peeled and roughly chopped

2 garlic cloves, crushed
2 jalapeño peppers, split, ribs and seeds discarded

3 green bell peppers, split,
ribs and seeds discarded
2 tablespoons olive oil

1 cup dry white wine
1 cup heavy cream
¼ teaspoon salt

This sauce accompanies "Crab Cakes," as seen in *A Taste For All Seasons*.

- Sauté the onion, garlic, and peppers in the olive oil 4 or 5 minutes. Add the white wine, and simmer 5 minutes. Add the cream and salt, and simmer another 5 minutes. Purée in a food processor and set aside, keeping warm until ready to serve.

ℒEMON-CREAM SAUCE

1 shallot, minced
4 tablespoons unsalted butter
¼ cup dry white wine
2 tablespoons lemon juice
1 tarragon sprig, chopped

4 thyme sprigs, chopped
1 pint heavy cream
¼ teaspoon salt
⅛ teaspoon white pepper

This sauce accompanies "Breast of Chicken," innovated by Alan R. Gibson, formerly chef of The Pillar House, as seen in *The Pillar House Cookbook*. (It is also excellent tossed with freshly cooked pasta.)

- Sauté the shallot in half of the butter for 3 minutes. Add the wine, lemon juice, and herbs, and simmer until reduced by two-thirds. Strain.
- Add the cream, and continue simmering until reduced by half. Cut the remaining butter into ¼-inch cubes, and add to the sauce, stirring continuously until fully incorporated. Season with salt and pepper, and strain. Cover and set aside in a warm place until ready to serve.

ℳANGO-PORT SAUCE

1 ripe mango, peeled, pitted, and puréed in a food processor
1 shallot, minced
½ cup port wine
¼ teaspoon sugar

2 cups heavy cream
4 tablespoons unsalted butter, cut into ¼-inch chunks
salt and white pepper to taste

This sauce accompanies "Grilled Breast of Duckling," innovated by Alan R. Gibson, formerly chef of The Pillar House, and seen in *The Pillar House Cookbook*.

- Simmer the shallot and port wine until about 2 tablespoons remain. Add the mango purée and sugar, and continue cooking until the sugar is dissolved. Add the cream, blend well, and simmer until reduced by a third, or until the sauce reaches the desired thickness.

- Add the butter and blend continuously, until fully incorporated. Season with salt and pepper, then set aside in a warm place until ready to serve.

MARSALA CREAM

1 shallot, minced
1 tablespoon unsalted butter
1 cup dry marsala wine
1 teaspoon fresh thyme
  leaves

1 cup heavy cream
2 tablespoons unsalted
  butter, cut into ¼-inch
  cubes
salt and white pepper to taste

- Sauté shallot in the butter, covered, for 5 minutes. Add the marsala and thyme, and reduce until about 2 tablespoons of liquid remain.
- Add the cream, and continue simmering until reduced by half. Add the butter, and stir continuously, until fully emulsified. Season with salt and pepper. Set aside, keeping warm until ready to serve.

This sauce accompanies "Medallions of Veal, Ragout of Wild Mushrooms," innovated by Alan R. Gibson, formerly chef of The Pillar House, as seen in *The Pillar House Cookbook.*

MISO SAUCE

stems of 12 shiitake
  mushrooms
1 shallot, minced
6 tablespoons dry white wine
2 cups heavy cream

2 tablespoons light miso
  paste
1 teaspoon soy sauce
¼ teaspoon white pepper

- Simmer the stems, shallots, and white wine in a small saucepan until 2 or 3 tablespoons remain. Add the remaining ingredients, and continue simmering until reduced by half. Cover and set aside, keeping warm until ready to serve.

This sauce accompanies "Grilled Shiitake Mushrooms" as seen in *A Taste For All Seasons.*

Miso is a fermented and aged soy bean paste unique to Japanese cuisine. It has a very high protein content, and is often used as a substitute for meat and meat juice reductions. Miso can be purchased in any health food market.

𝒫ARSLEY SAUCE

1 bunch fresh parsley, well washed, stems removed
1½ cups heavy cream
½ cup fish stock
½ cup dry white wine
salt and white pepper to taste

- Blanch the parsley in boiling salted water for 3 minutes. Drain, and purée in a food processor with a little of the cream.
- Simmer the stock and the wine in a small saucepan until reduced by two-thirds. Add the remaining cream and simmer until reduced by half. Stir in the parsley purée, and season to taste with salt and pepper. Set aside, keeping warm until ready to serve.

——— • ———

This sauce accompanies "Ocean Sausages with Salmon Caviar," as seen in *A Taste For All Seasons*.

𝒫OACHED SEA TROUT, PURPLE BASIL SAUCE

4 6-ounce sea trout fillets
salt and white pepper as needed
¼ cup melted butter
2 large shallots, minced
2 ripe medium tomatoes, peeled, seeded, and diced
6 large mushrooms, sliced
1 tablespoon chopped parsley
1 cup dry white wine
1½ cups heavy cream
2 tablespoons unsalted butter
10 purple basil leaves, cut into fine julienne

- Preheat oven to 350°F.
- Lightly butter an ovenproof baking dish.
- Season the fish lightly with salt and pepper, and place it in the dish.
- Sprinkle the shallots, tomatoes, mushrooms, and parsley over the fish. Drizzle the melted butter over this, and pour in the white wine. Cover, and place into the preheated oven for 12 minutes, or until the fish is tender.
- Pour the liquid from the fish into a small saucepan. Simmer until reduced by half. Add the heavy cream, and again simmer until reduced by half.
- Place the fillets on serving plates, top with some of the sauce, and sprinkle with julienned basil leaves.

——— • ———

Purple basil is one of at least a dozen different varieties of *Ocimum basilicum*, and a member of the mint family. The purple variety is used here primarily for its color, but its flavor is nearly the same as the green variety, and can be substituted if the purple variety is unavailable.

Sea trout belong to the drum family of fish, so named for a drumming sound made by the male species. True sea trout is found in European waters, and is similar to our salmon in that it returns to the fresh waters from which it came, often traveling considerable distances to do so. The record for the longest homing run—more than 600 miles—is reportedly held by a Polish sea trout.

Sea trout in the United States is often called weakfish, so named for weak mouth tissues that are easily torn by fish hooks. They are found in the Atlantic, from Massachusetts to Florida, close to shore in the summer months, migrating south and offshore during winter months.

This recipe can be found in *A Taste For All Seasons*.

Roasted Garlic Sauce

1 garlic bulb
¾ cup dry white wine
1 shallot, minced

1½ cups heavy cream
salt and white pepper to taste

- Preheat oven to 325°F.
- Place the garlic bulb on a small roasting pan, with enough water to almost cover it.
- Simmer the wine and shallot in a saucepan, until 2 tablespoons remain. Break up the garlic bulb and squeeze the individual cloves into the pan. Add the cream, and simmer until reduced by half. Purée the sauce in a blender, strain, and season to taste with salt and pepper. Set aside, keeping warm until ready to serve.

This sauce accompanies "Asparagus and Forest Mushrooms in Phyllo," as seen in *A Taste For All Seasons*.

Roquefort Sauce

This sauce accompanies "Sirloin Steak," innovated by Alan R. Gibson, formerly chef of The Pillar House, as seen in *The Pillar House Cookbook*.

1 shallot, minced
¼ cup dry white wine
2 cups heavy cream

3 tablespoons crumbled Roquefort cheese
pinch of salt

- Simmer the shallot and wine until nearly dry. Add the cream, and continue simmering until reduced by half. Add the cheese and salt and set aside, keeping warm until ready to serve.

Roquefort cheese is produced in the French town of the same name. A mold, introduced into the milk and cream at a certain point in its creation, produces the blue veins for which it is well known. If unavailable, any variety of blue cheese can be substituted.

ℛOSEMARY-POMMERY SAUCE

2 tablespoons unsalted butter
1 shallot, minced
½ cup petit sirah, or other light-bodied red wine
2 sprigs fresh rosemary, chopped
1 sprig fresh thyme, chopped

1 bay leaf
1 pint heavy cream
1 heaping tablespoon Pommery or other grainy mustard
salt and white pepper to taste

This sauce accompanies "Roast Rack of Lamb," innovated by Alan R. Gibson, formerly chef of The Pillar House, as seen in *The Pillar House Cookbook*.

- Sauté shallot in the butter, covered, for 3 minutes. Add the wine and herbs, and simmer until reduced to about 2 tablespoons of liquid. Add the cream, and continue simmering until reduced by half. Stir in the mustard, season with salt and pepper, and strain. Set aside, keeping warm until ready to serve.

ℳUSSEL BARQUETTES, SAFFRON SAUCE

20 barquette pastry shells
1 small shallot, minced
1 cup dry white wine
1 sprig fresh thyme
20 large mussels, debearded and well rinsed

pinch of saffron
1 cup minced leeks, white part only
1 cup heavy cream
¼ cup chives, sliced paper thin

- Bring the shallots, wine, and thyme to a boil. Add the mussels, cover, and simmer until all the mussel shells are open. Remove the mussels from the pan.

- Ladle off the bulk of the liquid and place in a clean saucepan, discarding the last remaining bit (in the event any sand was expulsed into this liquid). Add the saffron and leeks, and simmer until reduced by three-fourths. Add the cream and continue simmering until reduced by half, or until the sauce is thick and creamy.

- Remove the mussels from their shells and add them to the sauce. Stir, then remove from the fire. Place a teaspoon of the sauce into each barquette shell, and top with a mussel. Heat in a 350°F oven for about 5 minutes, sprinkle with chopped chives, and serve.

This recipe is from *A Taste For All Seasons*.

A barquette is a small boat-shaped tart shell, made of short-crust pastry (pie dough), and filled with sweet or savory ingredients, and served hot or cold as hors d'oeuvres, appetizers, garnishes, or desserts.

Saffron and Green Peppercorn Sauce

1 large shallot, minced	½ teaspoon saffron
3 tablespoons olive oil	½ cup dry white wine
1 teaspoon green peppercorns, mashed	1½ cups heavy cream
	salt and white pepper to taste

This sauce designed to accompany "Steamed Flounder," as seen in *A Taste For All Seasons*.

- Sauté the shallot in the olive oil over medium heat, for 3 or 4 minutes. Add the peppercorns, saffron, and white wine. Simmer until reduced by half. Add the cream, and continue simmering until again reduced by half. Season to taste with salt and white pepper, then set aside, keeping warm until ready to serve.

Sea Scallops with Saffron and Pepper Cream

1½ pounds sea scallops	1 large shallot, minced
salt, black pepper, and flour as needed	1 garlic clove, pressed
2 tablespoons olive oil	2 pinches saffron
¼ cup dry white wine	2 cups heavy cream
	black pepper as needed

- Pat the scallops dry with a clean towel. Sprinkle them lightly with salt and pepper, and dust lightly with flour. Sauté in the olive oil over high heat for 1 minute, browning them all over. Remove with a slotted spoon and set aside. Wipe out the pan with a clean paper towel.
- Place the wine, shallot, garlic, and saffron in the pan, and simmer until reduced by half. Add the cream, and continue simmering until reduced again by half.
- Strain the sauce, then nap 4 individual serving plates with sauce and arrange the scallops in the center of each plate. Top with fresh grated black pepper on and around the scallops, and serve.

This recipe is from A Taste For All Seasons.

PRAWNS WITH TANGERINE AND RIESLING

2 shallots, minced
2 tablespoons unsalted butter
2 tablespoons olive oil
16 large prawns, shelled, deveined, tails removed
1 cup Riesling wine
juice of 1 tangerine

1 cup heavy cream
salt and white pepper to taste
12 sprigs watercress
12 tangerine segments, trimmed and seeded

- Sauté shallots in the butter and olive oil for 3 minutes. Add the prawns and sauté for another minute or two. Remove the prawns and set aside.
- Add the wine and tangerine juice, and simmer until 2 or 3 tablespoons of liquid remains. Add the cream and reduce by half. Return the prawns, bring to a simmer, and season to taste with salt and pepper.
- Arrange 4 prawns radially on each of 4 serving plates. Top with the sauce, and garnish with watercress and tangerine segments.

VERGÉ SAUCE

½ cup crème fraîche
2 tablespoons Dijon-style mustard

juice of ½ lemon
2 tablespoons fresh chives, minced

This sauce accompanies "Asparagus," innovated by Alan R. Gibson, formerly chef of The Pillar House, as seen in *The Pillar House Cookbook.*

....

This sauce accompanies "Salmon Tortellini," innovated by Alan R. Gibson, formerly chef of The Pillar House, as seen in *The Pillar House Cookbook.*

....

- Combine all the ingredients, and place over medium heat, stir continuously until hot and thoroughly blended. Set aside, keeping warm until ready to serve.

VODKA CREAM

1 shallot, minced	2 teaspoons Dijon-style
1 large garlic clove, pressed	mustard
2 tablespoons butter	1 cup crème fraîche (or sour
2 tablespoons vodka	cream)

- Sauté the shallot and garlic in the butter for 3 minutes. Add the vodka and mustard, and blend thoroughly. Add the crème fraîche, stir to blend thoroughly. Bring to a boil, them remove from the fire.

CRÈME FRAÎCHE

2 cups heavy cream	½ cup sour cream or yogurt
½ cup buttermilk	¼ teaspoon salt

- Combine all the ingredients in a clean saucepan, and bring to a temperature of 100°F.
- Place into a clean stainless steel bowl, cover, and set into a cold oven overnight (12 hours).
- Refrigerate for 24 hours. Carefully remove thickened top part (this is the crème fraîche), and discard any liquid left at the bottom. Cover and refrigerate until ready to use.

Crème fraîche is sort of a French version of sour cream, though it has a considerably higher fat content and a different flavor (difficult to describe). It can be used in a myriad of ways—worked into salad dressings, savory and sweet sauces. It is also excellent as a design medium for dessert Arabesques (see section on sauce painting, chapter 16).

WILD MUSHROOM CREAM SAUCE

2 tablespoons unsalted butter
1 small shallot, minced
4 sprigs fresh thyme, tied together
½ pound fresh shiitake, chanterelle, or oyster mushrooms (or other variety, in any combination thereof)

¼ cup dry white wine
¼ cup brandy or Cognac
1½ cups heavy cream
3 tablespoons unsalted butter, cut into quarter-inch cubes
salt and white pepper to taste

- Heat a sauté pan over a medium flame. When fairly hot (not too hot), add the butter, and sauté shallots, thyme, and mushrooms 3 or 4 minutes. Add the white wine and brandy or Cognac. Remove the mushrooms with a slotted spoon and set aside. Reduce the liquid until approximately 2 tablespoons remain.
- Add the cream, bring to a simmer, and reduce by half. Return the mushrooms to the cream, and continue simmering until it reaches the right thickness.
- Add the butter and work in to the sauce by stirring continuously over the medium flame.

———— • ————

Wild mushroom cream sauce is ideally served with any poultry or light game— chicken, duck, pheasant, quail, partridge, etc.

————————

WATERCRESS SAUCE

1 tablespoon unsalted butter
1 small shallot, minced
¼ cup dry white wine
2 cups heavy cream
pinch of salt

pinch of white pepper
leaves of 1 bunch watercress, rinsed, dried, and finely minced

- Sauté shallots in the butter about 3 minutes. Add the white wine, blend, and reduce until nearly dry.
- Add the heavy cream, salt and pepper. Simmer until reduced by about half. Add the minced watercress, and continue reducing until desired viscosity is reached. Adjust seasoning with salt and white pepper.

The primary attraction of watercress for culinary uses is its peppery pungency. Medicinally, like other *cruciferae* (mustard family), it functions as a stimulant, diuretic, and antiscorbutic (prevents scurvy). Since cooking quickly alters that pungency, the cress here is added near the end, retaining as much of its flavor as possible.

CHAPTER 9

BUTTER SAUCES

SOME BACKGROUND ON BUTTER

Butter is composed of approximately 80 percent fat, 18 percent water, and 2 percent milk solids (milk solids include naturally occurring salt, casein, and whey proteins). In the United States, we are familiar primarily with two varieties of butter—salted and unsalted. Yet there are many different varieties, made from varying degrees of quality of cream, and representing numerous styles of production. There is also a long and intriguing history associated with butter, and in modern times a great battle between the dairy industry and the modern manufacturers of margarine.

At the age of 15, I spent a summer as a "farm cadet," working on a dairy farm on the northern border of New York State. I was involved in all activities of farm life, which included rising at 4:30 A.M. every morning, seven days a week, performing peripheral tasks in the milking of their herd of dairy cattle. Throughout the summer, there was a regular supply of unpasteurized and unhomogenized milk, served at mealtimes, as well as fresh butter churned from the cream that rose to the top of those pitchers. Though I didn't know then that I would eventually choose the food service industry as a career route, the experience afforded me an understanding of the fundamentals of the dairy industry, as well as firsthand knowledge of how butter is made. I find it curious today that many of my culinary students have nary a clue as to what butter is or how it is created.

Butter has historically been produced in the cold northern parts of the world, where long sunless winters meant an absence of important dietary nutrients, particularly vitamins A and D. With limited exposure to sunlight (human skin manufactures vitamin D when exposed to the sun), and a short growing season, dairy products provided those two essential vitamins, as well as calcium, phosphorus, and some trace minerals. Southern Europe and the more temperate locales bordering the Mediterranean, on the other hand, have traditionally preferred olive and walnut oils in their cooking. An ancient Greek poet, mocking a fourth century Thracian wedding, once described the guests at that wedding as "butterophagous gentry." In fact, as late as the eighteenth century, the people of Mediterranean lands believed that butter was the cause of leprosy, which seemed to be more prevalent in the cold north. And it is well known that the indigenous peoples of the Orient have long been lactose intolerant, even though all humans are born with the enzyme lactase, which enables us to digest mother's milk. Except for areas of the world where dairy foods are consumed as a source of essential nutrition, the human body's ability to manufacture lactase is lost shortly thereafter. It is further interesting to note that when the Japanese first came into contact with Europeans, they were appalled by their foul body odor, a consequence of their consumption of animal flesh and fats. The Japanese called them *bata-kusai,* or "butter-stinkers."

In the northern European countries where butter is an integral part of the diet, the cream is handled or treated before churning to give it additional character. Germany, Austria, Belgium, Switzerland, France, Holland, and Denmark variously add a bacterial culture, creating "ripe butter." Another method involves allowing the cream to "ripen," anywhere from three to seven days, before churning it into butter. Interestingly, archaeological digs in Ireland, Scotland, and Scandinavia have uncovered barrels of ancient butter buried in the cool, antiseptic environment of peat bogs. Though it is believed that this practice was a means of safekeeping butter from enemies during times of war (trees were sometimes planted to mark a burial site), it was also a way to ferment, or "ripen" the butter, making it more delicious. The French create a piquant and tart-flavored butter by fashioning it from *crème fraîche,* a cultured cream product similar to our sour cream. And finally, butter production is not limited to cow's milk. In the African and Asian countries that do produce some dairy products, the milk of buffalo, camel, donkey, goat, sheep, and yak is used, creating butter of even stronger and more unique flavor.

The color and flavor of butter is intrinsically related to the diet of the dairy animals from which the butter is produced. Butter produced in the winter tends to be pale and less distinctively flavored, since winter diet consists of stored hay and grain; butter produced in summer months tends to be brighter yellow and stronger flavored, since the herds graze on fresh pastures, which may include yellow-tinted wildflowers such as buttercups (hence the origin of that flower's name).

No discussion of the intricacies, history, and subtle differences among butters is complete without some mention of margarine. In 1913, chemist Michel Chevreul isolated a substance from animal fat that formed pearl-shaped drops. He named this substance *margaric acid,* deriving it from the Greek word for pearl, *margaron.* In the mid-nineteenth century, Europe experienced a disastrous cattle plague, which precipitated a serious shortage of both butter and animal fats required for the production of industrial lubricants and soap. Napoleon III offered a prize for the formulation of a synthetic edible fat, and in 1869, chemist and pharmacist Hippolyte Mège-Mouriés was awarded the prize for his new spread. He was not the first chemist to give suet a spreadable texture, but he was the first to add a small amount of milk, giving the spread some palatability. From a gastronomic point of view, there really is no place for what Margaret Visser once termed "the most adulterated product in the history of man." (Ms. Visser discusses the fascinating and intense historical battle between dairy producers and the manufacturers of "marge" in her informative work, *Much Depends On Dinner*, c. 1986, Collier Books.)

Of the two varieties of butter most available to us, the unsalted variety is superior, since it is fresher than the salted variety, and overall less adulterated. A European style butter is now available in the United States, though it is expensive and difficult to find. Another way to obtain butter is through a technique I learned from Peter Van Erp, one of the most knowledgeable professional chefs I have had the good fortune to work with. At the rustic private club where I worked under his tutelage many years ago, we discovered several quarts of heavy cream in the walk-in refrigerator that were well past the expiration date stamped on the package. Examining their contents, I found that they had indeed turned sour, although "ripe" is the word used where strong-flavored dairy products are held in high esteem. I was preparing to discard the cream when the chef stopped me and instructed me to pour all of the cream into a large mixing bowl, and whip it until it curdled. I whipped it well past whipped cream until it all sort of clumped together, leaving a mass of butter, and a white, watery liquid at the bottom of the bowl. I removed the mass of coagulated fat to a large sheet of muslin, and massaged it for some time, until most of the water contained within was squeezed out. What remained was a most delicious tasting, piquant butter, which the chef later used for sauces, sautéing, pastries, and so on. I have used this same technique on occasion, both as a means of recovering a use for soured heavy cream and as an effective way to demonstrate to students from where butter is derived.

BUTTER SAUCES

When heat is applied to butter, the result is four distinct products, three of which are considered a form of sauce. At the moment when butter first reaches melted form, foaming up slightly, it is called *beurre fondu*—melted butter, a sauce that in earlier times qualified a dish as "à la Hollandaise" (see note following *Dutch Sauce*).

The next stage is *beurre clarifié*—clarified butter, produced with a larger quantity of butter, allowing it to simmer a bit longer beyond the first stage, then separating the fat from the milk solids, and carefully straining it. Clarified butter is used for sautéing (it has a higher smoking point with the solids removed), as an important component in roux, and for making cooked-egg emulsified sauces.

The third stage is *beurre noisette*—brown butter, possessing a golden brown color and a slightly nutty flavor and aroma when the milk solids caramelize (noisette also means "nut," a reference to both the color and aroma of the butter). If left on the fire a little longer, the result is *beurre noir*—black butter, an obscure and today rarely used sauce accompaniment. Even more obscure are some of the dishes with which black butter is served—among them poached skate and calves' brains.

Until recently, small butter sauces were categorized under the mother sauce heading of Hollandaise, and nearly all were variations of the cooked-egg emulsified sauce named after the Netherlands. Because of contemporary innovations based on beurre blanc, the Hollandaise heading has been changed to *Butter Sauces*, then further expanded into two sub-headings: Hollandaise (cooked emulsified egg sauces), and Beurre Blanc. We take some liberty with the French "beurre blanc," since it would be misleading to name a subdivision "butter sauce," under a heading of the same name.

Within Escoffier's sauce system, Hollandaise has served as a mother sauce, from which various smaller sauces could be made. The variations between small sauces, though subtle, are important. Béarnaise, for example, is not accurately a Hollandaise finished with a reduction of tarragon, vinegar, shallot, and pepper. It does include yolks, butter, and salt, but the lemon juice of Hollandaise is substituted with the tarragon reduction. Béarnaise then serves as a base for several other derivatives.

Beurre noisette is typically served with braised, pan-fried, or deep-fried offal; sautéed fish roe (such as shad or cod); and grilled or sautéed fish.

Guidelines for Preparation of Butter Sauces

There are some important differences between Hollandaise and beurre blanc, and some important steps to consider in their preparation. Hollandaise is easily translated from recipe form to actual practice, and can be made before kitchen production begins. It should be placed in a clean stainless steel container and held in a warm area, generally on a shelf above the cooking range. The temperature there averages 110—120°F, and will maintain the warmth of the sauce. If there is insufficient heat, the butter will begin to solidify; if there is too much heat, the sauce will separate. At any point in it's production or holding storage, a broken Hollandaise can be reemulsified by whipping the curdled mix, using a clean bowl and whip, into two tablespoons of warm water. Be sure to pour the broken sauce very slowly at first, while whipping continuously.

There are also important concerns with holding Hollandaise at the temperature that keeps it warm, but is not hot enough to break it. The warm, moist, dark environment Hollandaise is stored in is an excellent breeding ground for bacteria, particularly if the eggs are contaminated with salmonella. Preparing Hollandaise with clean, sterilized utensils is one way to prevent such a problem. It is also a good idea to know the source of the eggs. Salmonella and other bacteria breed in unsanitary conditions, where the hens are cooped up in small pens, and their movement in and out of those pens is restricted. Recent consumer concerns over the presence of salmonella in eggs and chicken products have given rise to the marketing of "free-range" poultry. Ideally, restaurant operators should purchase only fresh eggs, solely from producers who are aware of the dangers that come with antiquated facilities and obsolete techniques. For the retail consumer, "free-range" is one way of assuring that such products are safe for their consumption. The freshness of eggs is very important, not only for their superior qualities of taste and sanitation, but for their lecithin content as well. Lecithin, a naturally occurring element in egg yolks, is a natural emulsifier. The older the egg, the more its lecithin content declines.

The level of heat used for the initial cooking of the yolks is also important. They should be beaten in a clean stainless steel bowl, over barely simmering hot water. This will take 5–10 minutes, depending on the quantity. If the water is too hot, the eggs will curdle (like scrambled eggs), and there is no way to reverse that. The curdled eggs must be discarded, and the sauce started over again with a new batch of eggs.

The eggs will be fully cooked when they have thickened slightly, and their volume has approximately doubled. They are then removed from the fire, and the hot clarified butter, lemon juice, and seasoning are added. It is a good idea to accomplish this by placing a damp clean cloth over the top of the pot of hot water, then placing the bowl over this. This helps to maintain the heat of the sauce, and also frees the saucier's hands for the task, since the bowl sits securely in the damp cloth. This may not seem important, but from my experience in busy kitchens, there are times when the pace is fast and furious, and there are literally no co-workers available to stand and hold a bowl of cooked eggs while another pours in and incorporates the butter.

Finding the right balance of viscosity and taste is also a matter of experience. Eggs vary in their ability to emulsify the sauce. Lemon juice not only adds the tart acidity to balance out the fat, it also thins the sauce. An experienced saucier can accomplish this easily and with expedience, perhaps by alternating the lemon juice with hot water to help achieve this balance. It is also interesting to point out (depending on which text one refers to) that the acid in classical Hollandaise is often a white wine and cracked pepper reduction. In actual contemporary practice, however, lemon juice is almost exclusively used, while the reduction approach is used for Béarnaise and a handful of derivatives.

 ᗪUTCH SAUCE
(Sauce Hollandaise)

5 large egg yolks	pinch of cayenne pepper
2 tablespoons water	1 pint clarified butter
pinch of salt	juice of one lemon

- In a stainless steel bowl, over a saucepan of barely simmering water (bain marie), beat the yolks, water, salt, and pepper with a whip until thick (about 5 minutes).
- Remove from heat, lift up the bowl, and place a clean damp towel over the top and down under the saucepan. Set the bowl on top of the saucepan, over the cloth, and pour the butter in a slow steady stream, while beating continuously. As the mixture thickens, alternate the butter with some of the lemon juice. Continue until all of the butter and lemon juice are emulsified. Adjust the thickness of the sauce by beating in additional hot water. Set aside in a warm area until ready to use.

———————————— • ————————————

When cooking and whipping the yolks, be careful that the water beneath them is just barely simmering. If it is too hot, the eggs will cook too fast and turn into scrambled eggs.

Sauce Matrix IV
Dutch Sauce and Its Derivatives

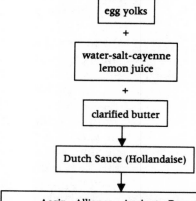

egg yolks

+

water-salt-cayenne
lemon juice

+

clarified butter

Dutch Sauce (Hollandaise)

Aegir   Alliance   Ancient   Bavarian
Champagne   Chantilly (Mousseline)   Flowerette
Daumont   Divine   Dunant   Flemish   Hazelnut
Lombard   Maltese   Marguery   Marquise
Maximilian   Mussel   Omega   Piccalilli
Rubens   Unequaled   Uzés   Waterfish

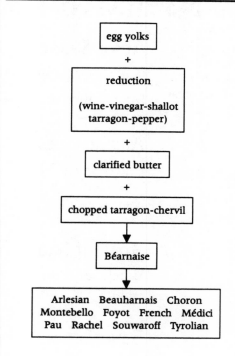

egg yolks

+

reduction

(wine-vinegar-shallot
tarragon-pepper)

+

clarified butter

+

chopped tarragon-chervil

Béarnaise

Arlesian   Beauharnais   Choron
Montebello   Foyot   French   Médici
Pau   Rachel   Souwaroff   Tyrolian

The clarified butter should be 130–140°F (no hotter than 150°F). Be sure to incorporate the butter into the cooked egg yolks in a slow, steady stream. If the butter is added too fast, the yolks cannot absorb the butter fast enough, and the sauce can break. If this happens, take another clean bowl and whip, and put in 2 tablespoons of warm water. Add the broken sauce, very slowly, in very small amounts, whipping continuously. Add the remaining butter and lemon juice.

The only clue we find as to why a cooked emulsified egg sauce is named Dutch Sauce (*Hollandaise* is a French word meaning "Dutch style") is that in earlier times, *à la Hollandaise* indicated a dish served with melted butter, a reflection of the importance of butter in Dutch cookery. From this then evolved a melted butter sauce more securely thickened using egg yolks.

Hollandaise is typically served with soft-boiled or poached eggs; poached fish; steamed vegetables.

TRADITIONAL DERIVATIVES OF DUTCH SAUCE

A mustard-flavored Dutch sauce is typically served with grilled fish and meat, and breaded, pan-fried meat.

Aegir Sauce (Girondin Sauce)

Dutch sauce seasoned with dry or prepared mustard.

Alliance Sauce

Dutch sauce flavored with a reduction of tarragon vinegar, white wine, cayenne and white pepper, garnished with chopped chervil.

Ancient Sauce (Sauce Ancienne)

Dutch sauce garnished with diced sour gherkins, mushrooms (sautéed in butter and lemon juice, and drained), and truffles.

Bavarian Sauce (Sauce Bavaroise)

Dutch sauce beaten with crayfish butter, garnished with diced crayfish tails.

CHAMPAGNE SAUCE
(Sauce au Champagne)

1 shallot, minced
1 cup champagne (or
    sparkling chardonnay
    wine)
5 large egg yolks

pinch of salt
pinch of cayenne pepper
1 pint clarified butter
juice of one lemon

- Simmer the shallot and wine, until reduced to 3 table-spoons.
- In a stainless steel bowl, over a saucepan of barely simmering water (bain marie), beat the yolks, reduction, salt, and pepper with a whip until thick (about 5 minutes).
- Remove from heat, lift up the bowl, and place a clean damp towel over the top and down under the saucepan. Set the bowl on top of the saucepan, over the cloth, and pour the butter in a slow, steady stream, while beating continuously. As the mixture thickens, alternate the butter with some of the lemon juice. Continue until all of the butter and lemon juice is emulsified. Adjust the thickness of the sauce by beating in additional hot water. Set aside in a warm area until ready to use.

A Champagne Sauce can also be found under Demi-glaze and Béchamel.

Chantilly Sauce
(Sauce Mousseline)

Dutch sauce, with unsweetened whipped heavy cream folded in just before service.

Flowerette Sauce (Sauce Fleurette, called Isigny Sauce)

Thick Dutch sauce thinned with warmed heavy cream.

Daumont Sauce

Dutch sauce flavored with oyster liqueur, garnished with diced mushrooms (cooked in butter and lemon juice), truffles, and oysters.

Dishes qualified with *à la Daumont* date back to the French Restoration, probably named after the Duc D'Aumont. These consist of an eclectic garnish of fish quenelles, sliced truffle, crayfish tails in pastry shells dressed with Nantua sauce, baby mushrooms, and fish roe, all coated with bread crumbs, sautéed in butter, and accompanied by Normandy sauce beaten with crayfish butter.

Divine Sauce

Dutch sauce flavored with poultry glaze, finished with unsweetened whipped cream.

Dunant Sauce (also Dunand)

Dutch sauce flavored with truffle essence, beaten with langoustine (or lobster) butter, finished with unsweetened whipped cream.

Dunant (also Dunand) was a Swiss cook in charge of the kitchens of Prince de Condé. When he retired, his son inherited the post, and later attained some notoriety as Napoleon's personal chef (see Chicken Marengo, under Demiglaze).

Flemish Sauce (Sauce Flamande)

Dutch sauce seasoned with dry mustard, garnished with chopped parsley.

Hazelnut Sauce (Sauce Noisette)

Dutch sauce finished with finely ground, toasted hazelnuts.

Lombard Sauce

Dutch sauce garnished with diced mushrooms and chopped parsley.

Maltese Sauce (Sauce Maltaise)

Dutch sauce flavored with the juice of blood oranges, garnished with blanched orange zest.

---·---

Blood oranges are a sweet, aromatic orange with bright red pulp, indigenous to Spain and the island of Malta. Maltese sauce is typically served with poached or grilled fish. Mikado sauce, a variation using tangerine juice and zest, is typically served with steamed vegetables.

Marguery Sauce

Dutch sauce flavored with oyster liqueur, garnished with diced poached oysters.

---·---

Diamond Jim Brady, the super-salesman of railroad supplies, was a frequent patron of Rector's, a popular restaurant on New York City's Times Square opened by Charles Rector in 1899. Variously dubbed *Broadway's Cathedral of Froth,* the *Supreme Court of Triviality,* the *Bourse of Gossip,* and the *Clearing House of Rumor* by journalists of that time, it was in its day the favored hangout of playboys, prize fighters, actors, journalists, statesmen, and the like. Brady had just returned from a trip to Paris, where he had dined on Filet de Sole, Marguery, at the Parisian Restaurant Marguery, and had deemed it the supreme gastronomic experience of his life. Back in New York, he conferred with Charles Rector, who subsequently summoned his son George—then a law student at Cornell—and sent the boy to Paris to infiltrate the kitchen at Marguery. His father's instructions were "to return either with the sauce Marguery, or in it." Lacking restaurant experience, young Rector was unable to secure a position of employment there. Instead, he secured employment at the Café de Paris as an apprentice cook, eventually moving on to the dining room—first as a busboy, then as an apprentice waiter. A year later, he was accepted as an apprentice at Restaurant Marguery. For two years, fifteen hours a day, he worked as an apprentice under the seven master chefs who presided over the kitchen. It took that long to witness the dish, as carefully guarded as a state secret. As soon as he discovered the elements of the recipe, he returned stateside.

Awaiting him on the pier when young George disembarked were his father, Diamond Jim, and the orchestra from Rector's. That night, the dish was served to a table of gourmands assembled to judge the results of the three-year reconnaissance. Diamond Jim presided at the head of the table. With him sat Marshall Field, Adolphus Busch, Victor Herbert, John Philip Sousa, Dan Reed, Alfred Henry Lewis, and Sam Shubert. Upon tasting the dish, Brady reputedly exclaimed: "It is so good I could eat it on a Turkish towel."

When Diamond Jim passed away in 1916, Rector sadly grieved, "I've lost my four best customers." As for young George, his law studies long forgotten, he settled happily into the family business. Years later, he claimed that Filet de Sole Marguery, à la Diamond Jim and Crabmeat Mornay had brought Rector's at least a million dollars in business.

ℱILET DE SOLE, MARGUERY

2 large fresh flounders, filleted, bones and heads well rinsed in cold water, and set aside
1 small carrot, peeled and sliced
1 small leek (white part) chopped and well rinsed
3 parsley sprigs
10 peppercorns
1 bay leaf
1 sprig thyme
1½ quarts cold water
12 oysters, shucked
12 medium shrimp, peeled and deveined
½ cup white wine
4 egg yolks
¼ pound unsalted butter, cut into ¼-inch cubes
4 parsley sprigs

- Place the flounder bones and heads, vegetables, herbs, spices, and water in a large pot. Bring to a simmer, and skim. Simmer 1½ hours, then strain through a fine sieve. Return to a smaller saucepan and simmer until reduced by two-thirds (about 1 pint).

- Preheat oven to 325°F.

- Place the fillets in a buttered casserole dish and pour over the stock. Place in the oven for 5 minutes. Add the oysters and shrimp, and continue baking another five minutes.

- Carefully remove the fillets and shellfish to an ovenproof serving dish. Cover and set aside, keeping warm. Simmer the remaining liquid in a saucepan, along with the wine, and simmer until reduced by three-fourths (about ½ cup). Place the egg yolks into a stainless steel bowl and temper this liquid in by pouring it in a slow, steady stream, while whipping continuously. Return this mixture to the fire and bring up to a simmer, stirring continuously. Add the butter and continue stirring until completely emulsified. Nap the sauce over the fish, glaze under the broiler, garnish with parsley sprigs, and serve.

This is clearly an example of the "up-scale" and opulent food of another era, a style that has virtually disappeared. The poaching and subsequent reduction are certainly in line with contemporary styles, but the excessive fat content, as well as the manner of masking the whole dish with the sauce and then glazing, seems to invalidate the intensity and time required to prepare the dish. If the same dish were to be prepared today, one might see the fillets rolled, then poached, and served up on end. The oysters might be placed on top of the rolled fillets, topped with the sauce, and glazed. The shrimp could be arranged alongside these, along with steamed turned potatoes (pommes vapeur) and two fresh seasonal vegetables.

Marquise Sauce

Dutch sauce blended with fine caviar just before service.

Maximilian Sauce

Dutch sauce blended with anchovy essence.

Mousseline Sauce (also Chantilly)

Mousseline is typically served with poached fish and steamed vegetables.

Dutch sauce with unsweetened whipped heavy cream folded in just before service.

Mussel Sauce

Mussel sauce is typically served with poached fish.

Dutch sauce blended with reduced mussel stock, garnished with poached mussels.

Omega Sauce

Dutch sauce garnished with chopped chervil.

Piccalilli Sauce

Dutch sauce garnished with chopped mustard pickles.

———————————— • ————————————

Piccalilli is an English condiment consisting of mustard-pickled cauliflower, carrots, gherkins, shallots, and other vegetables, served with cold roasted ham and pork.

————————————————————

.... # *R*UBENS SAUCE

½ cup dry white wine	pinch of salt
½ cup fish stock	pinch of cayenne pepper
¼ cup mirepoix, finely chopped	2 anchovy fillets, mashed
4 large egg yolks	1½ cups clarified butter
	2 tablespoons crayfish butter

- Simmer the wine, stock, and mirepoix until reduced by three-fourths. Strain.
- Prepare the Dutch sauce in the usual manner (see recipe on page 176), adding a tablespoon of the reduction and the anchovy to the egg yolks when cooking. When adding the butter, alternate with the remaining reduction. Adjust the thickness of the sauce by beating in additional warm water, and adjust the seasoning with salt and pepper.

Sabayon Sauce

Sabayon is a French version of the Italian zabaione—a cooked-egg emulsion without the butter. The Italian version is always sweet, and served as a dessert or dessert sauce (see Dessert Sauces). The French sabayon is almost exclusively savory, most often consisting of egg yolks combined with a fish essence or glaze, herbs, and champagne wine, then beaten rapidly over high heat (just like zabaione), and served as a sauce. It is typically served with poached fish. A recipe follows.

*B*eggar's Purses, Avocado Sauce, p. 354

*S*autéed Scallops, Three Bell Pepper Purées, p. 356

. . . . *S*pinach Ravioli, Crimson Sauce, p. 359

$\mathcal{P}$oached Shrimp with Scallop Mousse,
Lobster Sauce, p. 363

*S*pring Vegetable Râgout, p. 365

*P*oached Chicken Ivory, p. 365

*G*rilled Tuna Steak, Black Bean Sauce, p. 366
*S*autéed Halibut, Orange-Lime Salsa, p. 367

Poached Sole, Pan-Pacific, p. 368

$\mathcal{B}$oiled Lobster, Bello Giorno, p. 369

*P*oached Salmon, Sorrel Sauce, p. 370

.... *G*rilled Beef Medallion, Henri IV, p. 371

*G*rilled Veal Chop, Florentine, p. 372

*P*oire aux Poivre, p. 373

*S*easonal Berries in Pastry Tulip,
Three Fruit Sauces, p. 373

*P*OACHED SEA BASS, CHIVE SABAYON

4 6-ounce fillets sea bass
¾ cup dry white wine
¼ cup champagne vinegar
1 cup fish fumet
1 shallot, minced
1 bay leaf
¼ teaspoon salt
½ teaspoon white peppercorns, cracked and
tied up in a small piece of muslin
1 cup champagne (or sparkling chardonnay wine)
8 large egg yolks
3 tablespoons chives, minced
1 bunch fresh chives

- Bring the wine, fumet, shallot, bay leaf, salt, and pepper to a simmer. Poach the sea bass for 5 minutes. Remove and set aside, keeping warm.
- Simmer the poaching liquid until reduced to ½ cup. Strain, and add to the champagne.
- Place the eggs into a medium stainless steel bowl, and whip until smooth. While continuously beating, add the reduction and chives (make sure that the reduction is not too hot). Place over a high flame (or a pot of moderately boiling water), and beat vigorously until the mixture is light and frothy.
- Place the sea bass on serving plates or platter (make sure the sea bass is hot), top with the sauce, garnish with fresh chives and small boiled potatoes.

Unequaled Sauce (Sauce Nonpareille)

Dutch sauce beaten with crayfish butter, garnished with diced crayfish tails, mushrooms, and truffles.

Uzés Sauce

Dutch sauce made with anchovy paste and Madeira wine.

Waterfish Sauce

Dutch sauce flavored with a reduction of freshwater fish stock, garnished with julienned carrots and orange zest, blanched in the stock.

ℬÉARNAISE SAUCE

⅓ cup dry white wine
⅓ cup tarragon (or white wine) vinegar
1 shallot, minced
2 tablespoons tarragon, minced
2 tablespoons chervil, minced

½ teaspoon cracked white pepper
5 large egg yolks
¼ teaspoon salt
⅛ teaspoon cayenne pepper
1 pint clarified butter
1 teaspoon tarragon, minced
1 teaspoon chervil, minced

- Simmer the wine, vinegar, shallot, herbs, and pepper, until reduced to about ¼ cup. Strain through a fine sieve.

- Place the egg yolks into a stainless steel bowl, along with a tablespoon of the reduction and the salt. Place this over a saucepan of barely simmering water (bain marie) and beat the yolks with a whip until thick (about 5 minutes).

- Remove from heat, lift up the bowl, and place a clean damp towel over the top and down under the saucepan. Set the bowl on top of the saucepan, over the cloth, and pour the butter in a slow, steady stream, while beating continuously. As the mixture thickens, alternate the butter with some of the reduction. Continue until all of the butter and the reduction are emulsified. Add the herbs, and season to taste. Adjust the thickness of the sauce by beating in additional warm water or vinegar. Set aside in a warm area until ready to use.

———————————— • ————————————

Béarnaise was created in the 1830s by Collinet at the restaurant Pavillon Henri VI, in Saint-Germain-en-Laye, in honor of Henri VI (the "Great Béarnais"). Montmireil, chef to the Vicomte de Châteaubriand, created a dish of a thick slice from the middle of a beef fillet, which he broiled and served with large turned potatoes cooked in butter and a brown sauce seasoned with white wine and lemon juice, and garnished with parsley and tarragon.

In modern times, châteaubriand is exclusively served with Sauce Béarnaise, as is any grilled, fried, or roasted meat.

———————————————————————————

Arlesian Sauce (Sauce Arlésienne)

Béarnaise sauce flavored with tomato purée and anchovy paste, garnished with diced tomatoes.

Beauharnais Sauce

Béarnaise sauce made without chervil, beaten with tarragon butter.

Recipes qualified as beauharnais are named after the Countess Fanny de Beauharnais, cousin by marriage of Empress Josephine. Sweet dishes in this style (based on bananas and rum) reflect the Creole origins of Napoleon's first wife.

Beauharnais sauce is typically served with grilled fish or meat, as well as a dish of soft-boiled eggs (served in artichoke bottoms, coated with beauharnais and demi-glaze).

Choron Sauce

Béarnaise sauce finished with tomato purée.

Montebello sauce is nearly the same as choron: equal parts béarnaise and tomato sauce, blended together.

Because a cooked egg emulsified sauce cannot be heated after it is prepared, the tomato ingredient must be heated before adding. Choron sauce is typically served with soft-boiled or poached eggs, grilled fish, or sautéed or grilled meat.

Foyot Sauce (also Sauce Valois, and Sauce Henri IV)

Béarnaise sauce flavored with meat glaze.

A béarnaise flavored with meat glaze is variously dubbed Foyot, Valois, and Henry IV. Foyot, former chef to Louis-Phillippe (1773–1850, king of France 1830–1848), purchased the Café Vachette in 1848. Since it was located close to the Palais du Luxembourg, the café was frequented by political leaders, and became well known for numerous dishes, among them Veal Chops Foyot, Pigeon Foyot, Lamb Shanks à la poulette, and Ernestine Potatoes. Valois was probably Marguerite de Valois, wife of Henry IV, for whom this sauce is also named.

Foyot sauce is typically served with grilled, sautéed, or fried meat.

French Sauce (Sauce Française)

French sauce is typically served with poached fish.

Béarnaise sauce flavored with fish glaze and tomato purée.

Médici Sauce

Béarnaise sauce flavored with tomato purée and a reduction of red wine.

Pau Sauce (Sauce Paloise)

Paloise sauce is typically served with grilled chicken or meat.

Béarnaise sauce made with mint instead of tarragon.

Rachel Sauce

Rachel was the stage name of a nineteenth-century actress, Elizabeth Félix, who was the mistress of Dr. Véron, a notable gastronome.

Béarnaise sauce flavored with demi-glaze, garnished with diced tomatoes.

Souwaroff Sauce

Béarnaise sauce flavored with meat glaze, garnished with julienned truffle.

This sauce is named after Prince Souvarov, a frequenter of Paris restaurants, and a descendant of the governor of the Crimea. Several dishes of game poultry (pheasant, partridge, woodcock, and quail), as well as dishes of goose liver (foie gras), are always prepared with truffles and served in a terrine sealed with a piece of dough. A petit four was also named for the prince, consisting of two round butter cookies (called sablés), sandwiched with apricot jam, and dusted with powdered sugar.

Tyrolian sauce is typically served with braised or baked fish; grilled or fried kidneys; and grilled chicken or meat.

Tyrolian Sauce (Sauce Tyrolienne)

Béarnaise sauce made with olive oil instead of butter.

CONTEMPORARY INNOVATION

....

*L*EMON-THYME SAUCE

3 sprigs fresh thyme
juice of 1 lemon
2 tablespoons dry white wine
2 tablespoons white wine
   vinegar

4 egg yolks
1 cup clarified unsalted
   butter, very warm
salt to taste

- Simmer the thyme, lemon juice, white wine, and vinegar until reduced by half. Strain and set aside to cool.
- Put the eggs and the liquid reduction into a stainless steel bowl, and place over a pot of barely simmering water. Whip this mixture while pouring in the butter in a slow, steady stream. Season to taste with salt. Cover and set aside in a warm place until ready to serve.

This sauce is served with "Poached Filet of Salmon," as seen in *The Pillar House Cookbook.*

BEURRE BLANC

A beurre blanc is a sauce consisting of a reduction of stock, wine, juice, and/or vinegar, plus aromatics, then thickened by finishing that reduction with nuggets of whole butter. This technique is akin to *monter au beurre,* a time-honored practice of adding whole butter to a sauce to improve its taste. Monter is a French verb meaning "to lift," and the lifting here is of a gastronomic nature.

Basic Beurre Blanc is also referred to as Nantes Butter (Beurre Nantais), since it is believed to be the birthplace of the sauce. A chef by the name of Clémence neglected to include eggs in a béarnaise sauce for a dish of pike he was preparing for his employer, the Marquis de Goulaine. The Marquis enjoyed the dish nevertheless, Clémence further refined the technique, and it became an established dish for the generations that followed. Some recipes for both beurre Nantais and beurre blanc include heavy cream as an added stabilizer for the emulsion. It is imperative for the reader to understand that *a proper beurre blanc does not require cream to stabilize the emulsion.* When cream is added to this sauce, it moves into the realm of cream sauce. The simplicity and uniqueness of a beurre blanc is lost when this unnecessary ingredient is added.

The best way to describe the nature of beurre blanc is to consider a dish prepared *à la meunière* (in the style of the miller's wife). Historically, it is a dish of fish—whole, fillet, or steak—dusted with flour, sautéed in clarified butter, then dressed with a beurre noisette—made by adding raw butter to the same pan, cooking it until it browns lightly, then pouring this over the fish. This is followed by a light sprinkling of lemon juice and chopped parsley. In contemporary practice, it is prepared a little differently. After the fish has been sautéed, it is transferred to a serving plate or platter, and set aside to remain warm. Into the same pan goes a spoonful of very finely minced shallots, and they are sautéed briefly. Then the lemon juice is added, sometimes augmented with white wine. This is simmered, until it is reduced to approximately 2 tablespoons of liquid. To this liquid is added 2 tablespoons of whole unsalted butter (cut into ¼-inch pieces), and a spoonful of finely chopped parsley. This is stirred vigorously until the butter becomes completely emulsified into the reduction. It is then poured over the fish, and served. This is one of the simplest and most elegant ways to prepare fresh fish (can also be applied to veal and chicken) and a perfect example of a beurre blanc.

Beurre blancs have become extremely popular in recent years, hence the modification of the mother sauce category (Butter Sauces + the subdivisions Hollandaise and Beurre Blanc). They are light, extremely flavorful, and invite endless variations. As for the fat content, obviously a steady diet of butter-based sauces is not recommended fare, no matter what one's cholesterol count. But as an occasional gastronomic experience, it is worth the indulgence.

The primary difference between a beurre blanc and an egg-emulsified sauce—aside from the inclusion of egg—is that it must be made at the moment of service ("à la carte" or "à la minute"). Lacking a stable starch liaison, the light viscosity of a beurre blanc will not hold up for more than 10 or 15 minutes. That it will not hold up for a long time doesn't mean it is not a good sauce. It's just a reflection of the true nature of the sauce.

The proportion of butter-to-liquid varies, though on average is three-to-one. As with all finished sauce production, an experienced saucier has a feel for the amount of butter a given reduction requires to become a beurre blanc. This final step, of incorporating the butter, also needs to be done fairly aggressively. It will not become an emulsion if the butter is simply simmered until it melts. There must be vigorous manual stirring and swirling for the emulsion to take place. It should also not become any hotter than a minimal simmer.

$\mathscr{B}$ASIC BEURRE BLANC

3 shallots, minced
1 cup dry white wine
¼ cup white wine (or champagne) vinegar
½ pound unsalted butter, cut into ½-inch cubes
salt and white pepper to taste

- Simmer the shallots, wine, and vinegar, until reduced by three-fourths.
- Add the butter, and incorporate into the reduction by stirring continuously, until fully emulsified. Season to taste with salt and white pepper.

———————————— • ————————————

This sauce can be changed to an herb beurre blanc by simply incorporating finely minced fresh herbs along with the butter.

A contemporary variation to beurre blanc involves substituting crème fraîche for the butter. The closest thing to crème fraîche we have in the United States is sour cream, though crème fraîche is higher in fat, and is created with a different bacterial culture. A facsimile can be made as follows.

CRÈME FRAÎCHE, AMERICAN STYLE

2 cups heavy cream   ½ cup sour cream or yogurt
½ cup buttermilk   ¼ teaspoon salt

- Combine all the ingredients in a clean saucepan, and bring to a temperature of 100°F.
- Place into a clean stainless steel bowl, cover, and set into an oven heated only by the pilot light (12 hours).
- Refrigerate for 24 hours. Carefully remove thickened top part (this is the crème fraîche), and discard any liquid left at the bottom. Cover and refrigerate until ready to use.

BASIC BEURRE ROUGE

A variation of this sauce (Pinot Noir Beurre Rouge) can be made using a Pinot Noir red wine. With the addition of 1 tablespoon minced fresh dill, it goes particularly well with grilled salmon.

1 tablespoon shallot, minced   pinch of white pepper
1¼ cup dry red wine   ½ pound unsalted butter,
pinch of salt   cut into ½-inch cubes

- Simmer the shallot, wine, salt, and pepper, until reduced by three-fourths (about ⅓ cup).
- Add the butter and stir continuously, until completely incorporated.

TRADITIONAL BEURRE BLANCS

BERCY SAUCE

1 shallot, minced   ¼ pound unsalted butter,
½ teaspoon cracked white   cut into ½-inch cubes
   pepper   1 tablespoon parsley, minced
1 cup dry white wine   ¼ cup diced beef marrow
1 heaping tablespoon meat   pinch of salt
   glaze

- Blanch the marrow in boiling salted water for 5 minutes. Drain and set aside.
- Simmer the shallot, pepper, and white wine until reduced by two-thirds. Add the meat glaze, and blend in thoroughly.

This recipe is a variation of Bercy sauce, also found as a derivative of Velouté.

• Add the butter and stir continuously, until completely incorporated. Finish with the chopped parsley and bone marrow, and season to taste with salt.

CHAMBERTIN SAUCE

2 tablespoons unsalted butter
¼ cup mirepoix, minced
1 small garlic clove, crushed
2 mushrooms, roughly chopped
2 white fish frames, roughly chopped, and well washed
4 parsley stems, roughly chopped

1 sprig thyme
1 bay leaf
6 white peppercorns, crushed
2 cups Chambertin wine (a dry red Burgundy)
3 tablespoons unsalted butter, soft
1 tablespoon all-purpose flour

• Sweat the mirepoix and fish bones in the butter for about 10 minutes. Add the herbs, spices, and wine. Simmer until reduced by almost half. Strain, and return to the fire.
• Mash the butter and flour together (beurre manié) until smooth. Beat this paste into the wine, and simmer for 10 minutes. Strain, and season to taste.

Spring Vegetable Beurre Blanc (Sauce Printanière)

Dishes prepared spring style (à la Printanière) are garnished with the exquisite baby spring vegetables, the first harvest of a new growing season. This sauce is an integral part of a Spring Vegetable Râgout (Râgout des Légumes, à la Printanière) prepared as follows:

Blanch a variety of scrubbed and trimmed miniature spring vegetables, sufficient to serve four persons, in 2 cups of chicken stock (such as artichoke hearts, Brussels sprouts, carrots, green peas, pearl onions, new potatoes, patty pan squash, string beans, turnips, zucchini, etc.), until al dente. Each vegetable variety should be blanched separately, since cooking times vary. Arrange the vegetables in a serving dish and set aside, keeping warm. Simmer the chicken stock until reduced to approximately one cup of liquid. Beat in 8 tablespoons unsalted butter, season to taste with salt and white pepper, pour over the vegetables, and serve.

Spring sauce is also served with soft-boiled or poached eggs, and poached or sautéed poultry.

SAXON SAUCE

··················

1 shallot, minced
½ cup dry white wine
1 cup fish stock
juice of 1 lemon
1 tablespoon prepared
  mustard

¼ pound unsalted butter,
  cut into ½-inch cubes
pinch of salt
pinch of white pepper

- Simmer the shallot, wine, and stock, until reduced by three-fourths. Add the lemon juice and mustard, and blend in thoroughly.
- Add the butter and stir continuously, until completely incorporated. Season to taste with salt and pepper.

CONTEMPORARY INNOVATIONS

BOURBON BEURRE BLANC

2 shallots, minced
1 garlic clove, minced
½ cup bourbon
½ cup apple cider

½ cup cider vinegar
juice of 1 lemon
½ pound unsalted butter,
  cut into half-inch chunks

This dish accompanies "Corn-Crusted Sea Scallops with Bourbon Sauce," innovated by Waldy Malouf, Hudson River Club, New York.

- Simmer all the ingredients except the butter until reduced by two-thirds.
- Add the butter, and incorporate into the reduction by stirring continuously until fully emulsified. Season to taste with salt and white pepper.

CHIVE SAUCE, WITH RED PEPPER PURÉE

2 red bell peppers
olive oil as needed
3 tablespoons chicken stock

1 small shallot, minced
1 bay leaf
1 small garlic clove, minced

1 tablespoon olive oil
2 tablespoons heavy cream
½ pound unsalted butter,
    cut into ½-inch cubes
salt and white pepper to
    taste

2 tablespoons minced fresh
    chives
24 fresh asparagus spears,
    peeled, and cut into
    4-inch lengths

- Preheat oven to 400°F.
- Rub the peppers lightly with olive oil. Place on a baking sheet, and roast until they begin to turn black. Remove from the oven, place in a bowl, and cover tightly with plastic wrap. Allow to sit 15 minutes.
- Cut open the peppers, and separate the skin and seeds from the flesh. Discard the skin and seeds.
- Remove the peppers and chicken stock to a food processor, and purée. Set the purée aside, keeping it warm.
- Sauté the shallot, bay leaf, and garlic in the olive oil for 3 or 4 minutes. Add the wine, and simmer until approximately 2 tablespoons remain. Add the cream, and bring the sauce back to a simmer. Add the butter, and stir continuously until all the butter is incorporated. Strain, add the chives, and season to taste with salt and pepper.
- Blanch the asparagus spears in boiling salted water 3 or 4 minutes, or until tender but still firm.
- Ladle the chive sauce onto four serving plates. Lay 6 asparagus spears onto the sauce, then drizzle 3 tablespoons of the pepper purée over and around the asparagus.

---·---

This sauce accompanies "Steamed Asparagus," as seen in *A Taste For All Seasons*.

.... # *G*INGER BEURRE BLANC

2 tablespoons grated ginger
    root
1 small shallot, minced
6 parsley stems, roughly
    chopped

1½ cups dry white wine
½ pound unsalted butter,
    cut into half-inch chunks
salt and white pepper to taste

- Simmer the ginger, shallot, parsley, and wine until reduced by three-fourths (about ⅓ cup). Add the butter, and stir continuously until fully emulsified. Strain through a sieve before serving.

GINGER-LIME BEURRE BLANC

2 tablespoons grated ginger
   root
1 small shallot, minced
6 parsley stems, roughly
   chopped

1 cup dry white wine
juice and zest of 2 limes
½ pound unsalted butter,
   cut into half-inch chunks
salt and white pepper to taste

- Blanch the lime zest in boiling salted water for 3 minutes. Drain and set aside.
- Simmer the ginger, shallot, parsley, and wine until reduced by three-fourths (about ¼ cup). Add the lime juice, and simmer another 3 minutes. Strain through a sieve.
- Add the butter and lime zest, stirring continuously, until fully emulsified.

RED WINE VINEGAR SAUCE

1 shallot, minced
1 garlic clove, minced
1 bay leaf
¼ cup dry red wine

¼ cup red wine vinegar
½ pound unsalted butter,
   cut into ¼-inch cubes
salt and white pepper to taste

- Simmer the shallot, garlic, bay leaf, red wine, and vinegar in a small saucepan, until reduced by half.
- Add the butter, and stir continuously until fully incorporated. Season to taste with salt and pepper, strain, and set aside, keeping warm until ready to use.

———— • ————

This sauce accompanies "Smoked Roasted Baby Chicken," from *A Taste For All Seasons*.

SOY-GINGER BUTTER

¼ cup dry white wine
3 tablespoons grated ginger
   root
1 shallot, minced

2 tablespoons soy sauce
½ pound unsalted butter,
   cut into ¼-inch cubes
salt and pepper to taste

- Simmer the white wine, ginger, and shallot in a small saucepan until almost dry. Add the soy sauce.
- Add the butter, stirring continuously until fully incorporated. Strain, and set aside, keeping warm until ready to use.

———— • ————

This sauce accompanies "Sea Scallops," as seen in *A Taste For All Seasons*.

CHAPTER 10

TOMATO SAUCES AND PESTOS

Though tomato sauce is the fifth and last of the five mother sauces, there are only a handful of classical derivatives within this category, making it somewhat different than the other four foundation sauces. In addition, the traditional French tomato sauce (as originally set forth in Escoffier's *Guide Culinaire*) is thickened with a butter roux. Since tomato sauces are most commonly associated with Italian cuisine, and in particular, as an accompaniment for pasta, the French-style roux-thickened tomato sauce has always seemed to be a contradiction to the true nature of tomato sauces. Not only is the presence of flour a redundant use of carbohydrate, the very essence of a hearty tomato sauce is a purée of the ingredients.

———————————————— • ————————————————

In the late eighteenth century, a New York food importer claimed duty-free status on a shipment of tomatoes from the West Indies. He argued that since tomatoes were anatomically a fruit, as per the import regulations of that time, they were not subject to import fees. The customs agent disagreed, and imposed a 10 percent duty on the shipment, designated as vegetables. The case went as far as the New York State Supreme Court, which decided in favor of the customs agency, on the grounds of traditional linguistic usage. Tomatoes, held the majority, are "usually served at dinner, in, with, or after the soup, fish, or meat, which constitute the principal part of the repast, and not, like fruits, generally as dessert."

Armed with the mother sauce matrix we were taught in culinary school, we later learned of the multitude of regional tomato sauce varieties, illustrating that Italian sauces were not organized in any fashion similar to the French sauce system. In fact, Italian sauces (and cooking) are not organized at all, but disorganized, passionate, and emotionally intense, a reflection, perhaps, of the collective personality and temperament of one of the world's oldest cultures. This is not a negative evaluation of the Italian cooking traditions. Rather, it is an embrace of a unique history that has fostered a passionate and spontaneous style of preparing the foods indigenous to the Mediterranean, one of the most bountiful regions of the world.

Tomato sauces were not a part of Italian cookery until the sixteenth century, when the Spanish explorers returned from the New World with them. Europeans were slow to accept the strange and acidic fruit, and it did not become common fare in Italy before 1830. So for the more than two millennia before the introduction of the tomato, there is considerable ground to cover, in order to gain an understanding of Italian sauces and how they fit in with Italian cooking styles.

———————————— • ————————————

Tomatoes were unknown in Europe until the sixteenth century, when Spanish explorers returned from South America with them. Spain's possession of the Kingdoms of Naples and Sicily, from 1500 until 1700, explains how *pomi dei moro* (Italian for "Moor's apples") migrated to the Italian peninsula. In the late eighteenth century, when it was introduced into Paris, to a Frenchman's ears, "pomo dei moro" sounded similar to *pomme d'amour*, hence the colloquial name "love apple."

A PHILOSOPHICAL LOOK AT ITALIAN COOKERY

In commercial cookery, there are a handful of tomato sauces that until recently have been passed along as the sauces typical of Italian fare, at least as they were transported to the New World. But just as chow mein is unknown in China, the Spanish paella rarely includes seafood (unless in the style of Valencia), and the best French food is that of the peasantry (historically unable to afford cream or butter), we can conclude that the Italian fare we know in the United States may be corruptions of true Italian cuisine. Of course, this has changed considerably in the last generation, partially due to a proliferation of very fine and technically accurate cookbooks and recipe collections.

Nevertheless, in the restaurant trade, sauces Amatriciana, Bolognese, Marinara, and Napoletana have long been standard restaurant offerings, and will probably remain as such, in spite of the fact that even the *true* ingredients of these dishes are eternally disputed and debated by cookbook authors of Italian origin. Typically, Amatriciana was the tomato sauce made with pancetta (rolled up Italian bacon); Marinara was quick and simple plus some seafood (sometimes); Napoletana was simple or complex (depending on the recipe version and the region), but definitely didn't have meat; and Bolognese was the one with meat.

A further study of the *true* nature of Italian cookery uncovered another level of dishes, among them Linguine Vongole (clam sauce), Fettucine Alfredo (created at Alfredo's, a restaurant in Rome), Spaghetti Carbonara (the charcoal maker's spaghetti), and Pasta Primavera (with miniature spring vegetables). These dishes, like the common sauces, were also corruptions of their true nature. I cannot speak for Senior Alfredo, since his is a fairly modern addition to the Italian repertoire, and I haven't had the pleasure of dining at Alfredo's. But Spaghetti Carbonara is the charcoal maker's mainstay, a dish prepared in the mountains where the charcoal makers retreat for days at a time to carefully burn the mountain hardwoods, creating charcoal drawing utensils for the artists of the world. They bring with them essentially nonperishable ingredients which become a dish these artisans subsist on during their retreats—spaghetti, olive oil, black pepper, pancetta, an egg or two, and a hunk of Parmesan cheese. There is no cream, butter, olives, or prosciutto in the dish, as many a restaurant insists on adding. Anything outside of the original dish, as it's made by the charcoal makers, should be given another name.

Pasta Primavera is another victim of restaurateurs' best intentions to make a beautiful dish "better" for their dining patrons. Primavera is like the French printinière, the young first growth of succulent miniature vegetables grown during the spring. Dishes (French or Italian) so named are a reverent celebration of the end of winter, and the start of another growing season. Sliced "horse" carrots, chunks of zucchini and yellow squash, and quartered mushrooms, bound in a flour-thickened white sauce, smothered with a mound of grated cheese, is as clear a case of gastronomic sacrilege as claiming that margarine possesses a "buttery taste."

The next major revelation regarding cuccina Italiano was that Parmesan cheese was not intended to be grated over absolutely everything in that realm. Bread crumbs, for example, often toasted in a pan with olive oil, were also an important seasoning element. A typically Sicilian dish, for example, was pasta with anchovies and bread crumbs. The sauce consisted of garlic fried in olive oil, blended with tomato paste and anchovies, and tossed with spaghetti. The bread crumbs, toasted by sautéing in olive oil, along with chopped parsley, were then sprinkled over the top.

Other dishes with intriguing sounding names had even more intriguing stories to go along with them. Pasta Puttanesca, or "harlot's pasta," got its name from the speed with which it could be made—that is, one that could be made between clients, or a quick dish made by a wife for her husband after an afternoon matinée with her lover. The sauce consisted of olive oil, garlic, plum tomatoes, olives, capers, salt, and parsley, all tossed with spaghettini (the thinner the pasta, the shorter the cooking time), and is prepared in about 15 minutes. Bucatini Briganteschi (Highwayman Style) was so named for a benevolent southern Italian outlaw known solely by the name Giuliano; Spaghetti alla Buccaniera (Buccaneer Style), Ravioli alla Zappatora (Ditch-digger's Style), Penne all'Arrabbiata ("Angry" style), and Maccheroni alla Carrettiera (Teamster's Style) are all dishes so highly spiced with both pepper and garlic that supposedly only a virile "he-man" could handle the heat.

There are stories behind the names of the pastas themselves as well. Spaghetti was derived from "spago," meaning cord, linguine came from "lingua," meaning tongue, refer ring to the oval shape of the noodle, and lasagna was derived from *lasanum*, meaning "big pot"; ravioli was derived from "rabiole," meaning scraps of little value, referring to the leftover food chopped up and wrapped in small pasta pillows by the sailors of Genoa during their longer voyages; tagliatelle was invented in 1487 by a Bolognese cook in imitation of the hair of Lucrezia Borgia.

The final chapter is the *pesto* movement, already a part of the west coast repertoire, which later picked up momentum as it was adopted in the East. In truth, pesto has no direct relation to basil, but is derived from the Latin word *pestare*, meaning "to pound," from which is derived pestle, the grinding tool used with a stone bowl (a mortar), and in which various herbs and spices are ground into a paste—a pesto. "Pistou," for example, a bean, pasta, and vegetable soup unique to Provence (southern France), includes an olive oil, tomato, garlic, and basil paste that is added to the soup just before serving. We can now find numerous herbal and nut pesto sauces used to dress any number of pasta dishes.

As for the quartet of tomato sauces most familiar in commercial cooking, they cannot be considered in the same way as the French mother sauces. They are simply commonly accepted corruptions of a handful of sauces from a cuisine that has emigrated into our melting pot cuisine. But we do begin to understand the nature of Italian cooking—sauces, pasta, and so on—that it is more a style and approach than a grand organized system. In fact, pasta, and the sauce that dresses it, represents a very creative moment in the kitchen. The choice of noodle must first be made, based on the character and texture of the sauce that accompanies it. And the number of choices are enormous, in spite of the fact that our choices are limited to the varieties which manufacturers and importers decide are the most popular. In Italy, every town and village boasts its own shapes and names for pastas unique to that area. But the ingredients for the sauce can be made up based on ingredients available at the time a dish is made. And that sauce can be created at the moment one decides to create it. Giuliano Bugialli, for example, divides his book *Bugialli on Pasta* into chapter titles as follows: Pasta with Beans, Pasta with Vegetables, Pasta with Fish, Pasta with Meat and Game (followed by regional and flavored pastas, a chapter on gnocchi, couscous and other grains, and desserts). In practice, there is no limit to the combinations and varieties of sauces that can be innovated. One works with inventiveness and imagination guided by availability of ingredients and one's own preferences.

When working with this palate of edibles, there are a handful of important guidelines that will ensure favorable results. These are as follows:

- Use only fresh, local ingredients.

- A quality dried pasta, made from durum semolina (the hard wheat that makes the best pasta), is generally superior to fresh pasta, which requires as little as 1 minute of cooking time. Fresh pasta lacks the chewy (al dente) quality that comes from semolina flour, and fresh pasta absorbs the juices and liquids of the sauce that dresses it too rapidly.

- "One should not indiscriminately sprinkle Parmigiano over everything if all dishes are not to melt into an unappealing sameness," writes Giuliano Bugialli. "Generally, cheese is not used with fish, game, or mushroom sauces—though there are a few exceptions—and rarely in dishes with hot red peppers."

- When using grated cheese, always grate your own.

- Pasta must be cooked in rapidly boiling, lightly salted water. It should be stirred for the first couple of minutes, to prevent the pasta from sticking to itself, until the water returns to a boil.

- Use plenty of water—1 gallon per pound of pasta.

- Cook the pasta just before it is to be served. Avoid precooking and reheating. (Large production houses cannot always afford this luxury.)

Olive oil is often added to the water for cooking pasta, based on the supposition that it will prevent the pasta from sticking together. This is a misconception, since the oil floats on top of the water and has little interaction with the noodles. The true reason for adding olive oil (or plain vegetable oil), is that it prevents the water from boiling over. In large production cooking (10 to 40 pounds of pasta at one time), this is a valid step, even with sufficient space between the water and the top edge of the pot. Nevertheless, the author recommends adding a small amount of olive oil (a tablespoon or two) to a pot of boiling water, as a spiritual ingredient, one of many mystical little tricks of the trade that adds a subtle and undefinable characteristic to a dish.

The recipes that follow offer a basic structure of tomato sauces. There is a basic French-style tomato sauce, without the roux, from which a handful of derivatives can be made. This includes contemporary innovations, followed by pestos and other puréed sauces, similar in that they are all puréed pastes of some kind.

TRADITIONAL TOMATO SAUCES

Basic Tomato Sauces

FRENCH STYLE

¼ cup olive oil
1 shallot, minced
1 medium Spanish onion, very finely diced
3 garlic cloves, pressed
½ cup dry white wine
¼ teaspoon salt

¼ teaspoon black pepper
2 pounds (3–4 cups) ripe tomatoes, peeled, roughly chopped
6 sprigs fresh thyme
1 bay leaf

- Sauté the onion, shallot, and garlic in the olive oil, over medium heat, covered, for about 10 minutes.
- Add the remaining ingredients and simmer, uncovered, very slowly, stirring frequently, 30–40 minutes. Remove the thyme and bay leaf, and adjust seasoning.

This sauce can be puréed in a food processor, if desired.

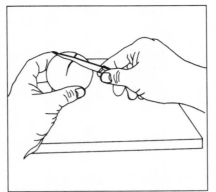 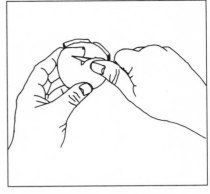

1. Scoring the bottom of a tomato.   *2. Peeling away the skin of the tomato (after blanching in boiling water and dipping in ice bath).*

Algerian Sauce (Sauce Algérienne)

Tomato sauce garnished with a julienne of green and red bell peppers, sautéed in olive oil.

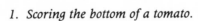

CREOLE SAUCE

¼ cup olive oil
½ cup Spanish onion,
   medium dice
½ cup celery, medium dice
¼ cup green bell pepper,
   medium dice
¼ cup red bell pepper,
   medium dice
4 garlic cloves, minced

3 cups fresh garden
   tomatoes, peeled and
   roughly chopped (or the
   equivalent of canned
   tomatoes in tomato juice)
¼ cup tomato paste
1 bay leaf
salt and pepper to taste

• Sweat the vegetables and garlic in the olive oil, over medium heat, for 10 minutes. Add the tomatoes, tomato paste, bay leaf, and a little salt and pepper. Simmer for 30 minutes.

———————— • ————————

The Creole cooking styles of the Louisiana delta are a unique blend of the French, Spanish, African, Caribbean, and native North American Indian cultures that influenced the cooking of that region. While Creole sauce is generally served with shrimp or crayfish, it represents a style of cooking unique in the world, and better represented by the regional specialties that can be found in New Orleans, among them gumbo and jambalaya. The presence of Creole sauce in any cookbook is more a way of acknowledging the uniqueness of that cuisine.

𝒩AVARESE SAUCE
(Sauce Navaraise)

¼ cup olive oil
1 shallot, minced
1 medium Spanish onion, very finely diced
8 garlic cloves, pressed
½ cup dry white wine
¼ teaspoon salt
¼ teaspoon black pepper
2 pounds (3–4 cups) ripe tomatoes, peeled and roughly chopped

6 sprigs fresh thyme
1 bay leaf
1 tablespoon basil leaves, minced
1 tablespoon sage leaves, minced
1 tablespoon oregano leaves, minced
1 tablespoon parsley, minced
3 tablespoons unsalted butter, cut into ½-inch cubes

- Sauté the onion, shallot, and garlic in the olive oil, over medium heat, covered, for about 10 minutes.
- Add the remaining ingredients and simmer, uncovered, very slowly, stirring frequently, 30–40 minutes. Remove the thyme stems and bay leaf. Add the chopped herbs, mount with butter, and adjust seasoning.

Richelieu Sauce

Tomato sauce flavored with meat glaze.

ℛOOSEVELT SAUCE

¼ cup olive oil
1 shallot, minced

1 medium Spanish onion, very finely diced

3 garlic cloves, pressed
½ cup dry white wine
¼ teaspoon salt
¼ teaspoon black pepper
1½ pounds (about 3 cups)
   ripe tomatoes, peeled and
   roughly chopped

3 sprigs fresh thyme
1 bay leaf
½ cup apple butter
¼ cup lemon zest, blanched

- Sauté the onion, shallot, and garlic in the olive oil, over medium heat, covered, for about 10 minutes.
- Add the white wine and simmer until reduced by half. Add the tomatoes, salt and pepper, and herbs, simmer, uncovered, stirring frequently, 30 minutes.
- Remove the thyme and bay leaf, and purée in a food processor.
- Return the sauce to the fire. Add the apple butter and lemon zest, and simmer briefly. Adjust seasoning.

———— • ————

Apple butter is apple sauce slowly cooked down in a heavy-gauge pan (a cast iron skillet is excellent for this) until thick, dark, and sweet. This can be accomplished in the oven, at 350°F, stirring frequently.

Saint Cloud Sauce

Basic French tomato sauce, mounted with tarragon butter and garnished with chopped tarragon.

*B*ASIC ITALIAN TOMATO SAUCE

¼ cup olive oil
1 medium Spanish onion,
   finely diced
¼ cup carrot, peeled and
   grated
8 garlic cloves, pressed
12 basil leaves, minced

3 cups fresh plum tomatoes,
   peeled and roughly
   chopped (or canned
   plum tomatoes, packed
   in juice)
½ teaspoon salt
½ teaspoon white pepper
¼ cup parsley, minced

———— • ————

Since sugar is not recommended for use in tomato sauces, the carrot, as well as the caramelizing of the carrot and onion, is included for its sweetness.

- Sauté the onion and carrot in the olive oil until lightly caramelized. Add the garlic and basil, and sauté another 3 minutes. Add the tomatoes, salt, and pepper, and simmer slowly, for 30–40 minutes.
- Purée in a food processor. Add the parsley, and adjust seasoning.

Regional Tomato Sauces

*A*MATRICIAN SAUCE
(Salsa Amatricana)

3 tablespoons olive oil
1 medium onion, finely diced
½ pound pancetta, cut into
  ¼-inch cubes
6 dried hot red chile peppers

3 cups fresh garden
  tomatoes, peeled and
  roughly chopped (or
  canned plum tomatoes,
  packed in juice)
salt and black pepper to taste

This dish, which originates from the town of Amatrice, is generally served with bucatini, a long pasta that is hollow in the center.

- Sauté the onion and pancetta in the olive oil for 10 minutes. Add the hot peppers, tomatoes, and some salt and pepper. Simmer for about 20 minutes, stirring frequently.

*B*OLOGNESE SAUCE

¼ cup olive oil
¼ pound prosciutto or
  pancetta, small diced
1 medium onion, small diced
1 medium carrot, peeled,
  small diced
1 celery stalk, trimmed,
  small diced
2 garlic cloves
6 ounces lean beef, ground
6 ounces lean boneless pork,
  cut into ¼-inch cubes
½ cup dry white wine

1 tablespoon marjoram or
  oregano leaves, minced
1 tablespoon parsley, minced
¼ teaspoon fresh grated
  nutmeg
½ teaspoon salt
½ teaspoon black pepper
1 pound fresh garden
  tomatoes, peeled and
  roughly cut (or canned
  plum tomatoes, packed in
  juice)
½ cup brown stock
¾ cup heavy cream

- Sauté the prosciutto, celery, carrot, and onion in the olive oil for 10 minutes, stirring frequently. Add the garlic, beef, and pork, and continue cooking another 10 minutes. Add the white wine, and simmer until nearly dry.
- Add the herbs, nutmeg, salt, tomatoes, and stock, and simmer, stirring frequently, for 20 minutes. Add the cream, and adjust the seasoning.

MARINARA SAUCE
(Salsa Marinara)

¼ cup olive oil
6 garlic cloves, minced
½ Italian parsley (flat leaf),
  roughly chopped
salt and pepper to taste

2 pounds fresh garden
  tomatoes, peeled
  and puréed (or canned
  purée)

- Sauté the garlic and parsley in the olive oil for 3 minutes. Add the tomatoes and some salt and pepper, and simmer about 20 minutes, stirring frequently. Adjust seasoning.

———————— • ————————

Marinara sauce is sometimes considered to be a simple tomato sauce, with seafood added, so named after the fishermen who included mussels, clams, squid, and so on. This is not necessarily the case, and the sauce is also known by the simple recipe here.

NEAPOLITAN SAUCE
(Salsa Napoletana)

¼ cup olive oil
3 garlic cloves, crushed
½ cup black Calamata olives,
  pitted and quartered
5 anchovy fillets, minced
2 tablespoons capers, drained

1 pound fresh garden
  tomatoes, peeled and
  roughly cut (or canned
  plum tomatoes, packed in
  juice)
½ cup tomato paste
¼ teaspoon black pepper

- Sauté the garlic in the olive oil until it begins to turn brown. Remove and discard.
- Add the olives, anchovy, and capers, and sauté a few minutes. Add the tomatoes, tomato paste, and black pepper, and simmer 20 minutes, stirring frequently.

Napoletana generally refers to a tomato sauce without meat. There are so many variations that it is difficult to arrive at one recipe that is *the* Naples style sauce. This recipe is one of numerous varieties.

*P*ASTA AGLIO E OLIO
(Pasta with Garlic and Oil)

2 garlic cloves, roughly
  chopped
1 pound spaghetti
¾ cup extra virgin olive oil
½ teaspoon hot red pepper
  flakes

salt and freshly ground
  pepper
25 sprigs Italian parsley,
  stems removed and
  coarsely chopped

- Sauté the garlic in the olive oil over medium heat for 2 minutes. Add the pepper flakes, salt, and pepper, and cook another 2 minutes.
- Cook the spaghetti in boiling salted water until al dente. Drain, and toss with the sautéed mixture and the parsley.

Bugialli, in whose book, *Bugialli on Pasta*, this recipe appears, suggests several variations of this dish. The garlic can be crushed, sautéed in the oil, then discarded. (This is not an uncommon practice, a way of infusing the oil with only the flavor of the garlic.) Other herbs can be included in this dish as well. These include rosemary (fresh or preserved in salt), which is cooked with the garlic, then discarded. Basil is also suggested, though torn basil leaves, sautéed with the garlic, can remain in the final dish. And finally, the author writes, "I cannot state strongly enough that grated cheese is *never* added to any *aglio-olio* dish."

CONTEMPORARY INNOVATIONS

.... ## 𝓑ARDELLI SAUCE

2 tablespoons olive oil
¼ cup prosciutto, minced
2 ounces unsalted butter
2 garlic cloves, minced
2 shallots, minced
1 cup mushrooms, sliced
   very thin

½ cup Neapolitan sauce
½ cup heavy cream
⅛ teaspoon salt
⅛ teaspoon white pepper
½ cup Parmesan cheese,
   grated

- Render the prosciutto in a heavy-gauge saucepan, over medium flame, until golden brown.
- Add the butter, garlic, shallots, and mushrooms, and sauté about 5 minutes.
- Add the tomato sauce, cream, salt and pepper, and bring to a boil. Adjust seasoning.
- Add the fettuccine and blend thoroughly. Serve topped with the grated cheese.

———————————— • ————————————

This dish was created by Charles Bardelli, late chef of Bardelli's, one of San Francisco's older restaurants (before Bardelli's it was known as Charles Fashion Restaurant). This sauce was designed to be served with Fettuccine Bardelli, and this recipe is sufficient to dress one pound of fettuccine.

————————————————————

.... ## 𝓒REAMED TOMATO SAUCE

1 tablespoon unsalted butter
1 large shallot, minced
1 large garlic clove, minced
3 tablespoons white wine
   vinegar
¼ cup dry white wine

1 cup drained canned
   tomatoes, chopped
1 cup heavy cream
2 tablespoons unsalted butter
salt and white pepper to
   taste

This sauce accompanies "Chicken Liver Mousse," innovated by Craig Claiborne and Pierre Franey. The recipe for the mousse follows.

- Sauté the shallot and garlic in the butter for 3 minutes. Add the vinegar and white wine, and simmer until reduced to roughly 2 tablespoons of liquid.
- Add the tomatoes and simmer for 5 minutes. Add the cream and simmer another 5 minutes.
- Remove the sauce to a blender or food processor, along with the remaining butter, and purée. Season to taste with salt and pepper and set aside, keeping warm until ready to serve.

CHICKEN LIVER MOUSSE

1 pound fresh chicken livers, trimmed of membranes, and roughly chopped
½ cup dry white wine
pinch of salt
pinch of white pepper
2 tablespoons Cognac

⅛ teaspoon freshly grated nutmeg
6 tablespoons unsalted butter, soft
1 cup heavy cream
butter as needed

- Marinate the chicken livers in the wine for one hour.
- Drain the wine, and discard. Place the livers, salt, pepper, Cognac, and nutmeg into a food processor. Purée, then add the butter, and purée again. Add the cream and blend in, using the pulse switch.
- Liberally butter 8 individual 6-ounce ramekins (similar to a small ceramic soufflé dish). Divide the liver mixture equally among the ramekins, and cover each one with a small circle of buttered paper (the paper that is used to wrap butter is excellent for this purpose).
- Place the ramekins into a steamer, or on a rack in a roasting pan, so that they sit above simmering water. Cover, and steam for 10 minutes. Turn the heat off, and let the ramekins sit for 15 minutes. Unmold carefully, and serve on a bed of the creamed tomato sauce.

ROASTED RED BELL PEPPER TOMATO SAUCE

8 large red bell peppers, split, seeds and connecting tissue removed

2 pounds fresh garden tomatoes, cores removed
10 garlic cloves, peeled

3 tablespoons olive oil
1 medium Spanish onion,
  medium dice
12 fresh basil leaves

¼ cup parsley, roughly
  chopped
3 cups tomato purée
salt and pepper to taste

- Preheat oven to 375°F. Place the peppers, tomatoes, and garlic on a roasting pan, and roast for 30 minutes.
- Remove the peppers, tomatoes, and garlic to a food processor.
- Sauté the onion in the olive oil for 5 minutes. Add the basil, and sauté another minute. Add this to the food processor, along with the parsley, and purée all.
- Remove the purée to a heavy-gauge saucepan, add the tomato, salt, and pepper, and simmer for 30 minutes.
- Strain through a screen sieve.

Tomato-Armagnac Sauce

3 tablespoons olive oil
1 shallot, minced
1 cup tomato, peeled,
  seeded, and medium-diced
1 teaspoon fresh thyme
  leaves

1 teaspoon fresh basil leaves,
  minced
¼ cup fish stock
salt and black pepper to taste
¼ cup Armagnac

- Sauté the shallot in the olive oil, covered, over medium heat for 5 minutes. Add the tomato, herbs, and fish stock. Simmer until reduced by half. Place the sauce in a food processor and purée. Return to the fire, add the Armagnac, and season with salt and pepper. Set aside, keeping warm until ready to serve.

This sauce accompanies "Lobster Strudel," as seen in *The Pillar House Cookbook.*

Tomato Coulis

1 quart canned whole
  tomatoes with their juice
⅓ cup olive oil
2 large shallots, roughly
  chopped
8 garlic cloves, crushed
1 bay leaf

1 cup extra-rich chicken
  stock (if extra-rich stock
  is not available, add
  1 tablespoon meat
  glaze (glace de viande,
  make with chicken or veal
  stock)
¼ cup balsamic vinegar

¼ cup fresh basil, parsley, and cilantro, minced

salt and black pepper to taste

- Sauté the shallots and garlic in the olive oil for 3 minutes. Add all of the remaining ingredients, except for the herbs, salt, and pepper.
- Simmer uncovered, for 30 minutes.
- Pass through a food mill, then add the herbs, and season to taste with salt and pepper.

PESTO SAUCES

·················· # ASPARAGUS SAUCE

1 pound asparagus
2 hard-boiled egg yolks
4 tablespoons unsalted butter
⅓ cup heavy cream

1 tablespoon lemon juice
pinch of salt
pinch of black pepper

———— • ————

Asparagus sauce is typically served with steamed vegetables, boiled potatoes, and hard-boiled or poached eggs.

————————

- Remove the bottom half of the asparagus (reserve for another use). Blanch the top half of the asparagus in boiled salted water, uncovered, until very tender. Drain, and purée in a food processor, along with the egg yolks.
- Place the asparagus purée, butter, and cream in a heavy-gauge saucepan and bring to simmer. Add the lemon juice, and season to taste.

·················· # BAGNA CAUDA, PIEDMONT STYLE

1 cup olive oil (from the sun-dried tomatoes)
6 anchovy fillets
5 garlic cloves, crushed
½ cup sun-dried tomatoes, packed in oil

¼ cup balsamic vinegar
½ teaspoon black pepper
1 cup Italian parsley, roughly chopped

- Place all ingredients, except for the parsley, in a food processor, and purée. Stir in the parsley, and remove to a chafing dish.

- Fire up the chafing dish, and serve with stalks and hearts of celery, cardoons, blanched artichoke hearts, and other fresh seasonal vegetables.

———————————— • ————————————

This specialty of the Piedmont region of Italy is traditionally served on Christmas Eve. It often includes white truffles, which have been substituted with sun-dried tomatoes here, since fresh white truffles are a rare commodity, even in Italy.

BASIL PESTO

leaves of 1 bunch of fresh
   basil, well rinsed and dried
¼ cup olive oil
½ cup pine nuts or walnuts
3 large garlic cloves, crushed

⅓ cup grated Parmesan
   cheese
¼ cup grated Romano cheese
salt to taste

- Place all ingredients, except the cheese, into a food processor, and purée. Remove the paste, add the cheese, then cover and refrigerate until ready to use.

———————————— • ————————————

Pignolias (pine nuts) are quite expensive, probably due to the fact that a pine tree started from seed will take 75 years to reach commercial levels of production. Walnuts are the most commonly used substitute in contemporary practice. One alternative is to sprinkle toasted pine nuts on top of a pasta tossed in the walnut-based pesto sauce.

GOAT CHEESE PESTO

1½ cups fresh basil leaves,
   rinsed and dried
4 garlic cloves
3 tablespoons pine nuts

pinch of salt
⅓ cup olive oil
¼ cup goat cheese (chévre)
pinch of black pepper

This recipe was borrowed with permission from *Marcella's Italian Kitchen*, by Marcella Hazan.

- Pound the basil, garlic, pine nuts, salt, and a tablespoon of the oil in a mortar (or purée in a food processor). Add the remaining oil, blending thoroughly. Remove the paste to a bowl, and blend in the goat cheese and pepper by mashing with a fork. Season to taste, and toss with freshly cooked pasta.

GREEN CLAM SAUCE

30 littleneck clams, shucked and reserved with their juice
½ pound dried linguine
⅓ cup olive oil
2 bay leaves
6 large garlic cloves, minced
1 medium Spanish onion, finely diced
½ teaspoon crushed red pepper
¼ cup dry red wine

3 tablespoons Italian parsley, minced
2 tablespoons fresh basil leaves, minced
2 tablespoons fresh chives, minced
2 tablespoons unsalted butter
½ cup grated Parmesan or Romano cheese
black pepper as needed

- Bring one gallon of water, a pinch of salt, and a tablespoon of olive oil to a boil. Add the linguine, stirring continuously until the water returns to a boil.

- In a large pan, sauté the bay leaves, garlic, onion, and red pepper in the olive oil over high heat for about 4 minutes, or until the garlic just begins to caramelize. Add the wine, clams and their juice, and the herbs, and simmer about 1 minute.

- When the linguine is cooked al dente, drain and add to the sauce, along with the butter, cheese, and some black pepper. Bring to a boil and serve.

This is a traditional recipe from Boston's North End, as seen in *Jasper White's Cooking from New England*.

MINT PESTO

15 large sprigs Italian parsley
15 large fresh mint leaves
5 large fresh basil leaves
1 teaspoon kosher salt
5 tablespoons unsalted butter, soft

1½ cups heavy cream
¼ cup Parmesan cheese, grated
salt and freshly ground black pepper to taste

- Pound the herbs and salt in a mortar until they form a paste. Transfer this to a bowl, and add the butter, cream, cheese, salt, and pepper. Blend thoroughly. Serve with just cooked green tagliatelle or other choice of pasta.

ᏢEANUT SAUCE I

2 tablespoons peanut oil
1 teaspoon sesame oil
3 tablespoons dry sherry
3 tablespoons white wine
  vinegar
¼ cup soy sauce
1 teaspoon hoisin sauce
1 cup chunky peanut butter

4 garlic cloves, minced
2 teaspoons red chile paste
2 tablespoons grated ginger
  root
3 tablespoons fresh cilantro,
  minced
3 scallions, sliced paper thin

- Blend all ingredients together thoroughly in a mortar or food processor. Cover and refrigerate, allowing it to marinate at least 24 hours. Serve with any grilled, roasted, or poached chicken dish.

ᏢEANUT SAUCE II

2 tablespoons peanut oil
¼ cup scallion, minced
2 garlic cloves, minced
1 teaspoon grated ginger root
1 tablespoon soy sauce
¼ cup chicken stock

1 teaspoon red chile paste
½ teaspoon ground cumin
1 cup chunky peanut butter
½ cup plain yogurt
¼ cup cilantro, minced

- Sauté the scallion and garlic in the peanut oil about 3 minutes. Add the grated ginger and sauté another 2 minutes. Add the soy sauce, stock, chile paste, and cumin. Blend thoroughly, and simmer until almost dry.
- Add the peanut butter, yogurt, and cilantro, and blend thoroughly. Serve with any poached or sautéed poultry dish.

ᏢARSLEY PESTO

1 large bunch Italian (flat
  leaf) parsley (leaves only),
  stems removed

¼ cup walnuts, roughly
  chopped
4 garlic cloves

¾ cup olive oil
¼ cup heavy cream

¼ cup Parmesan cheese,
   grated
salt and black pepper to taste

- Purée the parsley, walnuts, and garlic in a mortar or food processor. Add the olive oil in a slow, steady stream (using the pulse switch, if food processor is used). Repeat this with the cream. Stir in the cheese, and season to taste.

SAGE PESTO

1 bunch fresh sage leaves, rinsed, and stems removed.
½ cup olive oil

3 garlic cloves, peeled
⅓ cup toasted walnuts
⅛ teaspoon salt
⅛ teaspoon black pepper

- Combine all ingredients in a food processor and purée.

SUN-DRIED TOMATO PESTO

3 cups sun-dried tomatoes, soaked in boiling water
1 cup olive paste
6 garlic cloves

¾ cup olive oil
½ cup Romano cheese, grated

- Drain the tomatoes, discarding the water. Combine all in a food processor, and blend until puréed. Cover and refrigerate until needed.

TRAPINI PESTO

6 garlic cloves
1 teaspoon salt
1 cup basil leaves, rinsed, stemmed, and dried
1 cup slivered almonds
4 large ripe tomatoes, peeled, roughly chopped

½ cup olive oil
½ teaspoon freshly ground black pepper
1½ pounds bavette or spaghetti

- Pound the garlic, salt, and basil in a mortar until they form a paste. Add the almonds, and continue pounding.

- Purée the tomatoes in a food processor. Add the paste from the mortar, and the pepper, and incorporate the oil, using the pulse switch on the processor. Toss with the freshly cooked pasta and serve.

TUSCAN GREEN SAUCE

⅔ cup shelled walnuts
1½ cups Italian parsley leaves
¼ cup fresh basil leaves
2 garlic cloves
2 hard-boiled egg yolks
⅔ cup olive oil
⅛ teaspoon salt
⅛ teaspoon black pepper

Tuscan Green Sauce is served with "Beef Tongue," as seen in *Jasper White's Cooking from New England.*

- Place the walnuts, parsley, basil, garlic, salt, and pepper into a food processor and purée. Add the yolks, and purée again briefly.
- Using the pulse switch, add the oil in a slow, steady stream until it is completely emulsified. Set aside until ready to use.

WALNUT SAUCE

2 slices white bread, crusts removed, and soaked in ½ cup cold water for 20 minutes
2 garlic cloves, crushed
1 dozen walnuts, toasted and roughly chopped
¼ cup olive oil
¼ teaspoon salt
¼ teaspoon black pepper
¾ cup ricotta cheese
4 tablespoons unsalted butter, soft

- Squeeze the white bread dry. Place into a food processor with the garlic, walnuts, olive oil, salt, and pepper, and purée.
- Remove to a bowl, and blend in the cheese and butter. Toss with freshly cooked pasta.

CHAPTER 11

COLD SAVORY SAUCES

MAYONNAISE

It is believed that mayonnaise was created by the Duc de Richelieu (or his chef) in honor of the Duke's successful capture of Port Mahon on the island of Minorca in 1756. The sauce was subsequently dubbed *Mahonnaise*. Antoine Carême claimed that the word was derived from *manier*, a French verb meaning "to stir." Carême said, "Some people say *mayonnaise*, other *mahonnaise*, still others *bayonnaise*. It makes no difference that vulgar cooks should use these words, but I urge that these three terms never be uttered in our great kitchens and that we should always denominate this sauce with the epithet, *magnonaise*."

Other etymologists relegate the origin of mayonnaise to Bayonne, France, with the original name *Bayonnaise*. *Moyeu* was old French for "middle," and referred to the middle of an egg—the yolk. Bayonnaise eventually combined with moyeu, evolving into the name we currently use for this cold, egg-yolk-emulsified sauce. And Robert Sokolov, author of *The Saucier's Apprentice*, adds to the confusion with a theory of his own. ". . . it seems to me improbable that no one has yet proposed a fourth solution to the problem. Since most sauces are named after places (Béarnaise, Hollandaise, Piémontaise, Anglaise), it is logical that mayonnaise refer to one also. Unfortunately, there is no town of Mayonne; however, there is a city at the western edge of Normandy, called Mayenne. Who is to say that mayonnaise did not begin as mayennaise?"

ℬASIC MAYONNAISE

3 egg yolks
½ teaspoon dry mustard
2 to 3 tablespoons white
    wine vinegar or lemon
    juice

1 pint olive oil
salt and white pepper to taste

- Beat the yolks, mustard, and 1 teaspoon of vinegar or lemon juice in a stainless steel bowl, using a wire whip.
- Add the oil in a slow, steady stream, whipping continuously. Alternate the oil with the vinegar/lemon juice, as the sauce thickens.
- Season to taste with salt and white pepper.

Sauce Matrix V
Mayonnaise Sauce and Its Derivatives

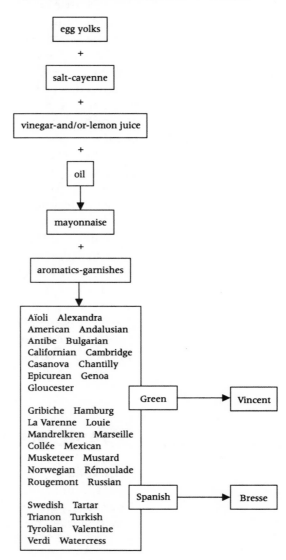

Escoffier's mayonnaise included both vinegar and lemon juice for the acid ingredients. A combination, or a choice of either, seems to be typical of older, traditional recipes, though lemon juice obviously adds a fresher element. Cook's choice applies.

The oil must be added in a slow, steady stream, in order for the eggs to properly emulsify (thicken) the oil. If added too quickly, the eggs cannot emulsify the oil fast enough, and the sauce can break. If this occurs, place one additional egg yolk into a clean bowl, and rewhip the broken sauce by adding it in a slow, steady stream. Follow with the remaining oil and acid.

Mayonnaise is typically served with the following items, served cold: hard-boiled eggs; calf's head; crudité (raw vegetables) and salads; poached fish and shellfish; cold meats.

TRADITIONAL DERIVATIVES OF MAYONNAISE

·················· **Aïoli**

4 to 6 large garlic cloves, split in two	pinch of white pepper
2 egg yolks	⅓ cup mashed potato
pinch of salt	juice of ½ lemon
	1 cup olive oil

- Pound the garlic in a mortar until it is a smooth paste. Add the yolk, salt, pepper, and potato. Continue pounding, while adding the oil in a slow, steady stream. Intersperse with the lemon juice. When the oil is completely emulsified, adjust the seasoning with salt and pepper.

The name aïoli is a combination of *ail* (garlic) and *oli* (Provençal dialect for oil). Léon Daudet (1867–1942), one of the greatest gastronomes of his time, contended that the culinary use of garlic achieved its peak of perfection in aïoli. Frédéric Mistral, who founded the journal "L'Aïoli" in 1891, wrote: "Aïoli epitomizes the heat, the power, and the joy of the Provençal sun. . . ." Grand Aïoli, a sumptuous Provençal dish eaten only two or three times a year, includes the sauce, served with poached salt cod, boiled beef and mutton, stewed vegetables (carrots, celery, green beans beets, cauliflower, chickpeas, etc.), snails, and hard-boiled eggs. Aïoli is also traditionally served with hard-boiled eggs (served cold); snails or poached fish (served cold); Bourride (a fish soup); steamed vegetables; and cold meat.

Alexandra Mayonnaise

Mayonnaise prepared with hard-cooked sieved egg yolks, seasoned with dry mustard, and garnished with chopped chervil.

American Mayonnaise
(Mayonnaise de Homard)

Mayonnaise blended with puréed lobster meat.

Andalusian Mayonnaise
(Mayonnaise Andalouse)

Mayonnaise blended with tomato purée, garnished with diced bell pepper.

Antibe Mayonnaise
(Mayonnaise Antiboise)

Mayonnaise blended with tomato purée and anchovy paste, garnished with chopped tarragon.

Bulgarian Mayonnaise
(Mayonnaise Bulgare)

Mayonnaise blended with thick, cold, puréed tomato sauce, garnished with diced celery root, poached in lemon and white wine.

Californian Mayonnaise
(Mayonnaise Californienne)

Heavy cream blended with tomato ketchup, seasoned with Worcestershire sauce, tabasco, paprika, and lemon juice.

CAMBRIDGE MAYONNAISE

2 hard-boiled egg yolks,
    pressed through a sieve
1 anchovy filet, well mashed
½ teaspoon dry mustard
⅛ teaspoon cayenne pepper
4 tablespoons white wine
    vinegar

1 cup olive oil
1 teaspoon tarragon, minced
1 teaspoon dill, minced
1 tablespoon parsley, minced
1 tablespoon small capers,
    drained
salt and white pepper to taste

- Beat the yolks, anchovy, mustard, cayenne, and 1 tablespoon of vinegar in a stainless steel bowl, using a wire whip.
- Add the oil in a slow, steady stream, whipping continuously. Alternate the oil with the vinegar as the sauce thickens.
- Add the herbs and capers, and season to taste with salt and white pepper.

Casanova Mayonnaise

Mayonnaise garnished with sieved hard-cooked egg yolks, chopped tarragon, and minced truffles.

Casanova de Seingalt, also known as Giovanni Jacopo, Italian adventurer, and libertine, was famous for his romantic and chivalrous exploits during the 1700s. He was also an attentive observer of gastronomic etiquette. Casanova is credited with inventing a special vinegar that accompanied hard-cooked eggs and anchovies, and for advocating Chambertin (a red Burgundy) as an accompaniment to Roquefort cheese. Famous pâtés, Genoese ceps, truffles, oysters, champagne, and other foods all owe their reputation as aphrodisiacs to him.

Chantilly Mayonnaise

Mayonnaise made with lemon juice, blended with unsweetened whipped cream just before serving.

Chantilly cream, heavy cream sweetened and whipped into an air-thickened emulsion, is the original use of the name of the château, which attained considerable notoriety in the mid-seventeenth century, under the supervision of the Swiss maître d', Vatel. In more recent times, any sauce can take on the name Chantilly by including whipped cream (sweetened or unsweetened) folded in near the time of service (see Chantilly Sauce under Velouté and Dutch Sauces).

Fritz Karl Watel, better known as Vatel, attained gastronomic notoriety in April 1671 when he was charged with the organization of a catered affair for 3,000 guests, in honor of Louis XIV. Upon learning that a shipment of dover sole had been delayed due to a storm over the English Channel, Vatel retired to his room and closed the door on the handle of a large knife, locking it into place. He subsequently impaled himself onto the knife. (Some accounts indicate that he simply ran a sword through his body.) More than two centuries later, August Escoffier was asked if he too would have committed suicide if he had been in the same situation. "No, I would have made a mousse of young chicken breasts and covered it with a fish velouté, and nobody would have known the difference."

Epicurean Mayonnaise (Mayonnaise Épicurienne)

Mayonnaise blended with puréed cucumber (seeded and peeled), anchovy paste, and puréed mango chutney.

Genoa Mayonnaise (Mayonnaise Génoise)

Genoa mayonnaise sauce is typically served with poached or grilled fish, served cold.

Mayonnaise made with lemon juice, blended with a paste made from pistachios, almonds, basil, sage, and parsley.

Gloucester Mayonnaise

Mayonnaise seasoned with Worcestershire sauce, garnished with diced or grated fennel root, and finished with sour cream.

.... # $\mathscr{G}$REEN MAYONNAISE
(Mayonnaise Verte)

1 cup mayonnaise
1 teaspoon tarragon leaves,
  minced
1 teaspoon parsley, minced

1 teaspoon watercress
  leaves, minced
1 teaspoon basil leaves,
  minced

- Combine all ingredients in a bowl and blend thoroughly.

———————————— • ————————————

    Mayonnaise Verte can be made with any combination of herbs, depending on the dish it is to be served with. A sole variety of herb can also be employed (such as dill, for example), or the herb(s) can be added in the form of a pesto (basil, cilantro, parsley, etc.). It is typically served with the following items, served cold: hard-boiled eggs, and poached fish or shellfish.

————————————————————————

Vincent Mayonnaise

1 part green mayonnaise blended with 1 part tartar sauce.

.... # $\mathscr{G}$RIBICHE SAUCE

2 hard-boiled egg yolks,
  pressed through a sieve
2 hard-boiled egg whites,
  cut into a fine julienne
½ teaspoon dry mustard
3 tablespoons white wine
  vinegar
1 cup olive oil

1 tablespoon minced
  tarragon leaves
2 sour gherkins, finely diced
1 tablespoon small capers,
  drained
1 tablespoon minced chervil
1 tablespoon minced parsley
salt and white pepper to taste

————— • —————

Gribiche sauce is typically served with the following dishes, served cold: poached fish or shellfish, and calf's head (Tête de Veau).

—————————

- Beat the yolks, mustard, and 1 tablespoon of vinegar in a stainless steel bowl, using a wire whip.
- Add the oil in a slow, steady stream, whipping continuously. Alternate the oil with the vinegar as the sauce thickens.

- Add the gherkins, capers, herbs, and egg whites. Season to taste with salt and white pepper.

Hamburg Mayonnaise (Mayonnaise à la Hambourgeoise)

Mayonnaise with the addition of lemon zest, a pinch of sugar, and a splash of Madeira.

Horseradish Mayonnaise (Sauce au Raifort Froide)

Mayonnaise blended with grated prepared horseradish (squeezed dry), flavored with a little lemon juice, and finished with chopped parsley.

— • —

Horseradish sauce comes in many different forms, both hot (see Béchamel) and cold (some include sour cream or crème fraîche). The following version was served with roast rib of beef at the Clift Hotel, San Francisco, during the late 1970s (I worked there as a Tournant).

*H*ORSERADISH SAUCE II

Cold horseradish sauce is typically served with potato or beet salad; crudités; smoked fish; cold meats.

½ cup heavy cream
2 slices fresh white bread, crusts removed, and shredded into crumbs

⅓ cup sour cream
4 tablespoons prepared horseradish, squeezed dry

- Combine all of the ingredients, and blend well. Cover and refrigerate 1 hour before serving.

*L*A VARENNE MAYONNAISE

1 small shallot, minced
3 tablespoons olive oil

½ cup mushrooms, roughly chopped

salt and pepper to taste
¼ cup dry white wine
1 cup basic mayonnaise
2 tablespoons mushroom
   duxelle

1 tablespoon parsley,
   minced
1 tablespoon chervil,
   minced

- Sauté the shallot in the oil for several minutes. Add the mushrooms, salt, and pepper, and continue sautéing. Add the white wine.
- Using a slotted spoon, transfer the mushrooms to a chopping board, and mince. Return to the sauté pan and simmer, stirring frequently, until the mixture is fairly dry. Set aside and allow to cool.
- Thoroughly blend together the mayonnaise, 2 tablespoons of the duxelle, and the herbs.

François Pierre La Varenne (1618-1678), began his career as *marmiton* (kitchen boy) in the home of the Duchesse de Bar, sister of Henri IV. Possessing great talents as a chef, he was the author of the first systematically planned books on cookery and confectionery, and showed how French cuisine had been influenced by Italian cookery during the previous 150 years.

La Varenne sauce is typically served with poached fish, served cold.

Leghorn Mayonnaise

Mayonnaise made with hard-cooked egg yolks, blended with anchovy paste, seasoned with a little nutmeg, and garnished with chopped parsley.

Louie Sauce

Mayonnaise blended with heavy cream and strained chili sauce (in proportions of 4-to-2-to-1), garnished with minced onion, green pepper, and seasoned with a touch of cayenne pepper and lemon juice.

Crab Louis is a dish originating in San Francisco, reputedly created by Louis Coutard. The salad is fairly consistently agreed upon (though rather boring): a bed of iceberg lettuce, topped with Dungeness crabmeat (or the shrimp and lobster variations), garnished with olives (usually black), and hard-boiled eggs. It is still found on the luncheon menus of many of San Francisco's restaurants, and the variations of "the original" sauce are endless.

Mandrelkren Mayonnaise

Mayonnaise made with pounded almonds blended with egg yolks, seasoned with a little salt and sugar, then beaten with oil and vinegar (as for mayonnaise).

Marseille Mayonnaise

Mayonnaise blended with a purée of sea urchins.

Mayonnaise Collée

Mayonnaise blended with liquefied meat aspic, in proportions of 2-to-1, then used as a coating for cold dishes.

The name of this preparation comes from *coller*, meaning "to paste, to stick." It is used in the same fashion as *chaud-froid*, to coat individual food items, as well as large roasts for service on a cold buffet. After the initial coating, the creamy ivory-colored base is decorated in some fashion with blanched vegetables, often in elaborate and colorful motifs. It is superior to chaud-froid in both ease of preparation and taste.

Mexican Mayonnaise

Mayonnaise blended with anchovy paste, garnished with diced red and green bell peppers.

$\mathcal{M}$USKETEER MAYONNAISE
(Mayonnaise Mousquetaire)

1 shallot, minced	¼ teaspoon cayenne pepper
½ cup dry white wine	1 cup mayonnaise
1½ tablespoons meat glaze	2 tablespoons chives, minced

- Simmer the shallot and wine until reduced to about 2 table-spoons of liquid. Add the glaze and cayenne, and stir until smooth. Set aside, and allow to come to room temperature.
- Add the reduction and the chives to the mayonnaise, and blend thoroughly. Serve with grilled or broiled meat or poultry.

Musketeer mayonnaise is typically served with cold meats.

$\mathcal{M}$USTARD MAYONNAISE

1 cup mayonnaise	2 tablespoons lemon juice
½ cup Dijon-style mustard	

- Combine all ingredients in a bowl and blend thoroughly.

Norwegian Mayonnaise
(Mayonnaise Norvegienne)

Mayonnaise made in the traditional manner, except that hard-boiled egg yolks are used in place of raw yolks.

While mayonnaise is traditionally made with raw egg yolks, it can also be made with hard-cooked egg yolks, as in the Norwegian sauce here. The same ingredient amounts as the raw variety apply.

Oriental Mayonnaise
(Mayonnaise Orientale)

Mayonnaise blended with a Middle Eastern style tomato fondue.

Orientale mayonnaise is typically served with poached fish (served cold).

ᴛomato Fondue
(for Oriental Mayonnaise)

¼ cup olive oil
1 shallot, finely diced
1 medium onion, small diced
3 garlic cloves
½ cup red and green bell
    peppers, medium dice
pinch of saffron

2 sprigs thyme
1 cup tomato purée
1 cup diced, peeled
    tomatoes, with their
    juice
salt and white pepper to
    taste

- Sweat the shallot and onion in the olive oil for 10 minutes. Add the garlic, peppers, saffron, and thyme, and sauté another 5 minutes. Add the tomatoes, and simmer about 20 minutes. Remove the thyme stems, season to taste, and allow to cool.

ᴿémoulade Sauce

1 cup mayonnaise
1 tablespoon Dijon-style
    mustard
1 anchovy fillet, mashed to a
    paste
1 tablespoon minced
    tarragon leaves

1 tablespoon minced chervil
    or parsley
2 sour gherkins, finely diced
1 tablespoon small capers,
    drained

- Combine all ingredients in a bowl and blend thoroughly.

Rémoulade, literally "sharp sauce," attributed to the addition of several salty and piquant ingredients, is commonly known in a very elegant dish, *Celery Rémoulade*, consisting of celery root (celeriac) cut into a very fine julienne, blanched briefly in boiling salted water, then blended with the sauce.

Rémoulade sauce is typically served with the following items, served cold: hard-boiled eggs; crudités and salad; poached fish; and cold meat.

Rougemont Mayonnaise

Mayonnaise seasoned with additional mustard, garnished with chopped tarragon.

RUSSIAN MAYONNAISE
(Mayonnaise à la Russe)

¾ cup mayonnaise
1 tablespoon Dijon-style
  mustard

3 tablespoons Beluga caviar
1 tablespoon tomalley
  (lobster liver)

- Press the tomalley through a sieve. Combine with the mustard, and 1 tablespoon of the caviar, and blend well. Sprinkle the remaining caviar on top of the sauce at service.

———————— • ————————

Dishes designated "à la Russe" generally refer to classic cuisine as practiced by French chefs under the Russian monarchy. They are not a true representation of Slavic culinary traditions.

Russian sauce is typically served with crudités, lettuce hearts, salads, and poached fish.

SARDAL SAUCE
(Sauce Sardalaise)

3 hard-boiled egg yolks
2 tablespoons heavy cream
2 tablespoons minced truffle
pinch of salt

pinch of white pepper
1 cup olive oil
juice of 1 lemon
2 tablespoons Cognac

——— • ———

Sardal sauce is typically served with grilled, broiled, or roasted meat.

- Beat the egg yolks, the cream, truffle, salt, and pepper with a wire whip. Add the oil slowly, beating continuously, alternating it with the lemon juice. Add the Cognac, and adjust the seasoning.

Spanish Mayonnaise
(Mayonnaise à l'Espagnole)

Mayonnaise seasoned with garlic, additional mustard, and paprika, and garnished with finely diced ham.

Bresse Mayonnaise

Spanish mayonnaise, flavored with Madeira and orange juice, seasoned with cayenne pepper, and finished with puréed sautéed chicken livers.

Swedish Mayonnaise

Mayonnaise blended with apple sauce that has been cooked with white wine, garnished with grated horseradish.

Swedish mayonnaise is typically served with pork.

Tarator Sauce

Toasted almonds or pine nuts, garlic, and white bread soaked in milk, pounded to a paste in a mortar, seasoned with salt and vinegar or lemon juice, beaten with oil as for mayonnaise.

TARTAR SAUCE
(Sauce Tartare)

Tartare sauce is typically served with the following items, served cold: hard-boiled eggs; rice; poached fish; oysters; and the following items served hot: deep-fried potatoes; braised, pan-fried, or deep-fried offal.

1 cup mayonnaise
2 tablespoons Spanish onion, minced

1 hard-boiled egg yolk, pressed through a sieve
2 tablespoons chives, minced

• Combine all ingredients in a bowl and blend thoroughly.

Trianon Mayonnaise

Mayonnaise blended with tomato purée and white onion purée, garnished with diced gherkins and red bell pepper.

Turkish Mayonnaise (Aïoli à la Turque)

Pressed garlic and white bread soaked in milk, pressed through a sieve, blended with egg yolks and vinegar, then beaten with oil as for mayonnaise.

Tyrolian Mayonnaise (Mayonnaise Tyrolienne)

Mayonnaise blended with tomato purée.

Valentine Mayonnaise

Mayonnaise seasoned with additional mustard, blended with grated horseradish and chopped tarragon.

VERDI SAUCE

1 cup fresh spinach leaves, well rinsed, blanched in boiling salted water, and squeezed dry
¾ cup mayonnaise

¼ cup sour cream
3 tablespoons sour gherkins, finely diced
2 tablespoons fresh chives, very finely sliced

- Pound the spinach leaves in a mortar, or chop into a very fine purée. Combine with the remaining ingredients.

WATERCRESS MAYONNAISE

(Mayonnaise Cressonière)

Watercress mayonnaise is typically served with soft-boiled or poached eggs, and specifically with a water-cress, parsley, and potato salad, topped with chopped hard-boiled eggs. (This sauce can also be prepared using hard-boiled egg yolks.)

1 bunch watercress leaves, well rinsed, stems removed
2 egg yolks

juice of 1 lemon
pinch of salt
pinch of pepper
1 cup olive oil

- Combine the watercress, yolks, half the lemon juice, salt, and pepper in a food processor.
- Use the pulse, or on/off switch, and incorporate the oil slowly and carefully, alternating it with the lemon juice. Adjust seasoning with salt and pepper.

CONTEMPORARY INNOVATIONS

ℋERB CREAM

....

½ cup mayonnaise
2 tablespoons white wine
  vinegar
1 teaspoon chopped fresh
  basil
1 teaspoon chopped fresh
  parsley

1 teaspoon chopped fresh
  tarragon
¼ cup half-and-half
salt and white pepper to
  taste

———— • ————

This sauce accompanies
"Roast Potatoes and Bell
Peppers," as seen in *A Taste
For All Seasons*.

- Combine all ingredients in a bowl and blend thoroughly.

ℋORSERADISH SAUCE

....

¾ cup gin
¼ cup juniper berries
1½ cups mayonnaise
½ cup half-and-half

2 tablespoons champagne
  vinegar
¼ cup prepared horseradish
pinch of salt
pinch of white pepper

———— • ————

This sauce accompanies
"Gin-cured Salmon," as
seen in *A Taste For All
Seasons*.

- Simmer the gin and juniper berries until reduced by two-thirds. Allow to cool, then strain into a food processor. Add the mayonnaise, half-and-half, vinegar, horseradish, salt and pepper, and purée. Cover and refrigerate overnight before serving.

ℒIME SAUCE

....

———— • ————

This sauce accompanies "Co-
lumbia River Caviar
Mousse," as seen in *A Taste
For All Seasons*.

1½ cups mayonnaise
5 tablespoons lime juice
¾ cup half-and-half

salt and white pepper to
  taste

- Combine all ingredients in a bowl and blend thoroughly.

MUSTARD-PECAN MAYONNAISE

¾ cup mayonnaise
4 tablespoons grainy
  mustard
½ cup toasted chopped
  pecans

juice of 1 lemon
salt and white pepper to
  taste

This sauce accompanies "Fried Catfish," as seen in *A Taste For All Seasons*.

- Combine all ingredients in a bowl and blend thoroughly. Season to taste with salt and pepper.

RED PEPPER AÏOLI

2 egg yolks
1 large red bell pepper
olive oil as needed
4 large garlic cloves,
  pressed

salt and white pepper to
  taste
1 cup olive oil
juice of 1 lemon

- Preheat oven to 400°F.
- Rub the pepper lightly with olive oil and roast on a pan until it begins turning black (15–20 minutes). Place into a plastic bag, and seal for 15 minutes. Remove the pepper, and separate the skin and seeds from the flesh.
- Purée the egg yolks, bell pepper, garlic, and a little salt and pepper in a food processor. Using the pulse switch, add the olive oil in a slow, steady stream, alternating with the lemon juice. Adjust the seasoning with salt and pepper.

This sauce is served with "Wild Mushroom Terrine," as seen in *A Taste For All Seasons*.

Also referred to as "Beurre de Provence" (butter of Provence), this is a variation of the Mediterranean French specialty, essentially a garlic-dominated mayonnaise. In Provence, Aïoli is the name of the dish itself, whether seafood or vegetables, served with this sauce.

Saffron-Rosemary Aïoli

¼ cup dry white wine
2 sprigs fresh rosemary,
　nettles removed from
　stems
¼ teaspoon saffron
5 large egg yolks

2 garlic cloves, minced
¼ teaspoon salt
⅛ teaspoon white pepper
1 pint olive oil
juice of one lemon

- Place the white wine and rosemary nettles into a small saucepan, cover, and simmer 5 minutes. Remove the cover, and continue simmering until reduced by approximately half. Strain into a small bowl, add the saffron, and set aside.

- When the rosemary infusion has cooled off, combine it with the yolks, garlic, salt, and pepper in a stainless steel or glass bowl. Whip with a whisk, while adding the olive oil in a slow, steady stream. Intersperse the oil with a portion of the lemon juice, until all the oil and lemon is fully incorporated.

According to Larousse Gastronomique, "Not all the ingredients we have enumerated . . . are absolutely essential. There is no set rule on this point. One should proceed according to one's tastes and the means at one's disposal." Recipes for aïoli—sometimes referred to as "Provençale butter"—vary in their inclusion of an acid ingredient. Mayonnaise (of which we can include aïoli as a family member) contains an acid (vinegar or lemon juice) both for palatability, and as a catalyst to strengthen the oil emulsification. Since the definition above allows some room for creativity, saucier's choice applies.

Sour Sauce
(Sauce Aigrelette)

2 egg yolks
1 tablespoon Dijon-style
　mustard

3 teaspoons lemon juice
1 cup olive oil
¼ cup dry white wine

2 tablespoon white wine
   or Champagne
   vinegar
1 tablespoon fresh chives,
   minced

1 tablespoon fresh tarragon
   leaves, minced
salt and white pepper to
   taste

- Using a wire whisk, whip the yolks, mustard, and one tea-spoon of lemon juice together in a stainless steel or glass bowl.
- Whip in the oil, pouring it in a slow, steady stream, while continuously whipping. Alternate the oil with the remaining lemon juice, the wine, and the vinegar. Finish with the herbs, salt, and pepper.

---•---

Aigrelette is a French term meaning slightly sour or tart.

SUN-DRIED TOMATO MAYONNAISE

1 cup mayonnaise
½ cup crème fraîche
½ cup oil-packed sun-dried
   tomatoes, drained, and
   cut into small dice

juice of ½ lemon
1 garlic clove, pressed
2 tablespoons basil leaves,
   minced

- Combine all ingredients in a bowl and blend thoroughly.

CRÈME FRAÎCHE

---•---

Sun-dried tomato mayon-naise goes exceptionally well with crudité. The rec-ipe for crème fraîche is an American facsimile of a cul-tured cream (similar to our sour cream), unique to France. It can be used in a myriad of ways—worked into salad dressings, savory and sweet sauces.

---

2 cups heavy cream
½ cup buttermilk

½ cup sour cream or yogurt
¼ teaspoon salt

- Combine all the ingredients in a clean saucepan, and bring to a temperature of 100°F.
- Transfer to a clean stainless steel bowl, cover, and set into an oven heated only by the pilot light (12 hours).
- Refrigerate for 24 hours. Carefully remove thickened top part (this is the crème fraîche), and discard any liquid left at the bottom. Cover and refrigerate until ready to use.

BELL PEPPER ROUILLE

2 red bell peppers
2 serrano chile peppers
½ cup dry white wine
2 tablespoons balsamic
  vinegar
1 bay leaf
¼ teaspoon red chile pepper
  paste

½ cup capers, drained
¼ cup chicken stock (or
  water)
1 large egg yolk
1 anchovy fillet
8 garlic cloves, crushed
1 cup cubed French bread
½ cup olive oil

- Rub the tomatoes and peppers lightly with olive oil, and roast in a preheated 400-degree oven until they begin turning black. Place in a bowl, cover with plastic wrap, and allow to sit 15 minutes. Separate and reserve the flesh from the skin, stems, and seeds.

- Simmer the peppers wine, vinegar, bay leaf, chile paste, capers, stock, and salt, for 10 minutes. Discard the bay leaf, and purée the mixture in a food processor. Remove this purée and set aside.

- Place the egg yolk, anchovy, garlic, and bread in the food processor, and purée. Add the olive oil slowly, and incorporate into the purée using the pulse switch. Add the pepper purée and blend thoroughly. Cover and refrigerate overnight before serving.

———————————————— • ————————————————

Rouille, literally "rust," is a traditional mayonnaise sauce spread on French bread croutons and served with a dish of boiled or poached fish or octopus (served cold), and Bouillabaisse, a rich Mediterranean fish stew. There are many simpler versions, including one made by pounding garlic, red chile peppers, and a boiled potato into a paste in a mortar and pestle. Fish bouillon is then added, until the paste becomes a smooth sauce.

———————————————————————————

VINAIGRETTE

The word *vinaigre*, literally "sour wine," is a combination of *vin* (French for wine, from the Latin *vinum*), and *aigre* (French for sour, from the Latin *acer*, meaning sharp).

Vinegar is actually more than just sour wine. It is a fermented product requiring nearly as much care as wine fermentation, though less time. White or red wine is fermented in oak barrels, using a "mother," a strain of bacteria that consumes the alcohol in the wine, turning it into acetic acid. This fermentation requires roughly 6 months. This is followed by a careful filtering of the vinegar, then adjusting the acid content by adding water and/or wine.

Orléans, France, an important wine transport center on the Loire River, is also the French vinegar capital (a vinegar merchant's corporation was established there in 1394). Today, the "Orléans method" is the name applied to the careful fermentation process, while the "German method" refers to industrially produced vinegar, a short distillation method requiring 1–3 days. The difference in flavor and aroma between the two, of course, is significant.

Balsamic vinegar, of Italian origin, is actually a white wine vinegar, also fermented. It takes on a dark hue as a result of the long fermentation in wooden casks.

*B*ASIC VINAIGRETTE

1 cup olive oil	⅛ teaspoon salt
⅓ cup red or white wine vinegar	⅛ teaspoon white pepper

- Combine the ingredients in a bowl, and blend thoroughly with a wire whip.

TRADITIONAL VINAIGRETTES

*L*EMON VINAIGRETTE

1 cup olive oil	pinch of salt
⅓ cup lemon juice	pinch of white pepper

- Combine the ingredients in a bowl, and blend thoroughly with a wire whip.

*M*USTARD VINAIGRETTE

1 cup olive oil
⅓ cup white wine vinegar
2 tablespoons water
1 heaping tablespoon
   Dijon-style mustard

1 small shallot, peeled and
   roughly chopped
handful of parsley sprigs
pinch of salt
pinch of black pepper

- Place all ingredients into a blender and purée. Adjust seasoning with water, salt, and pepper.

*R*AVIGOTE SAUCE

½ cup olive oil
¼ cup white wine vinegar
½ teaspoon Dijon-style
   mustard
½ teaspoon tarragon leaves,
   minced
½ teaspoon fresh chives,
   minced

½ teaspoon parsley, minced
½ teaspoon chervil, minced
2 tablespoons Spanish
   onion, very finely diced
1 teaspoon small capers,
   drained

- Blend all ingredients thoroughly in a stainless steel bowl.

Ravigoter is a French verb meaning to revive, to refresh. The sauce is typically served with the following items, served cold: poached fish or mussels; calf's head or brains; poached poultry; and cold meats; and these items served hot: braised or pan-fried offal; poached or pan-fried poultry; and grilled meat.

---

*W*INE VINAIGRETTE

1 cup olive oil
¼ cup red wine vinegar
¼ cup dry red wine
pinch of salt

pinch of black pepper
1 small shallot, peeled and
   roughly chopped
handful of parsley sprigs

- Place all ingredients into a blender and purée. Adjust seasoning with water, salt, and pepper.

CONTEMPORARY INNOVATIONS

.... ## $\mathscr{A}$PPLE CIDER MIGNONETTE

——— • ———

The Apple Cider Mignonette accompanies oysters on the half shell, as seen in *Jasper White's Cooking From New England*.

———————

1 tablespoon shallot, minced
3 tablespoons Granny Smith apple, chopped

1 tablespoon black pepper, coarsely ground
⅓ cup apple cider vinegar

- Blend all ingredients thoroughly in a stainless steel bowl. Cover and refrigerate for 1 hour, then serve with oysters on the half shell.

.... ## $\mathscr{A}$SIAN VINAIGRETTE

1 cup peanut oil
1 tablespoon sesame oil
1 tablespoon grated ginger root

1 garlic clove, crushed
¼ cup plain rice vinegar
2 tablespoons soy sauce
2 tablespoons water

- Place all ingredients into a blender and purée. Adjust seasoning with water, soy sauce, and vinegar.

.... ## $\mathscr{B}$LUE CHEESE VINAIGRETTE

1 garlic clove, cut in half
½ cup olive oil
3 tablespoons white wine vinegar

⅓ cup crumbled blue cheese
pinch of salt
pinch of white pepper

- Rub the garlic clove around the inside of a clean wooden bowl, then discard the garlic.
- Pour in the oil, vinegar, salt, and pepper, and blend thoroughly. Add the blue cheese, and blend again.
- Add a cut, washed, and dried quantity of romaine or butter lettuce, toss, and serve.

There is an excellent blue cheese created in the United States by the descendants of the same family known for their success with washing machines. Maytag Blue has been available since its development in Iowa in the early 1940s. If difficult to locate, local availability can be found by telephoning the dairy at 1-800-247-2458.

CORIANDER-LIME VINAIGRETTE

This sauce is served with a romaine, avocado, jicama, goat cheese, and tomato salad, a creation of Susan Wilkens, chef at Little City Antipasti Bar, San Francisco, California.

1 cup olive oil
¼ cup champagne vinegar
¼ cup lime juice
1 jalapeño pepper, seeds removed, and roughly chopped

½ cup cilantro leaves, well rinsed and dried
½ cup mint leaves, well rinsed and dried
½ teaspoon kosher salt
½ teaspoon black pepper

- Purée the ingredients in a blender. Cover and refrigerate until ready to use.

CREAM VINAIGRETTE

½ cup heavy cream
4 teaspoons red wine vinegar

⅛ teaspoon salt
⅛ teaspoon black pepper

- Blend all ingredients thoroughly in a stainless steel bowl. Toss with appropriate lettuce leaves.

GINGER VINAIGRETTE

2 cups olive oil
¼ cup white wine vinegar
juice of 1 lemon
½ teaspoon salt

¼ teaspoon white pepper
3 tablespoons ginger root, grated

- Blend all ingredients thoroughly in a stainless steel bowl. Toss with appropriate lettuce leaves.

ℒEMON-BASIL VINAIGRETTE

. . . .

——— • ———

This sauce is served with "Mozzarella, Prosciutto, and Tomato," as seen in *The Pillar House Cookbook*.

1 cup olive oil
¼ cup lemon juice
½ teaspoon lemon zest
3 tablespoons balsamic
  vinegar

2 tablespoon water
2 shallots, chopped
¼ teaspoon salt
¼ teaspoon white pepper

- Purée the ingredients in a food processor. Cover and refrigerate until ready to use.

𝒪YSTER MIGNONETTE

. . . .

2 tablespoons shallot, minced
1 tablespoon carrot, finely
  shredded
2 tablespoons parsley, minced

1 tablespoon black pepper,
  coarsely ground
¾ cup champagne vinegar

- Blend all ingredients thoroughly in a stainless steel bowl. Cover and refrigerate for 1 hour, then serve with oysters on the half shell.

——————————— • ———————————

Mignon means literally delicate, pretty, dainty, sweet. In culinary parlance, mignonette refers to coarsely ground pepper, or a small cheesecloth sachet filled with peppercorns used to flavor soups and stews. Escoffier created chicken mignonettes (similar to medallions or noisettes), consisting of round chicken supremes, barded with pickled tongue and truffle, and foie gras mignonettes—slices of goose liver, coated with chicken mousseline, coated with egg and bread crumbs, and sautéed. Potatoes cut into fat matchsticks, slightly larger than allumettes (shoe string, or match-stick potatoes), are also called mignonettes.

This sauce accompanies oysters on the half shell, as seen in *Jasper White's Cooking From New England*.

RASPBERRY MIGNONETTE

1 cup raspberry vinegar
¼ cup dry white wine
1 teaspoon black pepper,
 coarsely ground

1 teaspoon salt
1 shallot, minced
1 tablespoon fresh basil
 leaves, minced

- Blend all ingredients thoroughly in a stainless steel bowl. Cover and refrigerate for 1 hour, then serve with oysters on the half shell.

SAFFRON VINAIGRETTE

¼ teaspoon saffron threads
¼ cup white wine
1 cup olive oil
¼ cup champagne vinegar
1 small shallot, minced
1 garlic clove, pressed

1 tablespoon parsley, minced
½ teaspoon Dijon-style
 mustard
juice of 1 lemon
salt and black pepper to
 taste

- Simmer the wine and saffron until reduced by half. Set aside to cool.
- Blend all ingredients thoroughly in a stainless steel bowl. Season to taste with salt and pepper. Cover and refrigerate until ready to serve.

SUN-DRIED TOMATO VINAIGRETTE

¼ cup oil-packed sun-dried
 tomatoes, cut into ¼-inch
 dice
1 cup olive oil (from the
 tomatoes)
⅓ cup red wine vinegar

2 tablespoons water
1 small shallot, peeled and
 roughly chopped
handful of parsley sprigs
pinch of salt
pinch of black pepper

- Place all ingredients, except the diced tomatoes, into a blender and purée. Add the diced tomatoes, and adjust seasoning with water, salt, and pepper.

THREE-ONION VINAIGRETTE

¼ cup red onion, peeled and
    roughly chopped
1 large shallot, minced
½ cup champagne vinegar
1 cup olive oil

2 tablespoons water
salt and black pepper to taste
3 scallions, peeled, root and
    green tops removed, and
    sliced paper thin

- Place all the ingredients, except the scallions, into a blender, and purée. Add the scallions. Cover and refrigerate until ready to serve.

TOASTED CUMIN VINAIGRETTE

1 cup olive oil
½ cup sherry wine vinegar
2 tablespoons cumin seeds

2 tablespoons Dijon-style
    mustard
½ teaspoon kosher salt

- Toast the cumin seeds on a pan in a 350-degree oven for about 15 minutes. Grind to a powder with a mortar and pestle.
- Purée the ingredients in a blender. Cover and refrigerate until ready to use.

———————————— • ————————————

This sauce is served with a romaine, jicama, red bell pepper, cherry tomato, and pistachio salad, a creation of Susan Wilkens, chef de cuisine at Little City Antipasti Bar, San Francisco, California.

————————————————

TOMATO VINAIGRETTE

1 cup olive oil
¼ cup basalmic vinegar
2 tablespoons tomato paste
    dissolved in 2 tablespoons
    warm water

1 teaspoon thyme leaves,
    minced
1 teaspoon capers, drained
pinch of salt
pinch of black pepper

- Combine all the ingredients in a bowl, and blend thoroughly. Allow to marinate 1 hour before serving.

WALNUT VINAIGRETTE

⅓ cup walnut oil
⅔ cup olive oil
¼ cup white wine or
    champagne vinegar

juice of 1 lemon
2 tablespoons water
¼ teaspoon salt
¼ teaspoon black pepper

- Place all ingredients into a blender and purée. Adjust seasoning with salt and pepper.

OTHER COLD SAUCES

COCKTAIL SAUCE I

1 shallot, minced
½ cup dry white wine
1 cup ketchup or strained
    chili sauce
1 tablespoon Worcestershire
    sauce

2–3 tablespoons prepared
    horseradish, squeezed dry
2 tablespoons lemon juice
¼ teaspoon celery salt
¼ teaspoon tabasco sauce

——— • ———

This sauce is typically served with chilled poached shellfish—shrimp, crab, lobster, crayfish, clams, and oysters.

———————

- Simmer the shallot and wine until nearly dry. Blend together with the remaining ingredients. Cover and store overnight in the refrigerator before serving.

COCKTAIL SAUCE II

⅓ cup Spanish onion, finely
    chopped
2 garlic cloves
5 tablespoons frozen apple
    juice concentrate
¾ cup tomato paste

½ cup champagne vinegar
1 teaspoon Tabasco sauce
1 tablespoon Worcestershire
    sauce
2 tablespoons prepared
    horseradish, squeezed dry

——— • ———

This sauce was adapted from a sauce innovated by Alan R. Gibson, and served with oysters and littleneck clams on the half shell.

———————

- Purée all of the ingredients in a food processor. Cover and store in the refrigerator overnight before serving.

CUMBERLAND SAUCE

zest and juice of 1 orange
zest and juice of 1 lemon
1 shallot, minced
1 cup Port wine
½ cup red currant jelly

pinch of cayenne pepper
¼ teaspoon dry mustard
   (dissolved in a little of the
   port)
¼ teaspoon grated ginger

- Blanch the zest in boiling water for 5 minutes. Drain (discard the liquid), then combine with the remaining ingredients, and simmer for 15 minutes.

Cumberland sauce is typically served with all forms of ham, mutton, and game, as well as meat or game pâtés and terrines.

MINT SAUCE
(Sauce à la Menthe)

¾ cup champagne vinegar
¼ cup water
2 tablespoons sugar
pinch of salt

2 cups fresh mint leaves,
   rinsed, and cut into a fine
   chiffonade

- Bring the vinegar, water, sugar, and salt to a boil. Stir until the sugar and salt are dissolved. Place the mint leaves into a glass or stainless steel bowl, and pour the hot liquid over. Allow to marinate several hours.
- Strain the liquid, discarding the mint. Add the remaining cup of mint, and serve.

This mint sauce is the typical English accompaniment for roast leg of lamb.

CHAPTER *12*

COMPOUND BUTTERS

Beurre Composé

*C*ompound butters serve a variety of functions. They are used in the production of cold hors d'oeuvres and canapés; to fortify the flavor of sauces; and in place of sauces on certain grilled and fried foods.

In cold hors d'oeuvres and canapé production, a flavored butter may serve as a spread on a cracker or piece of toast, on which other components are placed. It can also be combined with soft cheeses, serving as a binder and flavoring agent for mousses and various pastes used in the making of hors d'oeuvres.

Some sauces call for a *montée* of a specific compound butter to complete that sauce. And beurre blancs require butter in some form, generally plain whole butter, though a compound butter can be used, as per the saucier's discretion. In the case where a butter mount is not specifically called for, the saucier may add it nevertheless. A Périgord sauce does not specifically call for a montée, but truffle butter beaten in at the end will obviously add a stronger flavor of truffle; the flavor of a champagne tarragon sauce is enhanced with the addition of tarragon butter; a horseradish sauce created from a cream sauce will be intensified by mounting it with horseradish butter, and so on.

Compound butters can serve as an accompaniment in lieu of a sauce. Half-inch slices are cut from the wrapped cylindrical shape into which they are formed, the wrapping is removed, and the slices placed into ice water at the production station. When a grilled steak (compound butter used in this way is almost always applied to grilled meat) is placed onto a serving plate, it is topped with a slice of the butter, which then slowly melts from the heat of the food on the way to the dining patron. Simple, uncomplicated, and very savory.

HOW TO MAKE COMPOUND BUTTERS

Long before the advent of food processors, food was puréed manually, using a variety of methods. One way was to chop thoroughly with a large knife. Another way was to pound the item, using a mortar and pestle. Some of the recipes that follow call for the use of a mortar and pestle. The advantage of using a mortar and pestle over a food processor is that the action of pounding or grinding ingredients is more effective than the indiscriminate high-speed action of the processor blade, or the

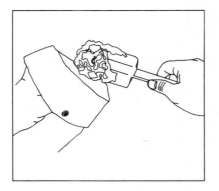

1. *Filling a pastry bag with a compound butter.*

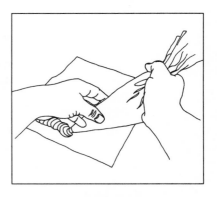

2. *Piping the butter out onto parchment paper.*

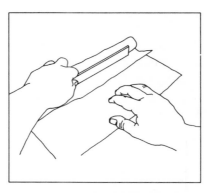

3. *Shaping the butter into a cylindrical roll.*

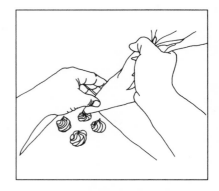

4. *Piping out rosettes.*

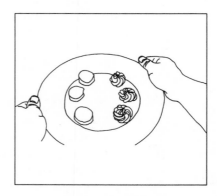

5. *Compound butter slices and rosettes.*

slow, tedious chopping with a knife. And since a mortar and pestle can be used to purée or grind so many different herbs, spices, and aromatics, it is wise to make the investment. They are available in many different shapes and sizes, fashioned out of metal, wood, stone, and ceramic, including a Japanese variety, called a *suribachi*. The marble and ceramic varieties (the latter unglazed on the interior) are among the best, since they are less porous than the wooden ones, allowing them to be cleaned after each use, and not contaminate the flavors of subsequent items.

Unsalted butter is preferred over the salted variety, since it is fresher and has less additives. It must be whipped, making it smooth and soft enough to blend with the herbs, spices, and aromatics that will be added. The whipping is done more quickly if the butter sits out at room temperature overnight, when it can then be beaten manually, or with the help of a hand mixer. When large quantities of butter are to be whipped, this is done in a commercial mixer, using the paddle attachment.

Once the butter is whipped, the flavoring agents are added. It should then be tasted, to determine if additional salt, pepper, or more of the other flavoring agents are required. The flavored butter is then transferred to the center of a sheet of wax paper or baker's parchment paper, using a rubber spatula. It is shaped into a long cylinder, roughly 1½ inches in diameter, and one edge of the paper is lifted over to enclose the cylinder. A ruler, or other straight-edged tool, is then used to press it into a uniform cylindrical form, by shimmying the straight edge up against the paper-wrapped butter (see illustration). It is then rolled up, the two ends twisted shut, wrapped in plastic wrap, and refrigerated. If the butter is specifically intended to be placed atop a grilled food item, a pastry bag fitted with a star tip can be filled with the butter, then piped out into rosettes onto a pan covered with a sheet of wax or parchment paper. These rosettes are then refrigerated until ready for service. The rosettes add an additional decorative touch. It should be noted here that all fats easily absorb other flavors from other foods in the refrigerator. This is why the cylinder form is wrapped airtight in plastic wrap. In the case of rosettes, they should be prepared the same day they are to be served. The cylinder can also be frozen, for as long as six months, though it must be wrapped with several layers of plastic, and clearly labeled.

TRADITIONAL COMPOUND BUTTERS

*B*ASIL BUTTER
(Beurre de Basilic)

½ pound unsalted butter, soft   1 garlic clove, pressed
1 cup fresh basil leaves,   pinch of salt
   minced very fine   pinch of white pepper

———— • ————

Basil butter is excellent
tossed with pasta.

- Whip all ingredients together thoroughly in an electric mixing bowl, using a paddle attachment. Shape into a cylinder measuring approximately 1½ inches in diameter, on baker's parchment or wax paper. Refrigerate.

*A*LMOND BUTTER
(Beurre d'Amandes)

½ pound unsalted butter, soft   pinch of salt
¾ cup slivered almonds   pinch of white pepper
1 tablespoon cold water

———— • ————

Almond butter is also used
in the preparations of petits
fours, cakes, and various
pastries.

- Toast the almonds on a baking sheet in a preheated 375°F oven, for 15–20 minutes, or until golden brown. Pound in a mortar, or place into a food processor along with the water, and process.
- Whip the puréed almonds, butter, salt, and pepper, then wrap and store as described.

*A*NCHOVY BUTTER
(Beurre d'Anchois)

½ pound unsalted butter, soft   1 tablespoon lemon juice
¼ cup anchovy fillets   pinch of white pepper

———— • ————

Anchovy butter is used in
the preparation of canapés
and hors d'oeuvres, and to
flavor various fish sauces.

- Rinse the anchovies well in cold water. Pat dry, and mince very fine.
- Whip all the ingredients together, then wrap and store as described.

ℬercy Butter

(Beurre Bercy)

2 shallots, minced
½ cup dry white wine
juice of 1 lemon
½ cup beef marrow, small
  diced

½ pound unsalted butter, soft
2 tablespoons chopped
  parsley
pinch of salt
pinch of white pepper

- Simmer the shallots, wine, and lemon juice until nearly dry (about 2 tablespoons liquid should remain). Set aside to cool.
- Poach the marrow in boiling salted water for about 10 minutes. Drain, and gently dry.
- Whip all ingredients together, until thoroughly blended, then wrap and store as described.

Bercy butter, also known as shallot butter, is named after a district of Paris, historically known for one of the largest wine markets in Europe. It is traditionally served with grilled or fried fish, fish stews, and is an essential part of a notable dish, Entrecôte (steak) Bercy.

𝒞urry Butter

2 shallots, minced
½ cup dry white wine
juice of 1 lemon
2 tablespoons curry powder
½ pound unsalted butter, soft

2 tablespoons cilantro,
  minced
pinch of white pepper
pinch of salt

- Simmer the shallot, white wine, lemon juice, and curry powder until nearly dry. Set aside to cool.
- Whip all the ingredients together, until thoroughly blended, then wrap and store as described.

The word *curry* is believed to be a corruption of *kari* or *karhi*, a southern Indian word for "sauce." Traditionally, however, curries evolved from a need to slow the spoilage of food within a hot climate. By experimenting with different spice combinations, blends were created that inhibited spoilage. And by virtue of the English occupation of India, the west was introduced to these exotic foods.

A curry blend needs to be cooked initially, to facilitate the release of its flavor. In the northern region, this is accomplished by heating the curry powder in ghee (clarified butter), while in the south, coconut oil is used. (Consider the use of butter in cold northern Europe, compared with the olive oil loving south.)

Within India, curry blends vary, as much as tomato sauces among the families of Sicily, or barbecue marinades in the regions of southeastern United States. Among the herbs and spices used in curry blends are: anise, cardamon, chile pepper, cinnamon, clove, coriander (seed and leaf), cumin, fennel (seed and root), fenugreek, garlic, ginger, lemon grass, mace, mustard, nutmeg, onion, saffron, tamarind, and turmeric.

CAVIAR BUTTER
(Beurre de Caviar)

½ pound unsalted butter, soft   pinch of white pepper
¼ cup fine quality caviar

- Pound the caviar to a paste in a mortar and pestle.
- Whip along with the butter and pepper until thoroughly blended, then wrap and store as described.

Any good quality of fish roe can be used to make this butter—from beluga and osetra, two of the finest imported sturgeon caviars, to salmon, shad, trout, or whitefish roe. Caviar butter is used in making canapés and cold hors d'oeuvres, and to flavor some fish sauces. (Information on North American varieties of caviar can be obtained by contacting Carolyn Collins Caviar, 925 West Jackson Boulevard, Chicago, IL 60607; (312) 226-0342, Rose Roberts, contact person.)

CHIVRY BUTTER

½ pound unsalted butter, soft
1 shallot, minced
1 tablespoon tarragon
   leaves, minced
1 tablespoon parsley, minced

1 tablespoon chervil, minced
1 tablespoon chives, minced
pinch of salt
pinch of white pepper

Chivry butter is typically used in preparing cold hors d'oeuvres, and used to flavor Chivry-style sauces.

- Blanch the shallot and herbs in boiling salted water, for 2 minutes. Drain, and squeeze dry.
- Whip all the ingredients together, until thoroughly blended, then wrap and store as described.

COLBERT BUTTER
(Beurre Colbert)

½ pound unsalted butter, soft
1 tablespoon meat glaze

2 tablespoons tarragon
   leaves, minced

- Whip all the ingredients together, until thoroughly blended, then wrap and store as described.

One of the most notable dishes qualified with the name Colbert is *Sole à la Colbert*, consisting of a whole Dover sole, gutted, skinned on the top (darker) side, and the fillets on that side separated from the skeleton in such a way that they remain attached at their outside edge. The upper edge of these fillets is then rolled outward. The backbone is cut at the top (where the fillets are rolled outward) and at the bottom. The whole fish is then dusted with seasoned flour, dipped in beaten egg, coated with bread crumbs, and deep fried. For serving, the backbone is carefully pulled out, revealing the tender white flesh of the underlying fillet, surrounded by the golden brown fried exterior, intending to imitate the lapels and white shirt of a tuxedo. A slice of Colbert butter is placed inside the cavity just before service.

Colbert butter, believed to be named after Jean-Baptiste Colbert, a minister of Louis XIV, can also be served with grilled or broiled meat or fish, fried oysters, and soft-boiled eggs.

CRAYFISH BUTTER
(Beurre d'Écrevisses)

1 shallot, minced
1 cup crayfish shells and trimmings
½ cup fish (or crayfish) stock
¼ cup dry white wine

½ pound unsalted butter, soft
¼ cup crayfish tails, finely diced
pinch of salt
pinch of cayenne pepper

- Pound the crayfish shells in a mortar and pestle, or purée in a food processor.
- Simmer the shallot, shells, stock, and wine, until nearly dry. Place into a fine strainer, or wrap in several layers of muslin, and squeeze out all the liquid.
- Whip the butter, crayfish essence, tail meat, salt, and pepper until thoroughly blended, then wrap and store as described.

Crayfish butter is used in the preparation of canapés, and in all fish and shellfish soups, stews, and sauces.

EPICUREAN BUTTER
(Beurre de Gastronome)

6 hard-boiled egg yolks
8 anchovy fillets, rinsed and dried
1 tablespoon chives, minced
1 tablespoon tarragon, minced

¼ teaspoon dry mustard
½ pound unsalted butter, soft
1 teaspoon gherkins, minced
pinch of white pepper

- Pound the yolks, anchovies, herbs, and mustard into a paste in a mortar and pestle.
- Whip all the ingredients together, until thoroughly blended, then wrap and store as described.

GARLIC BUTTER
(Beurre d'Ail)

½ pound unsalted butter, soft   pinch of salt
8 large garlic cloves   pinch of white pepper

- Blanch the garlic in boiling salted water for 8 minutes. Drain, dry, and pound in a mortar and pestle, or squeeze through a garlic press.
- Whip all the ingredients together, until thoroughly blended, then wrap and store as described.

——— • ———

Garlic butter is an excellent addition to any pasta dish.

———————

GREEN BUTTER
(Beurre Vert)

1 cup parsley leaves (stems removed), well rinsed and dried   ½ pound unsalted butter, soft
pinch of salt
pinch of white pepper

- Purée the parsley in a food processor, then continue mincing manually. Wrap in a double layer of muslin, and squeeze all the juice out.
- Whip this juice along with the remaining ingredients, until thoroughly blended, then wrap and store as described.

——————— • ———————

This butter can be prepared using the green juice of spinach, other herbs, or combination of herbs. The traditional method for making this colorful butter involves placing the raw juice into a hot bain marie, and heating until the liquid separates. It is then strained through multiple layers of muslin, and the green deposit remaining on the muslin is used as the coloring agent.

———————

HORSERADISH BUTTER

¼ cup grated fresh
  horseradish root
¼ cup dry white wine

½ pound unsalted butter, soft
pinch of salt
pinch of white pepper

- Simmer the horseradish and wine until nearly dry.
- Whip all the ingredients together until thoroughly blended, then wrap and store as described.

------- • -------

If fresh horseradish root is unavailable, substitute prepared horseradish, squeezing out excess juice before adding.

LEMON BUTTER

the zest and juice of 1 lemon
½ pound unsalted butter, soft

pinch of salt
pinch of white pepper

- Blanch the lemon zest in lightly salted boiling water for 5 minutes. Drain and dry.
- Whip all the ingredients together until thoroughly blended, then wrap and store as described.

LOBSTER BUTTER

(Beurre de Homard)

1 shallot, minced
1 cup lobster tail shells, legs,
  and trimmings
½ cup fish (or lobster) stock
¼ cup dry white wine
½ pound unsalted butter, soft

¼ cup lobster meat, finely
  diced
the tomalley (green-tinted
  liver, found inside the
  cavity of the crustacean)
pinch of salt
pinch of cayenne pepper

- Pound the lobster shells in a mortar and pestle, or chop finely with a knife or in a food processor.
- Simmer the shallot, shells, stock, and wine, until nearly dry. Place into a fine strainer, or wrap in several layers of muslin, and squeeze out all the liquid.
- Whip the butter, lobster essence, tail meat, tomalley, salt, and pepper until thoroughly blended, then wrap and store as described.

------- • -------

Crab and shrimp butters can be made in the same way, and like Lobster butter are used in the preparation of canapés, and in fish and shellfish soups, stews, and sauces.

MAÎTRE D'HÔTEL BUTTER
(Beurre Maître d'Hôtel)

This is one of the best known classic compound butters, and can be served with any variety of grilled meat, fish, and poultry.

½ pound unsalted butter, soft
3 tablespoons parsley, minced

2 tablespoons lemon juice
pinch of salt
pinch of white pepper

- Whip all the ingredients together until thoroughly blended, then wrap and store as described.

MONTPELLIER BUTTER

1 shallot, minced
1 cup of roughly equal quantities of the following items: watercress leaves, parsley sprigs, chervil sprigs, tarragon leaves, and spinach leaves
½ pound unsalted butter, soft
¼ cup olive oil
1 tablespoon chives, minced
1 garlic clove, pressed

1 anchovy fillet, rinsed, dried, and minced
1 teaspoon sour gherkins, minced
1 teaspoon capers, minced
1 hard-boiled egg white, minced
1 hard-boiled egg yolk, pressed through a sieve
1 raw egg yolk
pinch of cayenne pepper

This butter is served with poached fish, served cold, and is used to decorate whole poached fish.

- Blanch the shallot, herbs, and spinach in boiling salted water for 5 minutes. Drain, squeeze dry, and mince very fine.
- Whip all the ingredients together until thoroughly blended, then wrap and store as described.

MUSTARD BUTTER

Any variety of mustard can be used to prepare Mustard butter, including herb-flavored or grainy mustard.

½ pound unsalted butter, soft
3 tablespoons Dijon-style mustard

pinch of white pepper

- Whip all the ingredients together until thoroughly blended, then wrap and store as described.

PAPRIKA BUTTER

½ pound unsalted butter, soft   pinch of white pepper
3 heaping tablespoons
   ground paprika

- Whip all the ingredients together until thoroughly blended, then wrap and store as described.

———————————— • ————————————

Paprika is the Hungarian name for a Hungarian sweet chile pepper, which looks very much like an elongated red bell pepper. It is dried and ground into a seasoning used to flavor stews, sauces, soups, soft cheeses, and butter. Though an essential ingredient in Hungarian cookery, particularly in stews such as goulash and paprikas, it has only been as such since the nineteenth century. It is believed to be native to the Americas, though has been known in Europe since the fifteenth century.

PIEDMONT BUTTER

½ pound unsalted butter, soft   ⅛ teaspoon freshly grated
½ cup Parmesan cheese,   nutmeg
   grated   pinch of salt
zest of 1 lemon   pinch of white pepper

- Whip all the ingredients together until thoroughly blended, then wrap and store as described.

PISTACHIO BUTTER

½ pound unsalted butter, soft   ½ cup pistachio nuts
2 tablespoons water

- Toast the pistachios on a baking sheet in a preheated 375°F oven for 15 minutes. Pound in a mortar and pestle, along with the water, until a smooth paste.
- Whip this paste along with the butter, until thoroughly blended, then wrap and store as described.

RED PEPPER BUTTER

(Beurre de Piment)

1 large red bell pepper
olive oil as needed
½ pound unsalted butter,
    soft

pinch of salt
pinch of white pepper

- Rub the pepper thoroughly with the olive oil, then roast in a preheated 400°F oven for 20–30 minutes, or until it begins to turn dark brown and black. Remove from the oven, and place into a container with a tightly fitting lid. Leave covered for 10 minutes.
- Remove the pepper, and separate the flesh, discarding the skin and seeds. Pound the pepper flesh in a mortar and pestle. Whip along with the butter, until thoroughly blended, then wrap and store as described.

SALMON BUTTER

——— • ———

This butter can also be made with smoked or dry-cured salmon (gravlax).

———————

½ pound unsalted butter,
    soft
½ cup poached, flaked
    salmon

1 tablespoon dill, minced
pinch of salt
pinch of pepper

- Whip all the ingredients together until thoroughly blended, then wrap and store as described.

SARDINE BUTTER

½ pound unsalted butter,
    soft

½ cup skinless, boneless
    sardines, drained of oil

- Whip all the ingredients together until thoroughly blended, then wrap and store as described.

TARRAGON BUTTER

½ pound unsalted butter, soft
1 cup tarragon leaves

pinch of salt
pinch of white pepper

Herb butters can be prepared
with virtually any single
herb, or combination of
herbs, then used to flavor a
specific sauce, soup, or any
dish that would harmonize
with the flavor of that herb(s).

- Blanch the tarragon leaves in boiling salted water, for about 2 minutes. Drain, and pat dry. Pound them in a mortar and pestle, or mince very fine.
- Whip this paste along with the remaining ingredients until thoroughly blended, then wrap and store as described.

ᴛRUFFLE BUTTER

½ pound unsalted butter, soft   pinch of salt
¼ cup chopped black truffle   pinch of pepper
2 tablespoons heavy cream

- Pound the truffle and cream in a mortar and pestle until they form a paste.
- Whip this paste along with the remaining ingredients until thoroughly blended, then wrap and store as described.

Truffles are one of the most prized gastronomic foods in the world. Along with mushrooms and morels, under the botanical heading of Fungi, they are also among the most primitive of our foodstuffs. Related to molds and yeasts, they are *saprophytic,* meaning that they are unable to photosynthesize sugars, and must live on the decaying remains of other organisms. The rich meaty flavor of fungi, and their ability to intensify the flavor of foods they accompany, is largely due to a high content of glutamic acid, which makes them a natural version of monosodium glutamate (the function of MSG as a flavor enhancer is due to its ability to open the taste buds).

Truffles are mushrooms that produce their fruiting bodies (the edible part) underground. They have a symbiotic relationship with trees such as beech, hazelnut, oak, poplar, and willow. Because they never break above ground, they must be smelled out by pigs, trained dogs, or goats. Truffles contain a musky chemical that is also secreted in a male pig's saliva, and which prompts mating behavior, hence a pig's keen ability to ferret out truffles. (This may also explain the acclaimed aphrodisiac properties of the truffle.) The white truffle (Alba truffle) is found in the Piedmont and Emilia regions of Italy. The black truffle (Périgord truffle) is found primarily in the Dordogne region of southwestern France, and in parts of Spain, Germany, and Italy.

𝒯UNA BUTTER

½ pound unsalted butter, soft

½ cup poached fresh tuna, drained, chilled, and finely minced.

- Whip all the ingredients together until thoroughly blended, then wrap and store as described.

𝒲INE MERCHANT BUTTER
(Beurre Marchand de Vin)

1 shallot, minced
1 cup dry red wine
1 cup rich brown beef or
  veal stock, or consommé

1 tablespoon parsley, minced
½ pound unsalted butter, soft
pinch of white pepper

- Simmer the shallot and wine until reduced by half. Add the stock or consommé, and continue reducing until nearly dry (2 tablespoons of liquid should remain).
- Whip the reduction along with the remaining ingredients until thoroughly blended, then wrap and store as described.

Marchand de vin indicates a dish seasoned with a red wine and shallot reduction. Any grilled or broiled meat, or a dish of kidneys, can be garnished with this rich butter. Whiting or Sole à la Marchand de Vin is poached in a red wine and shallot court bouillon, later reduced, and mounted with butter to create a sauce.

A tablespoon of meat glace can be used in place of the stock or consommé.

CONTEMPORARY INNOVATIONS

.... ### ℬLUE CHEESE BUTTER
(Beurre de Fromage Bleu)

½ pound unsalted butter, soft   pinch of white pepper
½ cup Maytag blue cheese

- Whip all ingredients until thoroughly blended, then wrap and store as described.

------------------ • ------------------

Though Maytag is a name most often associated with washing machines, Elmer Maytag, son of the founder of the company, pursued an interest in cheese making in the 1920s. His son Frederick continued this work, and began production of a blue cheese innovated and patented by the University of Iowa. Commercial production began in 1941 (when the price of milk in Iowa was 10 cents a quart), and the same painstaking manual process first employed is still used today. (For the name of a retail store where Maytag Blue Cheese can be purchased, telephone 1-800-247-2458.)

.... ### 𝒞LIFT HOTEL BUTTER
(for Sautéed Shrimp)

1 shallot, minced
1 garlic clove, pressed
¼ cup dry white wine
juice of 1 lemon
½ pound unsalted butter, soft
1 tablespoon chives, minced
1 tablespoon parsley, minced
1 heaping tablespoon paprika
1 tablespoon Worcestershire sauce
2 tablespoons all-purpose flour

- Simmer the shallot, garlic, wine, and lemon juice, until nearly dry.
- Whip this reduction along with the remaining ingredients until thoroughly blended.

This butter is part of a dish that was prepared at the Poissonier station (where all sautéed and poached fish dishes were prepared) at the Clift Hotel, San Francisco, many years ago when I worked there as a Tournant (Swing Cook). It is unique in that it contains a small portion of flour, which effectively creates a slightly thickened sauce. A recipe for the dish follows.

*S*AUTÉED SHRIMP, CLIFT HOTEL

24 U-12 shrimp, peeled, and deveined
⅓ cup clarified butter

1½ cups dry white wine
¾ cup Clift Hotel Butter
(Yields 4 servings)

- Sauté the shrimp in a hot sauté pan, in the clarified butter, no longer than 1 minute. Add the white wine, then remove the shrimp using a slotted spoon, and set them aside. Simmer the wine until reduced by half. Add the butter and the shrimp, and stir until the butter is completely emulsified with the wine. Correct the thickness and quantity of the sauce if necessary, using white wine and additional butter, and serve over rice pilaf.

U-12, literally "under 12," is a size designation, indicating that there are 12 or less of this particular size of shrimp per pound.

*E*DIBLE FLOWER BUTTER

½ pound unsalted butter, soft
¼ cup edible flowers, minced

½ teaspoon salt
¼ teaspoon white pepper

- Whip all the ingredients together until thoroughly blended, then wrap and store as described.

Edible flowers can be used in a variety of dishes, particularly in, but not limited to, salads. Many varieties are *UNSAFE* to consume, either because they are naturally poisonous—like azalea, daffodil, oleander, poinsettia, and wisteria—or because they have been sprayed with insecticides. Nonpoisonous varieties include apple blossoms, chrysanthemum, marigold, nasturtium, pansy, and violet.

Escargot Butter

½ pound unsalted butter, soft
1 shallot, minced
2 large garlic cloves, minced
2 tablespoons Pernod
2 tablespoons parsley, minced

⅛ teaspoon nutmeg, freshly
   grated
pinch of salt
pinch of white pepper

- Whip all the ingredients together until thoroughly blended, then wrap and store as described.

---•---

This dish is the creation of Peter Van Erp, former Chef-Instructor at the Culinary Institute of America, Hyde Park, New York. The snails can be prepared either in the shell, or in mushroom caps, baked with a large portion of the butter joined with each snail.

Mustard-Marjoram Butter

½ pound unsalted butter, soft
2 tablespoons fresh
   marjoram leaves, minced

3 tablespoons Dijon-style
   mustard
½ teaspoon salt
¼ teaspoon white pepper

- Whip all the ingredients together until thoroughly blended, then wrap and store as described.

Roasted Garlic and Herb Butter

3 garlic bulbs, cloves
   separated
olive oil as needed
½ pound unsalted butter, soft
⅓ cup minced fine herbs
   (basil, tarragon, parsley,

cilantro, sage, oregano,
   and/or thyme)
½ teaspoon salt
½ teaspoon white pepper

- Preheat oven to 350°F.
- Lightly coat the garlic cloves with olive oil. Place on a roasting pan, and roast for 1 hour. Remove and allow to cool.
- Squeeze the garlic from the roasted cloves into a bowl. Whip this, along with the remaining ingredients, until thoroughly blended, then wrap and store as described.

$\mathcal{S}$AFFRON BUTTER

. . . .

1 shallot, minced	1 sprig thyme
1 garlic clove, minced	pinch of salt
1 cup dry white wine	pinch of white pepper
½ teaspoon saffron	¾ cup unsalted butter, soft
1 bay leaf	

———— • ————

This butter accompanies "Lamb Medallions," as seen in *A Taste For All Seasons*.

————————

- Place all the ingredients except the butter into a saucepan. Simmer until reduced to approximately 3 tablespoons. Remove and discard the bay leaf and thyme.
- Whip the reduction along with the remaining ingredients until thoroughly blended, then wrap and store as described.

$\mathcal{S}$MOKED SHRIMP BUTTER

. . . .

———— • ————

This butter accompanies "Barbecued Bluefish," created by Gordon Hamersley, proprietor of Hamersley's Bistro, Boston, Massachusetts.

————————

¼ pound unsalted butter, soft	1 tablespoon parsley, minced
1 small shallot, minced	1 tablespoon lemon juice
1 garlic clove, minced	⅛ teaspoon salt
4 medium smoked shrimp, finely chopped	⅛ teaspoon white pepper

- Whip the reduction along with the remaining ingredients until thoroughly blended, then wrap and store as described.

$\mathcal{T}$OMATO-CORIANDER BUTTER

. . . .

¼ pound unsalted butter, soft	1 tablespoon dry white wine
½ cup tomato, peeled, seeded, and small diced	pinch of salt
2 tablespoons fresh cilantro leaves, minced	pinch of white pepper

From "Grilled Swordfish" as seen in *The Pillar House Cookbook*.

- Whip all the ingredients together until thoroughly blended, then wrap and store as described.

WILD MUSHROOM BUTTER

1 cup chanterelle, oyster, and morel mushrooms, brushed clean, and minced
2 shallots, minced
½ cup dry white wine

juice of ½ lemon
½ pound unsalted butter, soft
½ teaspoon salt
¼ teaspoon white pepper

- Simmer the mushrooms, shallots, wine, and lemon juice, until nearly dry. Allow to cool.
- Whip the reduction along with the remaining ingredients until thoroughly blended, then wrap and store as described.

CHAPTER 13

MARINADES

A marinade is a liquid, seasoned with various aromatics, into which meat, poultry, game, or vegetables are steeped. They are generally made up of one or more of the following ingredients:

OIL   ACID   AROMATICS

While their function is primarily to flavor, some tenderizing takes place by virtue of the acid ingredient (vinegar, citrus juice, and/or wine). When only the flavor of the aromatics is intended, they should be tied up in cheese cloth (spice sachet) so that they can be removed before the marinating food is cooked. Oil + aromatics, or even just aromatics alone, are also considered a form of marinade. Some marinades are cooked before applied to a food, and others are uncooked. Marinating should be done in noncorrosive vessels, such as stainless steel, glass, or ceramic (avoid plastic and aluminum). The length of time a food should be marinated will vary according to the type of food marinated. A sauerbraten may marinate refrigerated for three days. A chicken breast, marinated in olive oil, garlic, chopped fresh herbs, and lemon juice; or cubed lamb (for shish kabob), will need to sit at room temperature, covered, for only a few hours. Gravlax, a Swedish dry-cured salmon, is a good example of a dry marinade, using primarily herbs and spices.

𝒮AUERBRATEN

1 quart dry red wine
1½ quarts water
1 pint red wine vinegar
1 tablespoon salt
1 large Spanish onion, sliced
1 large carrot, peeled and
  sliced
2 stalks celery, roughly
  chopped
3 garlic cloves, crushed
¼ cup fresh thyme, chopped
1 bay leaf

2 cloves
½ teaspoon juniper berries,
  cracked
½ teaspoon black
  peppercorns, cracked
5 pounds beef bottom round
  or inner chuck
½ cup vegetable oil
3 tablespoons flour
1 cup tomato purée
1 cup gingersnaps, crushed

- Place all the ingredients (except the last four) into a ceramic crock, or other large noncorrosive vessel, and allow to marinate, refrigerated, for three days, turning the meat once a day. (Be sure the meat is completely immersed in the marinade.)

- Remove the beef from the marinade, and pat dry. Heat the vegetable oil in a large braising pan, and brown the beef on all sides. Remove the beef, pour off most of the oil, and add the flour, stirring until blended. Pour the marinade in, stir in the tomato purée, and simmer covered, for 1½ to 2 hours. Remove the cover, and continue simmering until the meat feels tender when pierced with a fork. Remove the beef, and set aside.

- Add the gingersnaps, and continue simmering until the sauce achieves the desired thickness. (Use additional gingersnaps to thicken, if necessary.) Strain, adjust seasoning, and serve with the sliced beef.

...................

2 cups kosher salt
¾ cup granulated sugar
3 tablespoons white
  peppercorns, crushed

2 2- to 3-pound salmon
  fillets, skin on
¼ cup Cognac
½ cup dill, minced
1 lemon, sliced very thin

- Combine the salt, sugar, and peppercorns. Sprinkle a thin layer of this onto a stainless steel pan or glass dish large enough to hold the salmon. Place the salmon fillets on this, skin side down.

- Rub the Cognac onto the salmon flesh. Sprinkle the remaining dry mix onto the fillets, and rub it in. Place the sliced lemon on top of the dry mix on one fillet, then turn one fillet over on the other. Cover with plastic wrap, and place a wooden board on top. Press the board down firmly, and set a weight on top of the board. Refrigerate this for 48 hours.

- Brush off some of the dry mix, and rub the dill onto the two fillets. Rewrap the fillets carefully, weight them down again, and leave at room temperature for 2 days.

- Gently brush off the dry mix, dill, and lemon, wrap, and refrigerate until ready to serve. Serve sliced on a horizontal bias, with a mustard-dill sauce, and small pieces of fresh rye bread.

Marinades are often used as the cooking medium, as in the case of sauerbraten, or a game dish intended for braising. This marinade may also be utilized in creating a sauce, since it has taken on much of the flavor of the food being braised.

The following marinade recipes offer a basic structure from which many varieties can be innovated. There is no limit to possible varieties, based on availability of ingredients, and saucier's inspiration.

BEER MARINADE

1 cup beer
juice and zest of 1 lime
4 garlic cloves, crushed
½ cup green onions, minced
¼ cup fresh cilantro, minced

6 dried red chili peppers
1 teaspoon powdered cumin
⅛ teaspoon salt
⅛ teaspoon black pepper

• Combine all the ingredients, and blend thoroughly. Suitable for marinating chicken, pork, or beef.

GIN MARINADE

½ cup olive oil
1 cup gin
juice of 12 limes
½ cup water
4 garlic cloves, pressed

2 sprigs fresh rosemary
½ teaspoon ground cumin
½ teaspoon salt
½ teaspoon white pepper

This marinade was created by Michael Ng, a student of the author's, at the City College of San Francisco, Hotel Restaurant program.

• Combine all the ingredients, and blend thoroughly. Particularly suited for marinating chicken intended for grilling.

LEMON MARINADE

juice and zest of 3 lemons
3 tablespoons olive oil
2 garlic cloves, crushed

1 sprig fresh thyme or
  rosemary
¼ teaspoon salt
¼ teaspoon black pepper

• Combine all the ingredients, and blend thoroughly. Suitable for marinating chicken, veal or fish.

*L*IME MARINADE

zest of 4 limes
juice of 6 limes
¼ cup olive oil

2 garlic cloves, pressed
1 teaspoon red chili paste
3 tablespoons soy sauce

- Combine all the ingredients, and blend thoroughly. Suitable for marinating chicken or veal.

*O*IL, LEMON, AND HERB MARINADE

1 cup olive oil
1 cup peanut oil
3 lemons, sliced paper-thin
6 garlic cloves, crushed

2 tablespoons cracked black pepper
1 cup basil, parsley, cilantro, and marjoram, roughly chopped

——— • ———

This marinade from "Grilled Chicken" as seen in *Jasper White's Cooking From New England.*

———————

- Combine all ingredients in a stainless steel bowl. Cut up a chicken into 8–10 pieces, marinate for 24 hours, then grill.

*R*ED WINE MARINADE

1 cup dry red wine
1 small Spanish onion, cut in half lengthwise, then sliced very thin
1 garlic clove, crushed

1 tablespoon parsley, roughly chopped
1 bay leaf
¼ cup olive oil
¼ teaspoon salt
¼ teaspoon black pepper

- Combine all the ingredients, and stir until the salt is dissolved. Suitable for marinating beef or lamb.

*R*ED WINE MARINADE II

2½ cups dry red wine
½ cup red wine vinegar
½ cup water

1 small Spanish onion, peeled, sliced

1 medium carrot, peeled,
   sliced
1 rib celery, roughly chopped
2 garlic cloves, crushed
2 bay leaves

1 bunch parsley stems, tied
   together
1 teaspoon black
   peppercorns
8 juniper berries
1 tablespoon kosher salt

- Bring the ingredients to a boil. Remove from the fire and allow to cool to room temperature before utilizing. Suitable for a heavy variety of wild game (venison, boar, mutton, goose, or duck).

*S*OY SAUCE MARINADE

½ cup soy sauce
½ cup mirin (sweet
   Japanese wine)
1½ tablespoons sesame oil
1 clove garlic, pressed

1 heaping tablespoon
   gingerroot, cut into fine
   julienne
5 scallions, green tops
   removed, cut on the bias
   very thin

- Combine all ingredients and allow to marinate 1 hour. Marinate bluefish, mackerel, or other high-fat fish (such as salmon, shad, swordfish, tuna, etc.) fillets for 30 minutes before grilling.

*S*ZECHUAN GRILLING MARINADE

¾ cup soy sauce
¼ cup water
¾ cup dry white wine
3 garlic cloves, crushed
1 tablespoon grated
   gingerroot
1 teaspoon Szechuan
   peppercorns, crushed

1 star anise, crushed
2 tablespoons medium dry
   sherry
1 teaspoon sesame oil
2 tablespoons dark brown
   sugar

———— • ————

This marinade was innovated by Timothy T. Hanni, Master of Wine, Beringer's Vineyards, St. Helena, California.

————————

- Simmer all ingredients in a saucepan for 10 minutes. Set aside and allow to cool. Use as a marinade for grilled poultry, beef, lamb, or pork.

✐OY MARINADE II

¼ cup soy sauce
¼ cup oyster sauce
3 tablespoons sugar
¼ cup dry sherry

3 tablespoons sesame oil
8 garlic cloves, pressed
2 tablespoons gingerroot,
    grated

- Blend all ingredients together well. Use as a marinade for poultry, marinating for several hours before grilling.

✐OMATO MARINADE

1 cup tomato juice
1 small Spanish onion, cut
    in half lengthwise, then
    sliced very thin

1 tablespoon basil leaves,
    minced
1 bay leaf
¼ teaspoon salt
¼ teaspoon black pepper

- Combine all the ingredients, and blend thoroughly. Suitable for marinating veal or pork.

✐OGURT MARINADE

1 cup yogurt
2 tablespoons cilantro,
    minced
zest of 1 lemon

1 garlic clove, pressed
¼ teaspoon salt
¼ teaspoon black pepper

- Combine all the ingredients, and blend thoroughly. Suitable for marinating chicken or fish.

BARBECUE SAUCES

✐ARBECUE SAUCE I

¼ cup duck or chicken fat
1 medium Spanish onion,
    peeled, and minced

1 bunch scallions, green tops
    removed, and minced
½ green bell pepper, minced

5 garlic cloves, pressed
2 cups ketchup
¼ cup Worcestershire sauce
¼ cup cider vinegar
½ cup beer

2 tablespoons Dijon-style
  mustard
3 tablespoons dark brown
  sugar
1 teaspoon red chile paste
1 teaspoon cumin

- Sauté the onion, scallions, pepper, and garlic in the fat, without browning. Remove to a large stainless steel bowl.
- Add the remaining ingredients and blend thoroughly. Cover and refrigerate 24 hours, or until ready to use.

ℬARBECUE SAUCE II

¼ cup olive oil
½ cup dry white wine
1½ cups tomato ketchup
¼ cup dark brown sugar
3 tablespoons orange
  marmalade
2 scallions, sliced paper thin
4 garlic cloves, pressed

1 tablespoon grated
  gingerroot
1 tablespoon soy sauce
¼ cup water
2 tablespoons red chile paste
juice and zest of 1 lemon
¼ cup parsley, minced

Both barbecue sauces are intended for marinating beef or pork ribs, or chicken.

- Combine all ingredients in a stainless steel bowl. Add the item intended for marinating, blend well, cover, and marinate refrigerated for 2 days.

𝒮WEET & PUNGENT SAUCE

peel of 1 orange, roughly cut
1 garlic clove, crushed
2 tablespoons peanut oil
½ cup red wine vinegar
½ cup rice wine vinegar
1½ cups pineapple juice
½ cup dark brown sugar

½ cup tomato ketchup
2 tablespoons soy sauce
2 tablespoons sesame oil
2 level tablespoons
  cornstarch, dissolved in ¾
  cup cold water

- Sauté the orange peel and garlic in the peanut oil for 3 or 4 minutes.
- Add all of the remaining ingredients, except for the cornstarch, and bring to a boil.

- Add the cornstarch, and bring to a boil. Strain, and adjust the seasoning to taste by using vinegar, sugar, and/or water. Set aside, keeping warm until ready to use.

This sauce can be used as both an accompaniment for any sweet and pungent dish (pork, chicken, shrimp, fish, etc.), or as a marinade for meat or poultry intended for the grill. When used as a sauce, the garnish, usually a combination of pineapple chunks and cherry tomatoes, and lightly blanched green bell peppers and thinly sliced carrots, should be added to the sauce at the time of service.

CHAPTER 14

ACCOMPANIMENTS OUTSIDE THE REALM OF SAUCE

he names to which all of the dishes in the following section are applied—chutney, compote, coulis, glaze, pickle, relish, and salsa—do not represent strict interpretations of each category. Though we like to be precise in such a specialized area as sauces and sauce accompaniments, in actual practice, personal style, philosophy, and individual interpretation inhibit such precision. One chef's chutney is another chef's compote, is another chef's relish, is another chef's salsa, and so on.

The recipes that follow are a combination of the author's innovations, gleaned from his own experience, combined with the innovations of other chefs and culinary practitioners. Because each of these are unique creations, and reflect the inventor's own definition of the category under which it falls, it is virtually impossible to exactly define the differences between these subsections. As we have pointed out, there are no absolutes in the culinary universe.

What is clear, however, is the use of various chutneys, relishes, salsas, pickles, and so on as accompaniments, which break from traditional sauces derived from the French sauce system. This is a positive development in the evolution of American cooking practices—a reflection of both creativity and an effort to incorporate other ethnic dishes and techniques into our eclectic melting pot cuisine. It is the culinary community's effort to think globally, and act locally.

The guidelines for using such dishes are fairly simple: consider the color, texture, flavor, and aroma of a given accompaniment to a given dish, and if it is harmonious with that dish, then employ it. The reader is encouraged to consider the dishes that follow, and experiment as the palate and creativity dictate.

CHUTNEYS

chutney: A sweet-and-sour condiment, made of fruit and/or vegetables, cooked in vinegar with sugar and spices, until it has the consistency of jam. The word is a corruption of the Sanskrit *chatni*, meaning "to lick." Chutneys may contain exotic fruits (mango, coconut, pineapple, tamarind), as well as temperate ones (eggplant, tomato, onion, melon, grapes, cherries, apple, etc.). Some are reduced to a purée, others retain recognizable pieces of their ingredients; all are characterized by a syrupy and sometimes highly spiced juice which coats the ingredients.

Fruit Chutneys

.... ## *A*PPLE, PEAR, AND RAISIN CHUTNEY

2 unripe red Bartlett pears
2 Granny Smith apples
juice of one lemon
½ cup light brown sugar
½ cup water
¼ cup cider vinegar
½ cup raisins

zest of 1 orange
zest of 1 lemon
zest of 1 lime
pulp of 1 orange, peeled,
   seeded, and cut into
   ½-inch chunks

- Peel and core the pears and apples, cut them into ½-inch chunks, and place into a lemon bath (1 pint water plus the lemon juice).

- Simmer the sugar, water, and vinegar for 10 minutes. Add the raisins and zest, and simmer another 10 minutes. Drain the apples and pears, add to the syrup, and simmer 5 minutes. Add the orange pulp, and simmer another 5 minutes. Remove from the fire, allow to cool, then cover and refrigerate until ready to serve.

.... ## *A*PRICOT CHUTNEY

1 pound dried apricots,
   quartered
½ cup sugar
½ cup water
¼ cup white wine
   vinegar

¼ cup shelled pistachio nuts,
   chopped
1 tablespoon pine nuts
1 teaspoon fresh mint
   leaves, minced

- Simmer the apricots, sugar, water, and vinegar in a covered saucepan for 30 minutes.

- Add the nuts and mint, and simmer uncovered 5 more minutes. Serve with Shash-Lik (grilled skewered chicken) or Shish Kabob (skewered lamb).

CHUTNEY SAUCE

Chutney sauce is the accompaniment for chicken or shrimp, deep-fried in beer batter.

1 cup mango chutney
1 cup prepared horseradish, squeezed dry
1 cup fresh or canned pineapple chunks

- Purée all three ingredients in a food processor. Cover and refrigerate until ready to serve.

CRANBERRY-FIG CHUTNEY

12 ounces fresh or whole frozen cranberries
zest and juice of 1 orange
juice of 1 lemon
¼ cup water
1 tablespoon grated gingerroot
3 dried red chile peppers
1 cinnamon stick
¼ teaspoon ground cinnamon

½ teaspoon dry mustard
1 teaspoon ground cumin
1 cup sugar
¼ teaspoon salt
⅓ cup unsalted, roasted cashews, roughly chopped
10 dried Calimyrna figs, stemmed, and cut into half-inch pieces

- Combine all the ingredients in a saucepan, bring to a boil, cover, and simmer for 8 minutes. Add the figs, and simmer uncovered another 5 minutes. Remove from the fire, add the cashews, allow to cool, then transfer to a storage container.

The cranberry, the largest species of several tart berries native to North America and Europe, is unique to North America. Smaller varieties are known as foxberry in England, and in various parts of the United States, the red whortleberry, partridge berry, whimberry, mountainberry, rockberry, and cowberry (the Latin word for cow being vaca, and the botanical name for the American cranberry, Vaccinium macrocarpon).

Cranberries were first introduced to New England settlers by the Wampanoag tribe of Massachusetts. Pemmican—the berry crushed with dried venison and bear fat—became a significant food staple for surviving the rugged New England winters. The colonists initially called these tart berries "craneberries" because of their pink blossoms that resembled the heads of cranes.

In 1677, when they began minting their own coins, the colonists appeased the crown's outrage over such an act of independence by shipping ten crates of cranberries, along with some codfish and Indian corn, to Charles II. In 1787, when James Madison wrote to Thomas Jefferson in France for background information on constitutional government to use at the upcoming constitutional convention, Jefferson shipped the requested information to Madison, in exchange for Pippin apples, pecans, and cranberries. By this time, cranberries had become so popular in New England that one Cape Cod town imposed a fine of one dollar on anyone picking more than a quart of cranberries before September 20 of a given year.

𝓛IME CHUTNEY

6 limes
½ cup dried sultanas (golden raisins)
1 Granny Smith apple, peeled, cored, and cut into ¼-inch dice
¼ cup gingerroot, peeled, and cut into fine julienne

2 garlic cloves, pressed
1 teaspoon red chile pepper paste
½ cup light brown sugar
½ cup white wine vinegar
½ cup water

- Remove the zest from the limes, using a zester, and set aside. Cut the remaining peel from the limes, and discard. Cut the remaining limes into roughly ¼-inch dice.

- Combine all the ingredients in a saucepan, and simmer for 15 minutes, stirring frequently. Allow to cool, then cover and refrigerate until ready to use.

𝓕IG CHUTNEY

½ cup water
juice of 1 lemon

1 tablespoon sugar
½ teaspoon salt

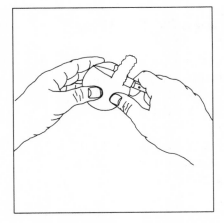

1. *Peeling away the zest from an orange (lemon, lime).*

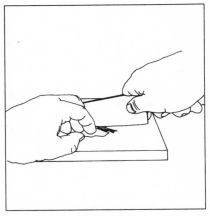

2. *Cutting the zest into a fine julienne.*

3. *Removing zest with a zester.*

1 teaspoon toasted ground cumin
3 dried hot red chile peppers

12 dried Calimyrna figs, stems removed, and cut into ¼-inch pieces

- Place the water, lemon, sugar, salt, cumin, and chile peppers into a saucepan, and simmer until the salt and sugar are dissolved.
- Add the figs, and simmer uncovered, 5 minutes.
- Cool, cover, and refrigerate until ready to use.

GRAPE CHUTNEY

¼ cup raisins
1 garlic clove, pressed
¼ teaspoon kosher salt
¼ cup brown sugar
juice of 1 lemon
½ teaspoon dry mustard
1 tablespoon horseradish, grated
1 tablespoon gingerroot, grated
½ cup cider vinegar
2 cups seedless green or red grapes
2 Granny Smith apples, peeled, cored, and cut into ½-inch chunks

- Bring all the ingredients except the fruit to a boil, and simmer until the sugar is dissolved. Add the fruit and simmer, uncovered, for 30 minutes. Cool, cover, and refrigerate.

PEACH AND APPLE CHUTNEY

½ cup cider vinegar
¼ cup water
1 small Spanish onion, minced
¼ cup raisins
1 teaspoon gingerroot, grated
¼ teaspoon dry mustard
2 tablespoons brown sugar
½ teaspoon celery seed
1 small dried red chile pepper
¾ pound ripe peaches, peeled, pitted, and cut into ½-inch chunks
¾ pound ripe pears, peeled, cored, and cut into ½-inch chunks

- Bring all the ingredients except the fruit to a boil, and simmer until the sugar is dissolved. Add the fruit and simmer, uncovered, for 30 minutes. Cool, cover, and refrigerate.

PINEAPPLE CHUTNEY

1 medium unripe pineapple
1 medium Spanish onion, peeled, and small diced
2 tablespoons gingerroot, grated
juice and zest of 2 limes
¼ cup cider vinegar
¼ cup rum
¾ cup light brown sugar, firmly packed
1 tablespoon black peppercorns, crushed
⅛ teaspoon ground cloves

- Peel the pineapple, cut into quarters lengthwise, and remove the fibrous core. Cut the remaining quarters into ½-inch chunks.
- Place all of the ingredients into a heavy saucepan and simmer, uncovered, for 25 minutes, or until most of the liquid has evaporated and the mixture is thick.
- Cool, cover, and refrigerate until ready to serve.

𝒫LUM CHUTNEY

1 teaspoon grated
  gingerroot
10 paper-thin slices
  gingerroot
¼ cup dry white wine
  vinegar
1 heaping tablespoon
  granulated sugar
1 tablespoon orange zest

½ teaspoon white
  pepper
10 underripe Santa Rosa
  plums (or other red
  variety), washed, pitted,
  and cut into 16 wedges
  each
½ cup Bermuda onion,
  sliced lengthwise,
  paper-thin

- Place the plum wedges and onion into a stainless steel or glass bowl.
- Combine the first six ingredients, bring to a boil, and stir until the sugar is dissolved. Pour over the plums and onions. Allow to cool, then cover, refrigerate, and marinate at least three days before serving.

𝒫LUM AND GINGER CHUTNEY

1½ oranges, peeled,
  segments removed from
  the membrane, and
  roughly chopped
½ cup fresh squeezed orange
  juice
¼ cup sugar
1 heaping tablespoon grated
  gingerroot
2 tablespoons dried
  currants

1 teaspoon ground cloves
2 tablespoons water
1 teaspoon curry powder
½ cup apricot preserves
2½ pounds ripe Santa Rosa
  (or other variety)
  freestone plums, pitted,
  and cut into half-inch
  cubes

This chutney accompanies "Dungeness Crab Wontons," as seen in *A Taste For All Seasons*.

- Place all of the ingredients except the plums into a small saucepan. Simmer for 30 minutes.
- Add the plums, and simmer for another 15–20 minutes, or until the plums are soft. Cool, cover, and refrigerate.

RED ONION-APPLE CHUTNEY

1 pound red onions, peeled, and sliced very thin
3 Granny Smith apples, peeled, cored, and roughly chopped

¼ cup cider vinegar
1 cup dry red wine
2 tablespoons sugar

This chutney accompanies "Vinegar-braised Rabbit," as seen in *A Taste For All Seasons*.

- Simmer all of the ingredients over a very low fire, in a heavy-gauge saucepan, covered, for 2 hours. Cool, cover, and refrigerate for 24 hours before serving.

SUN-DRIED TOMATO CHUTNEY

3 cups sun-dried tomatoes
½ cup cider vinegar
½ cup water
½ cup dried currants or raisins
1 large Spanish onion, peeled, and cut into ½-inch dice

3 large garlic cloves, minced
½ cup light brown sugar
1 tablespoon grated gingerroot
1 teaspoon dry mustard
1 teaspoon curry powder
½ teaspoon ground cloves
½ teaspoon salt

- Place all of the ingredients into a heavy-gauge saucepan, and simmer for 30–45 minutes, stirring frequently, until the mixture is thick. Cool, cover, and refrigerate until ready to serve.

TOMATO-GINGER CHUTNEY

10 ripe medium tomatoes, peeled and diced
2 tablespoons peeled and grated gingerroot
2 teaspoons granulated sugar

pinch of salt
pinch of black pepper
2 tablespoons peanut oil
1 tablespoon sesame oil
¼ cup cilantro, minced

- Discard as many of the seeds from the tomatoes as possible. Place into a noncorrosive saucepan, along with the ginger, sugar, salt, and pepper. Simmer, uncovered, for about 10 minutes, or until it is fairly dry.

- Add the peanut oil, sesame oil, and cilantro, and blend thoroughly. Set aside until ready to use.

Savory Chutneys

. . . .

CILANTRO CHUTNEY

⅓ cup olive oil
grated zest of 2 lemons
juice of 1 lemon
4 shallots, very finely diced
1 garlic clove, pressed
1 large bunch Italian parsley, stems removed, well

washed, and roughly chopped
1 large (or two small) bunches cilantro, stems removed, well washed, and roughly chopped
salt and black pepper to taste

- Combine all ingredients in a stainless steel bowl, and blend thoroughly. Cover and refrigerate, and marinate overnight before serving.

—————————— • ——————————

Coriander is one of the oldest cultivated spices, dating back to 5000 B.C. Its seeds have been found in ruins on the Aegean Islands and in the tombs of Pharaohs, and it is known to have been grown by the Assyrians and Babylonians. Used by ancient and modern cultures throughout Europe and the British Isles, it became a mainstay in Latin American cooking after the Spaniards introduced it to the New World.

An anomalous member of the carrot family, coriander differs from its brethren in that its seed is not perishable and both the seed and leaf are used as herb and spice (respectively). The upper part of the plant, often referred to by its Spanish name, *cilantro*, bears two opposite types of leaves and flowers. Completely different from its seed, the flavor and aroma of the leaves are unique among herbs, variously likened to those of rubber, citrus peel, a mixture of cumin and caraway, and honey. Whatever the case, the flavor of cilantro is lively and spirited, though when dried, it loses virtually all of its punch. Used abundantly in Chinese, Italian, Spanish, and South American cuisines, cilantro is also referred to as Chinese or Italian parsley. It should, however, not be confused with flat leaf parsley, a cousin of the standard curly parsley.

𝓜INT CHUTNEY

leaves of 3 bunches fresh mint, rinsed, dried, and minced
1 bunch cilantro, stems partially removed, rinsed, dried, and minced

2 jalapeño peppers, minced
juice of 1 lemon
4 garlic cloves, minced
½ teaspoon salt

• Combine all ingredients and blend thoroughly. Cover, refrigerate, and allow to marinate 24 hours before serving.

Recommended as an accompaniment for grilled salmon, bluefish, or other high-fat fish.

𝓟EANUT-CILANTRO CHUTNEY

2 bunches cilantro, rinsed, dried, stems partially removed
½ cup roasted shelled peanuts, roughly chopped
2 jalapeño peppers, minced
3 garlic cloves, minced

2 tablespoons fresh coconut, grated
juice of 2 limes
1 teaspoon sugar
1 teaspoon toasted ground cumin
½ teaspoon salt

• Place the ground cumin on a baking pan and into a 350-degree preheated oven for 15 minutes.
• Chop the cilantro in a food processor. Transfer to a mixing bowl.
• Add the remaining ingredients and blend thoroughly. Cover, refrigerate, and allow to marinate at least 24 hours before using.

Remove and discard the bottom 2–3 inches of stems from the cilantro. The remaining stems can be included.

𝓨OGURT CHUTNEY I

1 cup plain yogurt
1 garlic clove, minced

¼ cup cilantro, minced

1 small jalapeño pepper,
minced
½ cup white onion, very fine
dice

1 teaspoon toasted cumin
powder
¼ teaspoon salt

- Combine all ingredients. Cover and allow to marinate 24 hours.

𝒴OGURT CHUTNEY II

2 cups plain yogurt
3 garlic cloves, minced

1 tablespoon fresh mint,
minced
½ teaspoon salt

- Blend all ingredients together thoroughly. Cover, refrigerate, and marinate 24 hours before serving.

𝒴OGURT-MINT CHUTNEY

1 cup plain yogurt
½ cup fresh mint, minced
2 bunches scallions, green
tops removed, minced
2 garlic cloves, minced

1 small jalapeño pepper,
seeds and ribs removed,
minced
2 tablespoons olive oil
¼ teaspoon salt

- Blend all ingredients together thoroughly. Cover, refrigerate, and marinate 24 hours before serving.

𝒴OGURT RAITA

2 cups plain yogurt
1 large cucumber, peeled,
split in half lengthwise,
seeded, and sliced very
thin

½ teaspoon salt
¼ cup fresh mint, minced
1 teaspoon toasted cumin
seeds, ground to a powder

- Spread the sliced cucumber out in a colander, and sprinkle lightly with salt. Allow to sit for 15 minutes.
- Combine the cucumber and remaining ingredients in a bowl, and blend thoroughly. Allow to marinate several hours before serving.

*T*ZAKIKI

1 cup plain yogurt
½ cup cucumber, peeled,
   seeded, and cut into fine
   julienne
2 garlic cloves, pressed

2 tablespoons mint leaves,
   minced
1 tablespoon oregano leaves,
   minced
salt and white pepper to
   taste

- Combine all the ingredients in a stainless steel bowl. Cover and refrigerate overnight.

•

Tzakiki accompanies falafel and souvlaki, both Middle Eastern specialties served in pita bread. This recipe was created by Steve Karapatakis, Chef-proprietor of Le Greque, a Greek-style café in Providence, Rhode Island.

COMPOTES

compote: From Old French *composte*, meaning "stewed fruit," technically, fresh or dried fruit, cooked whole or in pieces in a sugar syrup. They are similar to confiture, another word for jam, jelly, or marmalade, derived from the verb *confire*—to preserve; to pickle.

*A*PRICOT-ONION COMPOTE

30 dried apricots, cut into
   quarters
½ cup sugar
1 cup champagne
   vinegar
2 medium Spanish onions,
   cut into ½-inch dice

peel of 1 lemon
2 cinnamon sticks
¼ teaspoon ground cloves
¼ teaspoon ground nutmeg
¼ teaspoon salt

- Combine all the ingredients in a heavy-gauge saucepan, and simmer gently, covered, for 20 minutes. Allow to cool, then cover and refrigerate until ready to serve.

CRANBERRY COMPOTE

This compote accompanies "Grilled Swordfish, Ginger Sauce," as seen in *A Taste For All Seasons*.

1 cup whole fresh (or fresh-frozen) cranberries
2 tablespoons sugar

¼ cup Zinfandel or other dry red wine
zest of ½ orange
2 whole cloves

- Combine all the ingredients in a saucepan. Simmer for 10 minutes, then set aside and allow to cool.

RAISIN COMPOTE

2 cups seedless raisins
2 shallots, minced
½ cup dry white wine
juice of 1 lemon
1 tablespoon granulated sugar

1 tablespoon toasted ground cumin
½ teaspoon salt
½ teaspoon fresh ground pepper

- Bring the ingredients to a boil in a saucepan. Simmer very low, covered, for 1 hour. Cover and refrigerate until ready to use.

RHUBARB COMPOTE

1 cup strawberries, rinsed, hulled, quartered
1 cup rhubarb, rinsed, and cut into quarter-inch thick slices on the bias

3 tablespoons unsalted butter
3 tablespoons sugar
juice of 1 lemon
2 tablespoons water
1 teaspoon grated gingerroot

This compote accompanies "Duck Breasts and Sausages," as seen in *A Taste For All Seasons*.

- Sauté the strawberries and rhubarb in the butter for several minutes. Add the remaining ingredients, and simmer uncovered for 10 minutes. Remove from the fire, allow to cool, cover, and refrigerate until ready to use.

The name for rhubarb comes from the Greek *Rha*, an early name for the Volga River (on whose banks the fruit was grown), and Latin *barbarus* for barbarians, or *barbaria*, meaning foreign country. During World War I, Americans were encouraged to eat the leaves as a vegetable supplement, which resulted in several cases of poisoning. Oxalic acid was believed to be the culprit, until it was discovered that the stalks, as well as spinach, also contain significant amounts of oxalic acid. The leaf toxin is yet to be identified.

SHALLOT COMPOTE

4 cups shallots, sliced ¼-inch thick
¼ cup olive oil
5 tablespoons sugar
2 cups dry white wine

¼ cup cider vinegar
pinch of saffron
pinch of salt
pinch of black pepper

This compote accompanies "Roast Loin of Veal," as seen in *A Taste For All Seasons*.

- Sauté the shallots in the olive oil over medium flame, covered, for 10 minutes. Stir occasionally, and do not allow to brown.
- Add the sugar, and cook until dissolved. Add the remaining ingredients, and simmer until reduced by three-fourths. Remove from the fire, and set aside until ready to serve.

WHITE ONION COMPOTE

2 pounds white onions, peeled, cored, and sliced lengthwise ¼-inch thick
1 cup golden raisins
½ cup dark brown sugar

1 cup dry white wine
½ cup white vinegar
2 garlic cloves, crushed
¼ cup gingerroot, peeled, and sliced paper-thin

- Place all ingredients into a saucepan. Bring to a boil, and simmer very low, covered, for 2 hours. Cool, cover, and refrigerate until ready to use.

ℐHIITAKE MUSHROOM COMPOTE

⅓ cup olive oil
1 large Spanish onion, thinly
  sliced julienne
2 large shallots, minced
2 tablespoons garlic, sliced
½ pound fresh shiitake
  mushrooms, stems
  trimmed, brushed clean
  with a mushroom brush

or clean towel, and cut
  into ¼-inch dice
1 tablespoon lemon zest
¼ cup champagne vinegar
¼ cup rice wine vinegar
1 sprig fresh rosemary
2 sprigs fresh thyme
½ teaspoon salt
½ teaspoon black pepper

- Preheat oven to 375°F.

- Place a sauté pan over medium flame, and allow to become hot. Add the oil, and sauté the onions, covered, stirring frequently, until they are lightly caramelized. Add the shallot, garlic, and mushrooms, and continue sautéing for 5 minutes. Add the lemon zest, vinegar, herbs, salt, and pepper. Simmer about 5 minutes, stirring continuously.

- Transfer to an ovenproof vessel, and bake for 40 minutes, covered. Remove from the oven, and allow to stand for 1 hour. Remove the herbs before serving.

COULIS

In earlier times, a coulis (cullis) (pronounced "coo-lee") referred to the juices which ran naturally out of a roast during cooking. This juice was strained through a funnel-like device known as a *couloir*, hence the name. In modern times, a coulis refers to a liquid purée of cooked seasoned vegetables, or raw or cooked fruit.

ℐPRICOT-GINGER COULIS

12 ripe apricots, peeled and
  pitted
2 tablespoons grated
  gingerroot

½ cup fish stock
4 dashes Tabasco sauce
2 dashes white
  Worcestershire sauce

- Purée all ingredients in a food processor. Cover and refrigerate overnight before serving.

If fresh apricots are unavailable, canned or dried can be substituted. If dried are used, they should be soaked for 20 minutes in hot water, then drained. The fish stock can also be substituted with white wine, for example, or any other white stock.

This coulis accompanies "Beer-battered Shrimp," as seen in *A Taste For All Seasons*.

CILANTRO SAUCE

This sauce accompanies "Tillamook Cheese Croquettes," as seen in *A Taste For All Seasons*.

1 shallot, minced
½ jalapeño pepper, split and seeded
1 tablespoon unsalted butter
4 ripe medium tomatoes, peeled and cored
2 tablespoons tomato paste
1 bay leaf
1 teaspoon parsley, roughly chopped
½ cup fresh cilantro leaves, roughly chopped
¼ teaspoon salt

- Sauté the shallot and pepper in the butter for 4 or 5 minutes. Add the tomatoes, paste, and bay leaf, and simmer for 30 minutes.
- Remove the bay leaf and discard. Purée the sauce in a blender or food processor, along with the parsley, cilantro, and salt. Reheat when ready to serve.

CUMBERLAND SAUCE

Cumberland sauce is a chilled sweet and tart accompaniment, served with game, lamb, or pork, as well as all varieties of game pâtés.

juice and zest of 1 orange and 1 lemon
½ cup water
½ cup Port wine
¼ cup white wine vinegar
1 small shallot, minced
½ teaspoon dry mustard
3 tablespoons red currant jelly
pinch of salt

- Boil the zest in the water for 5 minutes. Drain, and return the zest to the pan. Add all of the remaining ingredients, except the jelly, and simmer for 5 more minutes. Add the jelly, and simmer briefly. Set aside and allow to cool.

Golden Pepper Coulis

2 large yellow bell peppers, seeded, and cut into 1-inch chunks
1 medium Spanish onion, peeled and roughly chopped
1 medium all-purpose potato, cut into 1-inch cubes

1 tablespoon grated gingerroot
1–1½ cups water (sufficient to cover the ingredients)
salt and white pepper to taste
¼ cup dry champagne

This sauce accompanies "Chilled Poached Halibut" or "Grilled Sea Scallops," created by Gloria Ciccarone-Nehls, chef de cuisine at The Big Four Restaurant, Huntington Hotel, San Francisco, California.

- Bring all the ingredients except the champagne to a boil, and simmer, covered, for 20 minutes. Remove to a blender or food processor, and purée. Blend in the champagne, season with salt and pepper, and set aside to cool. Cover and refrigerate until ready to serve.

Papaya-Yogurt Coulis

1 shallot, minced
½ cup dry white wine
1 teaspoon grated gingerroot

1 small ripe papaya, peeled, seeded, and roughly cut
¾ cup plain yogurt
salt and white pepper to taste

- Simmer the shallot, ginger, and white wine, until about 2 tablespoons of liquid remain. Add the papaya, and simmer for 2 minutes.
- Remove to a food processor, along with the yogurt, and purée.

Tomato Coulis I

3 tablespoons olive oil
½ cup celery, carrot, and onion, minced
1 sprig thyme
1 bay leaf
6 parsley stems, roughly chopped

6 basil leaves, roughly chopped
4 large ripe tomatoes, peeled, stemmed, excess seeds removed, and roughly chopped

- Sauté the mirepoix in the olive oil for 5 minutes. Add the remaining ingredients, and simmer for 15 minutes. Remove, discard the thyme and bay leaf, and purée in a food processor.

*T*OMATO COULIS II

1 quart canned whole
  tomatoes with their
  juice
⅓ cup olive oil
2 large shallots, roughly
  chopped
8 garlic cloves, crushed
1 bay leaf
1 cup extra-rich chicken
  stock (if extra-rich stock is
  not available, add

1 tablespoon meat
  glaze—glace de
  viande—make with
  chicken or veal
  stock)
¼ cup balsamic vinegar
¼ cup fresh basil, parsley,
  and cilantro, minced
salt and black pepper to
  taste

- Sauté the shallots and garlic in the olive oil for 3 minutes. Add all of the remaining ingredients, except for the herbs, salt and pepper. Simmer uncovered, for 30 minutes. Pass through a food mill, then add the herbs, and season to taste with salt and pepper.

*Y*ELLOW BELL PEPPER SAUCE

2 yellow bell peppers, cut
  into 8 pieces each
1 shallot, minced
1 garlic clove, crushed
½ teaspoon fresh thyme
  leaves

3 tablespoons olive oil
1 cup fish stock or clam juice
pinch of salt
pinch of white pepper

——— • ———

This sauce accompanies
"Halibut with Yellow Pepper
Sauce and Chive Flowers,"
as seen in *A Taste For All
Seasons*.

———————

- Sauté the pepper, shallot, garlic, and thyme in the olive oil, over a medium flame, for about 5 minutes.
- Add the stock, salt, and pepper, and continue cooking another 5 minutes.
- Remove to a food processor, purée, and strain. Set aside, keeping warm until ready to serve.

PICKLES

·················· ℬLACKBERRY KETCHUP

1 12-ounce jar of seedless
   blackberry jam
½ cup cider vinegar
½ teaspoon ground
   cinnamon

1 teaspoon grated gingerroot
½ teaspoon ground allspice
pinch of ground cloves
pinch of black pepper
½ teaspoon salt

- Bring all the ingredients to a boil in a small saucepan, and simmer for 20 minutes, stirring frequently. Remove from the fire, and allow to cool.

The word *ketchup* has its origins in the Chinese word *khe-tsup*, meaning "pickled fish sauce." In seventeenth-century England, ketchup referred to a fermented sauce made from mushrooms or walnuts. Since tomato is anatomically considered a fruit, it follows that a liquid pickle could be created from any fruit, such as the blackberry ketchup innovated here, which accompanies "Steamed Lamb Loin," as seen in *A Taste For All Seasons*.

Kim Chee   Kim Chee is a pickle of Korean origin that is served at practically all Korean meals. It tends to be *extremely* hot, perhaps too hot for some palates. This can be adjusted by reducing the amount of chile pepper and chile pepper paste. The following are several versions.

·················· 𝒞UCUMBER KIM CHEE

3 large cucumbers
1½ tablespoons kosher salt
1 bunch scallions, sliced very
   thin
3 garlic cloves, pressed

1 teaspoon red chile pepper
   paste
½ teaspoon kosher salt
½ cup water

Cucumbers are often coated with oil or wax. If you find this coating disagreeable, and impossible to remove by washing, remove the peel and discard.

• Wash the cucumbers thoroughly. Trim and discard the ends, and cut the remaining cucumber into 1½-inch lengths. Cut each of these pieces in half, lengthwise, then remove and discard the seeds. Place these into a bowl, sprinkle with the salt, toss, and allow to sit 15 minutes.

• Rinse and dry the cucumbers, then combine with the remaining ingredients, blending thoroughly. Place in a stainless steel or glass bowl, cover, and allow to ferment for 2 days in warm weather, 1 week in cold weather.

SPRING KIM CHEE

3 cups Chinese cabbage, cut into 1-inch squares, and well washed
3 tablespoons kosher salt
3 garlic cloves, sliced very thin

1 tablespoon grated gingerroot
½ cup scallions, cut into 1-inch lengths, then cut into quarters, lengthwise
1 tablespoon kosher salt
1½ cups water

Chinese cabbage is also called Napa or celery cabbage, looks like a cross between pale romaine lettuce and savoy cabbage, and is a close cousin to another popular Chinese vegetable, bok choy.

• Sprinkle the cabbage with the salt, toss well, and allow to sit for 15 minutes. Rinse and dry thoroughly. Place the cabbage, along with the remaining ingredients, in a stainless steel or glass bowl, and blend thoroughly. Cover, and allow to ferment for 1 day in warm weather, 5 days in cold weather.

TURNIP KIM CHEE

3 medium Asian white turnips
1 tablespoon kosher salt
3 jalapeño or serrano green chile peppers, split, seeded, and sliced into long thin strips

2 tablespoons gingerroot, cut into fine julienne
1 teaspoon candied ginger, minced
½ tablespoon kosher salt
water as needed

• Peel the turnips, and cut into cubes, measuring 1 inch on all sides. Sprinkle with the salt, toss, place in a noncaustic bowl, and allow to sit overnight.

• Slice the turnip cubes into ⅛-inch thick slices. Place these slices into a noncaustic bowl, along with the water that has drained from the turnips, the remaining ingredients, and sufficient water to cover the ingredients. Cover, and allow to marinate, refrigerated, for 2 weeks.

Winter Kim Chee

½ cup celery, cut ⅛-inch thick, on the bias

1 head Chinese cabbage, separated into leaves, and split down the center

1 cup daikon (Japanese icicle radish), cut into 1-inch squares, ⅛-inch thick

¼ cup garlic, sliced very thin

¼ cup kosher salt

1 bunch scallions, cut into 1-inch lengths, then cut into quarters lengthwise

3 jalapeño, serrano, or Thai chile peppers, cut into fine strips

¼ cup grated gingerroot, peeled, and sliced very thin

1 underripe Bartlett pear, cored, and cut into ½-inch dice

3 tablespoons hot chile pepper paste

⅓ cup kosher salt, dissolved in 1 quart water

1 quart water

- Dissolve the ¼ cup salt in the water. Add the celery, cabbage, daikon, and garlic, stir well, and allow to marinate for 1 hour. Drain and rinse well.

- Place these vegetables, along with the remaining ingredients, into a noncaustic bowl, and cover. Allow to marinate at room temperature for 1 week, stirring the mixture daily. Serve with grilled or roasted Asian-style meat, poultry, or game, or any dish that will go well with a highly spiced pickle.

Pickled Eggplant

2 large eggplants

1 cup fresh mint leaves, roughly chopped

10 garlic cloves, pressed

salt and balsamic vinegar as needed

½ cup olive oil

- Wash the eggplants, then slice them lengthwise, about ¼-inch thick (discard the two outermost slices from each eggplant).

- Place a slice of eggplant on the bottom of a glass casserole dish, with slightly angled sides, and measuring approximately 8 inches × 5 inches at its opening, and 3–4 inches deep. Spread the slice with some of the garlic, and sprinkle lightly with salt, vinegar, and some of the mint. Repeat this procedure, pressing down each subsequent slice gently, until all the eggplant is used up.

- Place another casserole dish (same size and shape), on top of the eggplant, and weight it down. Allow this to sit at room temperature for 24 hours, draining the pickle periodically (the salt draws out the moisture in the eggplant).
- Drain off any remaining moisture, and transfer the eggplant to a clean casserole dish. Pour the olive oil over the pickle, cover, and refrigerate until ready to use.

𝒫ICKLED GRAPES

1 cup seedless red grapes
1 cup seedless green grapes
2 bay leaves
1 bunch tarragon
5 garlic cloves, crushed

2 cups champagne vinegar
1 cup water, brought to a
   boil with . . .
1 tablespoon coriander seeds

- Place all the ingredients into a stainless steel or glass container. Cover and allow to marinate at room temperature for 24 hours. Allow to marinate another 24 hours refrigerated. Serve with Grilled Pork Tenderloin.

𝒢RILLED PORK TENDERLOIN

¾ cup chicken stock
2 tablespoons olive oil
2 garlic cloves, sliced very thin
½ cup red bell pepper, cut
   into ⅛-inch by 1-inch
   julienne
½ cup green bell pepper, cut
   into ⅛-inch by 1-inch
   julienne
½ cup yellow bell pepper,
   cut into ⅛-inch by 1-inch
   julienne

½ cup red onion, finely diced
½ teaspoon red pepper chile
   paste
juice of 1 lime
3 tablespoons unsalted butter,
   cut into ½-inch cubes
½ cup cilantro, minced
3 2½- to 3-pound pork
   tenderloins, trimmed
olive oil, salt, and pepper as
   needed

- Simmer the stock until reduced by one-third. Set aside.
- Sauté the garlic, peppers, and onion in the olive oil. Add the chile paste, stock, and lime juice, and simmer several min-

This recipe was innovated by Fred Halpert, chef at Brava Terrace, St. Helena, California.

utes. Mount with butter, finish with the cilantro, and set aside, keeping warm.

- Brush the tenderloins with the olive oil, and sprinkle with salt and pepper. Grill on all sides, approximately 15 minutes total cooking time. Spoon the vegetables onto serving plates. Top with the sliced tenderloin, then some of the sauce.

PICKLED RED CABBAGE

1 teaspoon salt	2 garlic cloves, crushed
½ small head red cabbage, sliced very thin	1 tablespoon fresh thyme leaves, minced
1 medium Spanish onion, sliced lengthwise very thin	1¼ cups champagne vinegar
1 bay leaf	¾ cup water
½ teaspoon ground cumin	2 heaping tablespoons brown sugar
1 tablespoon juniper berries, crushed	

- Place the cabbage and onions into a bowl, sprinkle with the salt, and toss. Set aside.
- Simmer the remaining ingredients for 5 minutes, then pour over the cabbage and onions. Allow to cool, tossing frequently. Cover and refrigerate until ready to serve.

PICKLED SHALLOTS

1 pound shallots, peeled, and cut into halves or quarters, yielding a fairly consistent size	¼ cup granulated sugar
	¾ red wine vinegar
	½ cup water
1 cup red wine vinegar	5 sprigs fresh thyme

- Combine all the ingredients except the shallots and thyme in a small saucepan. Bring to a boil.
- Place the shallots and thyme into a clean jar. Pour the vinegar over, cool, cover, and place in the refrigerator. Allow to marinate one week before using.

RELISHES

···················· ℬELL PEPPER RELISH

2 red bell peppers, cut into
  ¼-inch dice
2 green bell peppers, cut
  into ¼-inch dice
2 yellow bell peppers, cut
  into ¼-inch dice
water and salt as needed
1 medium Spanish onion,
  peeled and sliced
  paper-thin

¼ cup sugar
¾ cup champagne vinegar
¼ cup water
2 tablespoons mustard seed
1 tablespoon celery seed
1 teaspoon cumin seed
1 teaspoon black pepper

- Bring the water and salt to a boil. Add the diced peppers, and boil for 2 minutes. Drain, and set aside.

- Bring the sugar, vinegar, water, and spices to a boil, then add the diced peppers and onions. Simmer for 2 minutes, remove from the fire, and set aside to cool. Place in a covered container, and refrigerate until ready to use.

···················· 𝒞ORN RELISH

2 cups cider vinegar
½ cup sugar
1 tablespoon salt
½ teaspoon celery seed
½ teaspoon mustard
  seed
2 cups fresh-frozen corn
  kernels
¼ head white cabbage, cut
  into ½-inch pieces

1 large white onion, ¼-inch
  dice
1 green bell pepper, ¼-inch
  dice
1 red bell pepper, ¼-inch
  dice
½ jalapeño pepper, split,
  seeded, and sliced very
  thin

This relish is served with
"Chicken and Cream, with
Biscuits" as seen in *A Taste
For All Seasons*.

- Combine the vinegar, sugar, salt, celery, and mustard seeds in a saucepan. Bring to a boil, and simmer 5 minutes. Add the vegetables, and simmer another 5 minutes. Cool, cover, refrigerate, and marinate overnight before serving.

CRANBERRY RELISH I

zest of 1 orange
1 tablespoon unsalted butter
6 tablespoons sugar
1 cup dry sherry
1 cup dry white wine

½ cup fresh-squeezed
  orange juice
2 cups whole fresh (or
  whole-frozen) cranberries

This relish is served with "Gin-cured Salmon," as seen in *A Taste For All Seasons*.

- Sauté the zest in the butter for 3 minutes. Add all the remaining ingredients, except the cranberries. Simmer until reduced by half. Add the cranberries, and simmer until the mixture is thick and smooth and all the cranberries have opened. Cool, cover, and refrigerate until ready to use.

CRANBERRY RELISH II

¾ cup sugar
¼ cup water
1 navel orange, trimmed,
  then cut into quarter-inch
  dice
1 lime, trimmed, then cut
  into quarter-inch dice
½ cup sultana raisins

1 heaping tablespoon peeled
  and very thinly sliced
  gingerroot
¼ teaspoon ground
  cinnamon
¼ teaspoon fresh ground
  nutmeg
2 cups whole fresh (or
  whole-frozen) cranberries

- Bring the sugar and water to a boil, and dissolve the sugar completely.

- Add the orange, lime, raisins and gingerroot, and simmer for 5 minutes, stirring continuously. Add the spices and cranberries, and continue simmering and stirring for 10 minutes. Cool, cover, and refrigerate until ready to use.

CREOSAT RELISH

¼ cup cucumber, peeled,
  seeded, and cut into
  ¼-inch dice

¼ cup green bell pepper, cut
  into ¼-inch dice

Creosote is an oil distilled from beechwood tar. The use of this name is a round-about reflection of its use as an accompaniment to wood- or charcoal-grilled meat and poultry.

¼ cup red onion, cut into ¼-inch dice
¼ cup tomato, peeled, seeded, and cut into ¼-inch dice

2 tablespoons sour gherkins, cut into ¼-inch dice
2 tablespoons capers

- Combine all of the ingredients, cover, and refrigerate overnight, then serve with grilled red meat.

ℰGGPLANT RELISH

1 large eggplant, peeled, and cut into ½-inch dice
1 tablespoon salt
¼ cup peanut oil
2 bunches scallions, finely sliced

1 teaspoon red chile pepper paste
2 tablespoons gingerroot, grated
¼ cup soy sauce
¼ cup rice vinegar

- Place the diced eggplant into a bowl, sprinkle with the salt, and toss. Allow to sit for 30 minutes.
- Heat the peanut oil in a sauté pan until it begins to smoke. Squeeze excess moisture out of the eggplant, and sauté in the peanut oil for several minutes. Add the onion, and sauté another 5 minutes. Add the remaining ingredients, and continue cooking 5 minutes. Remove from the fire, and allow to cool several hours before serving.

𝒫APAYA-MINT RELISH

juice of 1 tablespoon grated gingerroot, squeezed through a piece of cheesecloth
1 ripe papaya, peeled, seeded, and cut into ¼-inch dice
2 tablespoons dry champagne

1 tablespoon champagne vinegar
juice of ½ lime
½ red bell pepper, ¼-inch dice
½ small red onion, ¼-inch dice
1 scallion, finely sliced
6 mint leaves, minced
pinch of white pepper

This relish accompanies "Poached Halibut," created by Gloria Ciccarone-Nehls, chef de cuisine at The Big Four, Huntington Hotel, San Francisco, California.

- Combine all the ingredients in a stainless steel bowl. Cover and refrigerate one hour before serving.

*R*OASTED VEGETABLE RELISH

¼ cup olive oil
1 medium Spanish
  onion, diced into
  ½-inch cubes
1 large carrot, diced into
  ½-inch cubes
1 fennel root, diced into
  ½-inch cubes
1 red bell pepper, diced into
  ½-inch cubes

2 stalks celery, diced into
  ½-inch cubes
¼ teaspoon salt
¼ teaspoon white
  pepper
½ cup olive oil
¼ cup red wine
  vinegar
½ teaspoon Dijon
  mustard
12 sprigs parsley

- Preheat oven to 400°F.
- Combine the oil, vegetables, salt and pepper in a bowl. Toss, coating the vegetables with oil and seasoning.
- Remove the vegetables with a slotted spoon, and place on a roasting pan. Roast for about 30 minutes, stirring three or four times.
- Remove the vegetables to absorbent paper. Place the remaining olive oil, vinegar, mustard, and parsley in a blender, and purée. Pour over the vegetables, cover, refrigerate, and allow to marinate 12 hours (overnight).

*T*OMATO RELISH

2 cups canned diced
  tomatoes
½ cup celery, cut into
  ¼-inch dice
½ cup Spanish onion,
  cut into ¼-inch
  dice
2 teaspoons salt
¼ cup sugar

1 bay leaf
2 sprigs fresh thyme
½ teaspoon cracked black
  pepper
¼ teaspoon ground
  nutmeg
1 cup champagne
  vinegar

- Combine all ingredients in a heavy-gauge saucepan, simmer gently, uncovered, for 20 minutes. Remove from the fire, cool, cover, and refrigerate overnight before serving.

TRI-COLOR CORN RELISH

½ cup frozen corn kernels, rinsed and drained
½ cup red bell pepper, cut into ¼-inch dice
½ cup green bell pepper, cut into ¼-inch dice
½ cup yellow bell pepper, cut into ¼-inch dice
½ cup red onion, cut into ¼-inch dice

2 garlic cloves, pressed
2 anchovy fillets, mashed
2 tablespoons cilantro leaves, minced
2 tablespoons parsley, minced
½ cup olive oil
¼ cup red wine vinegar
juice of 1 lemon

This relish was innovated by George Lacey, former Chef-Instructor at The San Francisco School of Cooking, and accompanies "Grilled Chicken Breasts."

- Combine all the ingredients in a bowl and blend thoroughly. Cover and refrigerate overnight.

SALSAS

AVOCADO SALSA

1 small cucumber, peeled, seeded, and cut into very fine dice
1 ripe tomato, peeled, seeded, and cut into very fine dice
1 small red onion, peeled, and cut into very fine dice

1 small yellow or red bell pepper, cut into very fine dice
½ cup fresh lime juice
¼ cup cilantro, roughly chopped
1 tablespoon olive oil
1 ripe Haas avocado

The diced vegetables should be cut very fine (⅛-inch). This salsa accompanies "Salmon with Grainy Mustard," as seen in *A Taste For All Seasons*.

- Combine all the ingredients except the avocado in a small bowl. Cover and marinate at room temperature for 2 hours.
- Peel the avocado, cut into ¼-inch dice, and mix thoroughly with the marinating vegetables. Set aside until ready to serve.

CHINESE SALSA

6 dried black Chinese mushrooms
3 ripe medium tomatoes, peeled, seeded, and roughly chopped

½ cup scallions, sliced paper-thin
½ cup cilantro leaves, roughly chopped
2 garlic cloves, pressed

1 tablespoon gingerroot,
  grated
3 tablespoons rice wine
  vinegar

1½ teaspoons sugar
½ teaspoon salt
2 tablespoons sesame oil
1 tablespoon peanut oil

This salsa was innovated by George Lacey, formerly Chef-Instructor at the San Francisco School of Cooking, San Francisco, California.

- Cover the mushrooms in boiling water, and allow to sit for 30 minutes. Discard the water and the ends of the stems, then chop the mushrooms into ¼-inch dice.
- Heat the vinegar, sugar, and salt, and stir until dissolved. Combine this with the remaining ingredients and blend well. Cover and refrigerate overnight.

FRESH SALSA I
(Salsa Fresca)

½ cup Spanish onion, finely
  diced
2 jalapeño peppers, seeded,
  and finely diced
1 Anaheim (or other mild
  green chile), roasted,
  peeled, and finely diced

½ cup cilantro, minced
2 large, ripe tomatoes,
  peeled, and small diced
¼ cup lime juice
¼ teaspoon salt

- Combine all ingredients and blend thoroughly. Cover and refrigerate until ready to serve.

FRESH SALSA II
(Salsa Fresca)

4 medium ripe tomatoes,
  peeled, seeded, and cut
  into ¼-inch dice
6 scallions, finely diced
1 tablespoon orange zest
1 serrano pepper,
  chopped

½ cup cilantro leaves,
  roughly chopped
2 tablespoons lemon juice
1 tablespoon sugar
½ teaspoon salt

- In a stainless steel bowl, dissolve the sugar and salt in the lemon juice. Add the remaining ingredients, cover, and refrigerate, until ready to serve.

GOLDEN TOMATO SALSA

6 to 8 large ripe golden
tomatoes, peeled,
seeded, and cut into
¼-inch dice
zest and juice of 1 lime
zest of 1 orange
¼ cup orange juice
3 garlic cloves, pressed
1 pinch saffron, dissolved in
½ cup champagne

vinegar, slightly
warmed
¼ cup cilantro, minced
¼ cup parsley, minced
¼ cup basil leaves,
minced
½ teaspoon salt
½ teaspoon white pepper

- In a stainless steel bowl, combine all the ingredients. Cover and refrigerate for 24 hours before serving.

GRAPEFRUIT SALSA

1 cup pink grapefruit juice
3 pink grapefruits, peeled,
and cut into
membrane-free segments
1 small red onion, peeled,
and finely diced

1 small jalapeño pepper,
seeded, and minced
½ cup cilantro, minced
¼ cup parsley, minced
¼ cup sorrel leaves, cut into
fine julienne
¼ teaspoon salt

- Combine all the ingredients together in a stainless steel bowl. Cover and refrigerate 24 hours before serving.

GREEN SALSA

(Salsa Verde)

1 small Spanish onion,
minced
2 garlic cloves
½ cup cilantro, minced
2 jalapeño peppers, seeded,
and finely diced

8 fresh tomatillos, husks
removed, parboiled, and
finely diced
2 tablespoons lime juice
¼ teaspoon salt

- Combine all ingredients, and blend thoroughly. Cover and refrigerate until ready to serve.

JUAN PAIZ' SALSA

This is a creation of Juan Paiz, native of El Salvador, and garde manger (pantry cook) at Restaurant Jasper, Boston, Massachusetts.

3 tablespoons radish, finely diced
3 tablespoons red onion, finely diced
3 tablespoons fresh cilantro leaves, minced
1 teaspoon jalapeño pepper, minced
juice of 6 limes

- Combine all the ingredients in a stainless steel bowl. Cover and marinate, refrigerated, for at least one hour, then serve with clams on the half shell.

MANGO SALSA

½ cup champagne vinegar
¼ cup water
1 tablespoon brown sugar
1 large ripe mango, peeled, and cut into ¼-inch dice
2 tablespoons scallion, sliced paper-thin
juice and zest of 1 lime
¼ cup mint leaves, cut into fine julienne
½ cup cilantro, minced
¼ cup parsley, minced
2 tablespoons gingerroot, grated

- Bring the vinegar, water, and brown sugar to a boil, and stir until the sugar is completely dissolved. Combine with all the other ingredients in a stainless steel bowl. Cover and refrigerate for 24 hours before serving.

ORANGE-LIME SALSA

5 oranges
5 limes
1 tablespoon cilantro, roughly chopped
½ cup red onion, cut into fine dice
½ jalapeño pepper, minced
juice of 1 lime

- Pare the oranges and limes with a sharp knife, making sure to remove all the pith. Holding the fruit over a small bowl (to catch the juice), remove the fruit segments by cutting on either side of the skin that separates them.
- Remove any seeds from the segments, add the fruit to the bowl, then squeeze the juice from the remaining pulp into the same bowl. Add the cilantro, onion, lemon juice, and jalapeño. Cover and refrigerate until ready to serve.

This salsa accompanies "Grilled Ling Cod," as seen in *A Taste For All Seasons*.

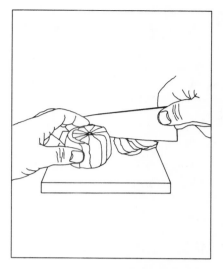

1. *Slicing the skin from a lemon (lime, grapefruit).*

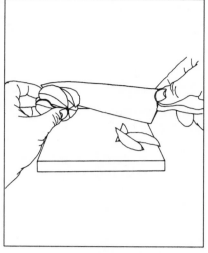

2. *Cutting the citrus flesh from between the membranes.*

𝒫APAYA SALSA

1 ripe papaya, peeled, seeded, and cut into ¼-inch dice
1 small red bell pepper, seeds and ribs removed, and cut into ¼-inch dice

½ red onion, diced
½ cup cilantro leaves, minced
¼ teaspoon ground cumin
juice of 2 limes

- Combine all the ingredients in a stainless steel bowl. Cover and marinate, refrigerated, for 24 hours before serving.

𝒫INEAPPLE SALSA

1 shallot, minced
2 garlic cloves, pressed
½ cup red onion, finely diced
1 small red bell pepper, finely diced

½ jalapeño pepper, seeded and finely diced
1 small ripe pineapple, peeled, cored, and cut into ½-inch cubes

¼ teaspoon saffron
¼ cup brown sugar
½ cup dry sherry
¾ cup rice wine vinegar

1 small bunch cilantro,
    stems removed, leaves
    roughly chopped

- Simmer all the ingredients, except the cilantro, in a small saucepan, for 15 minutes. Remove from the fire, and stir in the cilantro leaves. Cover, refrigerate overnight. Serve at room temperature, with Grilled Ahi Tuna and Risotto.

GRILLED AHI TUNA

3 tablespoons olive oil
2 garlic cloves, pressed
½ cup red onion, finely diced
½ jalapeño pepper, seeded
    and finely diced
1 shallot, minced
1 cup Arborio rice
¼ teaspoon salt
¼ teaspoon white pepper

½ cup dry white wine
2 cups fish stock, heated
    with a pinch of saffron
olive oil as needed
2 tablespoons coarse black
    pepper
salt as needed
6 7- to 8-ounce fresh Ahi
    tuna steaks

- Sauté the garlic, onion, and jalapeño pepper, covered, over medium heat, for 5 minutes. Add the rice, and sauté another 5 minutes. Add the wine and a half cup of the stock, and simmer, stirring occasionally. When the rice is nearly dry, add another half cup of the stock, and continue simmering and stirring. Repeat this process until all the stock is added, and the rice has absorbed all the liquid, but is still moist. Cover and set aside until ready to serve.
- Coat the tuna steaks with the olive oil, and sprinkle lightly with salt. Press the pepper into both sides of the tuna steaks, and grill over charcoal or wood, or broil, about 4 minutes on each side. Serve with the risotto and the salsa.

———— • ————

This recipe was innovated by Jonathan Waxman, Chef at Table 29, Napa, California.

————————

SPINACH SALSA

16 large spinach leaves,
    stems removed, well
    washed, dried, and minced

2 teaspoons hoisin sauce
1 teaspoon red chile pepper
    paste

This salsa was innovated by George Lacey, formerly Chef-Instructor at the San Francisco School of Cooking, San Francisco, California.

2 tablespoons soy sauce
¼ cup balsamic vinegar
2 tablespoons dry sherry
2 tablespoons sesame oil
2 teaspoons sugar
4 garlic cloves, pressed
2 tablespoons gingerroot, grated

1 tablespoon orange zest
¼ cup cilantro leaves, roughly chopped
¼ cup scallions, very finely sliced
2 tablespoons sesame seeds, toasted

- Dissolve the sugar in the vinegar. Combine all ingredients in a small bowl and blend well. Cover and refrigerate overnight. Serve at room temperature with assorted dim sum.

CHAPTER 15

DESSERT SAUCES

The word *dessert* is derived from *desservir*, meaning "to clear a table." Unlike the mother sauce structure for classic savory sauces, there is no such structure for dessert sauces.

The following sauces have been divided up into four headings: Caramelized Sugar Sauces, Chocolate Sauces, Egg-based Sauces, and Fruit Sauces.

CARAMELIZED SUGAR SAUCES

CARAMEL SAUCE I

1 cup sugar
2 tablespoons water
¾ cup boiling water

½ teaspoon lemon juice, strained

- Cook the sugar and water in a heavy-gauge saucepan, until it turns a light golden brown (8 to 10 minutes).
- Remove from the heat, then carefully and quickly add the boiling water, stirring well. Return to the heat, and stir continuously until dissolved. Add the lemon juice, blend in, then set aside to cool.

CARAMEL SAUCE II

½ cup sugar
1 tablespoon water
2 cups milk

¼ teaspoon cornstarch
1 tablespoon Kahlua
1 tablespoon Grand Marnier

- Dissolve the cornstarch in ½ cup of milk, and set aside. Heat the remaining milk with half of the sugar, stirring continuously so that it doesn't burn.
- Simmer the sugar and water until it begins to caramelize. Remove from the fire immediately, and add the two batches of milk. Bring to a boil, add the two liqueurs, and set aside until ready to serve.

CARAMEL SAUCE III

¾ cup sugar
3 tablespoons water

1 tablespoon lemon juice
¼ cup heavy cream

This sauce accompanies "Poached Apples," as seen in *A Taste For All Seasons*.

• Simmer the sugar, water, and lemon juice in a small sauce-pan, stirring continuously, until the mixture begins to turn light brown. Add the cream, and remove from the fire immediately. Stir until smooth. Set aside until ready to serve.

CHOCOLATE SAUCES

BASIC CHOCOLATE SAUCE

14 ounces imported
    semi-sweet chocolate,
    broken into small pieces
1 cup heavy cream

1 tablespoon vanilla extract
1 tablespoon brandy or
    Cognac

• Heat the chocolate in a double boiler until melted. Stir in the cream until smooth. Add the brandy or Cognac, and vanilla, and blend in until smooth and hot.

CHOCOLATE SAUCE II

5 tablespoons sugar
¾ cup light corn syrup
¾ cup heavy cream
½ pound imported
    semisweet chocolate,
    broken into small pieces

1 tablespoon vanilla extract
1 tablespoon Grand Marnier
1 tablespoon water

• Place the sugar, syrup, cream, and chocolate into a heavy-guage saucepan, over medium heat. Stir continuously until the chocolate is melted. Add the remaining ingredients, bring to a boil, and set aside until ready to serve.

CHOCOLATE CINNAMON SAUCE

1 cup milk
2 cinnamon sticks
4 ounces unsalted butter, cut
 into ½-inch cubes

½ pound dark semi-sweet
 chocolate, broken up into
 ½-inch pieces

- Place the milk and cinnamon sticks over a double boiler, and allow to steep over simmering water for 15 minutes. In the meantime, place the butter and chocolate in the double boiler, stirring occasionally, until melted and smooth. Remove the cinnamon, and pour the hot milk into the melted chocolate and butter. Stir until smooth.

CHOCOLATE GINGER SAUCE

½ cup sugar
2 tablespoons water
⅓ cup gingerroot, peeled
 and finely chopped

1¾ cup heavy cream
6 tablespoons cocoa powder

- Simmer sugar, water, and ginger, until the sugar just begins to caramelize. Add cream, and stir until thoroughly blended. Add cocoa powder, and blend. Strain through a sieve and serve.

CHOCOLATE RUM SAUCE

This sauce accompanies "Death by Chocolate," innovated by Marcel Desaulnier of The Trellis Restaurant, Williamsburg, Virginia, but it is appropriate for any chocolate confection.

¼ pound unsalted butter,
 softened
1 cup sugar
1 cup heavy cream
⅓ cup cocoa powder,
 unsweetened, sifted

2 teaspoons Myer's dark rum
⅛ teaspoon salt
1 tablespoon instant coffee
 granules
1 teaspoon vanilla extract

- Combine butter, sugar, cream, cocoa, rum, and salt in a heavy-gauge, noncorrosive saucepan over a medium flame. Stir continuously and simmer for five minutes. Remove from the fire, blend in the coffee and vanilla, and set aside.

*M*OCHA SAUCE

½ pound imported
  bittersweet chocolate
1 cup heavy cream
¼ cup freeze-dried coffee
  granules
¼ cup dark brown sugar,
  firmly packed

¼ cup corn syrup
1 tablespoon vanilla
  extract
¼ cup unsalted butter
3 tablespoons Cognac

- Place all of the ingredients except the butter and Cognac into a heavy-gauge saucepan, and place over medium heat. Stir continuously, until the chocolate is melted, and the mixture is smooth.
- Beat in butter, and blend in the Cognac. Bring the mixture up to a simmer, and set aside until ready to serve.

EGG-BASED SAUCES

*A*LMOND CREAM

1 cup milk
½ cup sliced almonds

3 large egg yolks
⅓ cup sugar

- Bring the milk and almonds to a boil, remove from the fire, and allow to sit, covered, for 30 minutes.
- Beat the eggs and sugar in a stainless steel bowl, until the sugar is completely dissolved, and the mixture is light yellow, and slightly thickened.
- Strain the almonds from the milk, and discard the almonds. Reheat the milk, then pour it very slowly into the egg mixture, while continuously beating. Return this mixture to the fire, and over medium heat, stir continuously until it is thick and smooth.
- Pour into a lightly buttered bowl, dab the top with a piece of butter (to prevent a skin forming), allow to cool, then cover and refrigerate until ready to serve.

———— • ————

This sauce accompanies "Poached Pears," as seen in *The Pillar House Cookbook*.

BOURBON SAUCE I

1 pint heavy cream
1 tablespoon sugar

1 small piece of vanilla bean
⅓ cup bourbon

- Simmer the cream, sugar, and vanilla, until reduced by half. Remove from the fire, remove and discard the vanilla bean, and blend in the bourbon. Set aside, keeping warm until ready to serve.

BOURBON SAUCE II

This sauce was introduced by George Lacey, former Chef-Instructor at the San Francisco School of Cooking. The Bread Pudding recipe follows.

¼ pound unsalted butter
1½ cups powdered sugar

2 egg yolks
½ cup bourbon

- Melt the butter and sugar over medium heat, stirring until thoroughly blended. Temper in the egg yolks, bring to a simmer, and remove from the fire. Blend in the bourbon. Serve warm with bread pudding.

BREAD PUDDING

6–8 cups stale bread, broken
    into 1-inch pieces
3 cups milk
1 cup half-and-half
2 cups sugar
8 tablespoons unsalted
    butter, melted
4 eggs, beaten

3 tablespoons vanilla
    extract
1 cup raisins
1 cup shredded coconut
1 cup chopped pecans
1 teaspoon cinnamon
½ teaspoon nutmeg

- Combine the bread, milk, and cream in a bowl, and allow to sit for 15 minutes. Add the remaining ingredients and blend thoroughly.
- Place this mixture into a buttered baking dish or casserole, and bake in a preheated 350-degree oven for 1 hour, or until the top is golden brown. Serve with the warm sauce.

CARAMEL SAUCE IV

3 egg yolks
2 cups milk
¼ teaspoon vanilla extract

1 cup confectioner's sugar
½ cup water

- Place the eggs in a stainless steel bowl, and set aside.
- Place the milk and vanilla in a saucepan, and heat over a low flame.
- Cook the sugar and water in a saucepan until it begins to turn a light golden brown. Remove from the fire, then whisk into the caramel as soon as it comes off the fire.
- Carefully whip the sugar/milk mixture into the yolks, by pouring it into the bowl in a slow, steady stream, while whipping vigorously.
- Return the mixture to the saucepan over a low flame, stirring continuously for about 5 minutes, or until thick and smooth. Serve with any dessert fritter.

COFFEE SAUCE

1½ cups strong black coffee
¼ cup sugar
1 teaspoon vanilla extract

2 tablespoons heavy cream
2 egg whites, beaten to stiff
  peaks

- Simmer the coffee, sugar, and vanilla, and reduce by half. It should be a little syrupy at this point.
- Remove from the fire, stir in the cream, then fold in the whipped egg whites.

COGNAC SAUCE

3 large egg yolks
½ cup sugar
1 teaspoon lemon zest

½ cup Cognac
¾ cup heavy cream, hot

- Beat the egg yolks, sugar, zest, and half of the Cognac over a double boiler.
- Beat in the hot cream, and finish with the remaining Cognac. Serve hot.

CRÈME ANGLAISE

½ cup vanilla sugar	pinch of salt
4 egg yolks	1 cup warm milk

- Whip the sugar, salt, and yolks in a stainless steel bowl, until slightly thickened.
- Pour in the milk in a slow, steady stream, while beating continuously. Return to the fire, and over medium heat, bring to a simmer, while stirring continuously. Strain, cool, and cover until ready to serve.

———————— • ————————

Vanilla sugar is made by placing a vanilla bean, split in half lengthwise, into a container of granulated sugar. Within a week, the sugar takes on the aroma and flavor infused from the vanilla bean. As the sugar is used, more sugar can be added.

Other variations can be applied to basic Crème Anglaise, such as the Gingered English Cream that follows. Orange or Lime English Cream, for example, can be made by adding orange or lime juice and zest.

GINGERED ENGLISH CREAM

4 egg yolks	1 tablespoon grated
⅓ cup sugar	gingerroot
	2 cups milk

- Whip the egg yolks, sugar, and ginger in a stainless steel bowl until they are thick and light lemon colored.
- Heat the milk is a saucepan until it just begins to simmer. Ladle it very slowly into the whipped eggs, stirring continuously. Return this mixture to the saucepan and heat over a medium flame, stirring continuously with a wooden spoon, until the mixture is lightly thickened and smooth, and coats the back of a spoon. Chill for 2 hours before serving.

——— • ———

This sauce accompanies "Peach Strudel," and "Bittersweet Chocolate Terrine," as seen in *A Taste For All Seasons*.

*P*EAR CUSTARD SAUCE

1 cup water
½ cup sugar
1 teaspoon lemon juice
3 ripe Bosc (or other
   variety) pears, peeled,
   cored, quartered, and

cut into quarter-inch
   chunks
2 cups half-and-half
4 egg yolks
2 teaspoons cornstarch

- Bring the water, sugar, and lemon juice to a boil. Add the pears, and simmer about 10 minutes, or until very tender. Remove the pears with a slotted spoon, and set aside.

- Heat the cream and half-and-half in a heavy-gauge, noncorrosive saucepan. While this is heating, whip the egg yolks and cornstarch vigorously in a stainless steel bowl, until the yolks have doubled in size.

- Bring the cream mixture just to the boil, then remove from heat, and pour very slowly into the yolks, while continuously stirring. Return this mixture to the saucepan, and simmer, while stirring continuously, for 5 minutes. (Be very careful not to scorch the bottom.) Remove from the fire, add the pears, and serve.

This sauce accompanies "Pear Fritters," as seen in *The Trellis Cookbook*, by Marcel Desaulnier.

*P*ISTACHIO SAUCE

3 egg yolks
⅓ cup sugar
1 cup milk

½ cup unsalted pistachios,
   shelled and roughly
   chopped

- Beat the egg yolks and sugar in a stainless steel bowl, until lemon colored and slightly thickened.

- Scald the milk in a small saucepan, then pour it slowly into the egg mixture, while continuously stirring. Return this sauce to the pan, and continue stirring over medium heat, until the mixture is smooth and thick. Remove from the fire, and add the pistachios. Set aside, keeping warm until ready to serve.

This sauce accompanies "Chocolate Pâté," as seen in *The Pillar House Cookbook*.

*R*UM-PRALINE SAUCE

½ cup sugar
¼ cup chopped raw almonds
2 cups heavy cream
½ teaspoon vanilla extract
pinch of salt

2 tablespoons unsalted
  butter, cut into ¼-inch
  cubes
2 tablespoons dark rum

- Cook the sugar and almonds, stirring continuously, until it turns golden brown. Remove from the fire, and pour onto a lightly buttered pan. Allow to cool and harden.

- Lift the slab of caramelized sugar and almonds from the pan, and break up into small pieces. Pulverize these pieces using a rolling pin, or in a food processor.

- Bring the cream, vanilla, and salt to a simmer, and reduce by half. Add the praline powder, and blend in. Mount with the butter, and set aside in a warm place until ready to serve.

*S*ABAYON SAUCE

5 egg yolks
⅔ cup sugar
1 cup dry white wine
1 tablespoon Kirsch

¼ teaspoon vanilla extract
½ teaspoon lemon zest
1 teaspoon orange zest

- Place all of the ingredients into a stainless steel (or copper) bowl, and set over a pan of barely simmering water. Whip the mixture continuously until it is thick and frothy (4–5 minutes).

———————————— • ————————————

Sabayon is the French version of the Italian Zabaione (see a savory Sabayon under Butter Sauces). In France it is generally savory, as an herb and stock flavored sauce for a variety of dishes, and only occasionally sweet. Champagne Sabayon is one such sweet version, served with poached peaches. It is made in the same fashion, substituting champagne for white wine, and a brandy for Kirsch.

———————————————————————————

ℤABAGLIONE
(Zabaione)

6 egg yolks
6 tablespoons sugar

2 tablespoons brandy or
   grappa
½ cup sweet Marsala wine

- Beat the first three ingredients vigorously, in a copper pastry bowl over a medium flame, or over a double boiler. When it has roughly doubled in volume, add the Marsala slowly, beating continuously.
- Serve immediately over fresh fruit, or individually as a separate dessert.

———————————— • ————————————

The American spelling *zabaglione* is considered archaic in Italy, where it is spelled *zabaione*.

The origin of the word is likely *sap* (Old Italian *zappa*), meaning "any essential bodily fluid; health, energy and vitality."

ℤABAGLIONE SAUCE (COLD)

5 egg yolks
⅔ cup sugar
1 tablespoon Kirsch
¼ teaspoon vanilla extract
½ teaspoon lemon zest

1 teaspoon orange zest
⅔ cup Marsala wine
½ cup heavy cream,
   whipped to stiff peaks

- Beat the first six ingredients vigorously in a copper pastry bowl over a medium flame, or over a double boiler. When it has roughly doubled in volume, add the Marsala slowly, beating continuously.
- Remove from the fire, and place in a large bowl of ice. Beat continuously, until the mixture has chilled.
- Fold in the whipped cream, then refrigerate until ready to use.

RUM ZABAGLIONE

6 egg yolks
6 tablespoons sugar

2 tablespoons brandy or
   grappa
½ cup dark rum

- Beat the first three ingredients vigorously in a copper pastry bowl over a medium flame, or over a double boiler. When it has roughly doubled in volume, add the Marsala slowly, beating continuously.
- Serve immediately over fresh fruit, or individually as a separate dessert.

--------------------•--------------------

Zabaglione can be made with virtually any variety of sweet wine, aperitif, or digestif: Amaretto, Benedictine, Cassis (black currant), Grand Marnier, Frangelica, Kahlua, and the like.

FRUIT SAUCES

APPLE CIDER CREAM

1½ cups apple cider
1 tablespoon apple brandy

½ Granny Smith apple,
   cored, peeled, and cut
   into 1-inch pieces
⅓ cup heavy cream

- Simmer the cider, brandy, and apple, stirring occasionally, until reduced by two-thirds. Add the cream, and simmer until reduced to 1 cup. Remove from the fire and strain.

APRICOT SAUCE

12 fresh ripe apricots, washed,
   pitted, trimmed, and cut
   into half-inch chunks

½ cup sugar
½ cup apricot Kirsch
¼ cup water

- Bring the ingredients to a boil, and simmer 20 minutes. Remove to a food processor and purée. Press through a sieve.

––––––––––––––––– • –––––––––––––––––

If fresh apricots are not available, canned or dried apricots can be substituted. The canned variety should be packed in sugar syrup, with subsequent modifications to sugar and liquid. If dried are used, soak in hot water first, then proceed as above.

This recipe can be utilized for virtually any variety of fruit sauce: cherry, kiwi, nectarine, peach, pineapple, and plum, to name a few.

–––––––––––––––––––––––––––––––

$\mathscr{B}$LACK CURRANT SAUCE

2 cups black currants, stemmed, and well washed (substitute frozen or canned if necessary)	½ cup sugar ½ cup water 3 tablespoons Cassis juice of 1 lemon

- Combine the currants, sugar, and water in a saucepan, and simmer for 20 minutes. Remove to a food processor, along with the Cassis and lemon juice, and purée. Strain through a sieve.

$\mathscr{B}$LUEBERRY SAUCE

2 cups fresh blueberries 2 tablespoons water ¼ cup sugar 1 tablespoon lemon juice	pinch of nutmeg 1 teaspoon cornstarch, dissolved in 2 tablespoons Kirsch

- Bring the blueberries, water, sugar, and lemon juice to a boil. Cover, and simmer for 10 minutes. Add the cornstarch dissolved in Kirsch, and while stirring, simmer for 1 minute. Press through a sieve, and set aside until ready to serve.

CRANBERRY-RASPBERRY SAUCE

2 cups whole fresh (or
   fresh-frozen) cranberries
¼ cup honey
¼ cup orange juice

1 pint dry-pack frozen
   raspberries
¼ cup Kirsch

- Simmer the cranberries, honey, and orange juice in a small saucepan 7 or 8 minutes. Add the raspberries, and simmer another 7 minutes. Remove from the fire.
- Purée the mixture along with the Kirsch in a blender or food processor. Strain through a fine sieve. Set aside until ready to serve.

This sauce accompanies "Buttermilk Baby Cakes," as seen in *A Taste For All Seasons*.

CALVADOS SAUCE

4 Granny Smith apples,
   peeled, cored, cut into
   half-inch chunks, and held
   in a lemon and water bath

(reserve the peels and
   cores)
½ cup water
½ cup sugar
1 cup Calvados

- Combine the peels, cores, and water in a small saucepan. Bring to a boil and strain, reserving the liquid, discarding the peels and cores.
- Return the liquid to the saucepan, and add the sugar and apple chunks (discard the lemon bath). Simmer for about 15–20 minutes, or until the apples are very soft. Remove to a food processor, along with the Calvados, and purée.
- Serve with baked apples, pancakes, crêpes, charlottes, etc.

A Pear Brandy Sauce can also be made following this same recipe. Substitute ripe pears for apples, and Clearcreek Pear Brandy (an exceptionally aromatic, clear pear brandy, distilled in Portland, Oregon) for the Calvados.

MELBA SAUCE

1 pint fresh, or frozen dry-pack
   raspberries (thawed)
¼ cup sugar

¼ cup water
¼ cup Chambord liqueur

- Bring the ingredients to a boil in a small saucepan, and simmer for 15 minutes.
- Remove to a blender or food processor, and purée. Press through a sieve, discarding the seeds.

Melba Sauce is actually an integral part of the Peach Melba (Pêche Melba), a vanilla-syrup poached peach served atop vanilla ice cream, with the puréed raspberry sauce poured over. It was created by August Escoffier in 1908, while chef at the Carlton Hotel, London, in honor of the Australian Diva Nellie Melba.

Strawberries or blackberries can also be substituted for raspberries, taking on the name, then, of the fruit substitution.

ORANGE SAUCE

zest and juice of 2 oranges
½ cup brandy
1 cup currant jelly

½ cup Grand Marnier (or other orange liqueur)

- Blanch the orange zest in the brandy for 3 minutes. Drain, discarding the brandy, and set the zest aside.
- Simmer the orange juice and currant jelly, until reduced by half. Remove from the fire. Add the Grand Marnier and zest, and blend thoroughly. Set aside, keeping warm until ready to serve.

ORANGE-BOURBON SAUCE

1 cup brown sugar
2 tablespoons unsalted butter

juice and zest of 1 orange
¼ cup bourbon

- Heat the brown sugar and butter, until the sugar is dissolved. Add the orange juice and zest, and blend well. Add the bourbon, blend, bring to a simmer, and remove from the fire.

PEACH-CARAMEL SAUCE

1 ripe medium peach,
  peeled, pitted, and puréed
¾ cup sugar
¼ cup water

½ cup heavy cream
2 teaspoons lemon juice
⅛ teaspoon vanilla extract

- Cook the sugar and water in a heavy-gauge saucepan, until it turns a light golden brown (8–10 minutes).

- Remove from the heat, then carefully and quickly stir in the heavy cream, peach purée, lemon juice, and vanilla. Set aside, and serve warm with poached peaches and/or ice cream.

𝒫INEAPPLE SAUCE

1 cup pineapple juice
1½ cups fresh pineapple, finely chopped

¼ cup sugar
½ cup water

- Simmer all the ingredients, stirring frequently, until reduced by one-third. Purée in a food processor, and serve hot over ice cream, or with any dish that would accommodate the flavor of pineapple.

ℛASPBERRY SAUCE

2 cups fresh (or frozen) raspberries
3 tablespoons sugar
1 tablespoon lemon juice

½ teaspoon cornstarch, dissolved in 1 tablespoon Kirsch

- Purée the raspberries in a food processor. Press through a sieve, discarding the seeds.
- Simmer the raspberry purée, sugar, and lemon juice for 10 minutes. Add the cornstarch dissolved in the Kirsch. Blend in and stir continuously, and simmer for 1 minute. Set aside until ready to serve.

ℛHUBARB SAUCE

½ pound fresh rhubarb, washed, trimmed, and roughly chopped

½ cup sugar
¼ cup Kirsch

- Simmer the ingredients in a saucepan, covered, for 5 minutes. Uncover, and continue simmering about another 8 minutes, or until very tender.
- Remove to a food processor, and purée. Strain through a sieve. Serve over any seasonal fresh fruit.

STRAWBERRY SAUCE

This sauce accompanies "Strawberry Mille-feuille," as seen in *The Pillar House Cookbook*.

If available, substitute 1½ cups fresh strawberries, rinsed, stemmed, and roughly chopped.

12 ounces frozen strawberries

1 tablespoon sugar
¼ cup kirsch

- Bring the strawberries and sugar to a boil in a small saucepan, and simmer until the sugar is dissolved. Remove to a food processor along with the kirsch, and purée. Strain through a sieve, and set aside.

CHAPTER 16

SAUCE ARABESQUES

*V*anessi's was a "Joe's style" restaurant in North Beach, San Francisco's Italian district. In San Francisco, "Joe's style" meant an open kitchen, situated right in the dining room, with seating at a counter that ran parallel to the open cooking range. Though both the style and size of the food servings was a kind of "refined peasant style," Vanessi's was the classiest of the genre, complete with Maître D' and wait staff dressed in tuxedos, and a distinctively elegant ambiance. I occasionally dined at that counter, taking in all of the activity, including the "dance" between the counter and the production range.

Tani, a native of Japan, was one of the performers behind the range during the night shift, and he would stop and chat with me briefly when there was a lull in the action. He had worked in Marseilles and the Orient, and we discussed all manner of things of a culinary nature. Tani was both knowledgeable and amiable, and he often shared a colorful proverb with me as we chatted in between kitchen orders. "Ordering . . . one calamari sauté, two veal doré!" Tani would pause to hear the order, then turn to me, and say, " 'Our lives are not in the hands of our Gods, but in the hands of our cooks.' Lin Yutang said that, but these waiters don't understand. They just bark their orders, expect us to push a button, and voilà, instant gourmet." Then he would ease back over to the cooking range, and begin preparing the order.

———————————— • ————————————

Vanessi's ceased operation at its original site in 1989, after nearly a half century of operation. A second site still remains, located on Nob Hill, San Francisco. Tani moved to Hawaii, where he opened his own restaurant.

—————————————————————

DEVELOPMENT OF A CHEF'S ARTISTRY

My interaction with Tani was an unchoreographed experience that led to important philosophical principles. From my conversations with him, I formulated an understanding that professional cooks could be measured on a scale that indicated varying degrees of artistic and mechanical tendencies. The artists are at one end of that scale, immersed in the creative possibilities of their transient medium and disdainful of the demands of day-after-day rote production; the mechanics are at the opposite end of the scale, maintaining a detachment from their work, thriving in the structure of continuous rote production. There is a little of each in every culinary practitioner, and both qualities are important in their own way. The artists are important for all the same reasons that art is an important form of expression, while the mechanics are essential in making restaurants work in the real, and demanding, world of restaurant business. The ideal, then, would be to build a restaurant around a kitchen brigade of professionals who relish the mechanical side of things, orchestrated by a knowledgeable chef who understands the creative side of designing a menu.

Tani seemed to represent the optimum balance of the two qualities. From our discussions, I knew he had the experience and knowledge to be profoundly creative, but in this particular setting, his work demanded a cadence of consistency and reliability, and he fulfilled that responsibility. At Vanessi's, he was the quintessential mechanic—always even-tempered, and calm, and very consistent in the dishes he prepared. He moved behind the range with self-assurance and ease, without ever raising his voice, without abrupt movements, always cool and calm.

At the other end of the spectrum was Luc Brondel, former chef-instructor at the Culinary Institute of America, and veteran of some of New York's most celebrated restaurants, circa 1960. As a student, I remember watching him stand in front of a reach-in box (a standing refrigerator), and noticed that his head would tip back while standing in front of the open door. When I later examined the inside of that reach-in to figure out why his head rotated back so far, I noticed that there was an open bottle of red wine from a banquet the night before.

An artist perceives his larder (the walk-in refrigerator) as a palate; the raw foodstuffs are paints; and the serviceware are the canvas. Artists of a culinary nature have the capacity to be temperamental, moody, sometimes arrogant, self-abusive, and occasionally unpleasant to the people around them. I was never exposed to the negative side of Brondel's personality, and always knew him as a highly creative—if maudlin—personality with a heart of gold. But Luc Brondel was definitely an artist. During the second year of school, I had the opportunity to visit his home, and some of Brondel's colleagues would also visit. They would all sit around the kitchen table, drinking wine, and discussing the paradoxes of human existence, intertwined with tales of past culinary experiences. After a while, Luc would start reciting some of his poetry. He'd get teary-eyed, and everyone would nod their heads in agreement, and then someone would fill the wine glasses once again. I just listened quietly, absorbing all the nuances and emotional displays, and considered the conclusions the "old timers" reached. The one principle that bounced around my conscious thought for the longest time was what seemed to be the ultimate dilemma for the culinary artist—working in such a transient medium. Could that explain why these fascinating characters were on occasion so maudlin and cynical about the business? Whatever the answer, I knew that I needed to watch my step, or I might very well end up in the same kind of predicament that these chef-artistes seemed to dwell in. In the back of my mind, I knew I was witnessing a hazard of the profession.

In 1980, I conceived a project to combine the *art* in *the art of cooking*, and compile it in written form. Six years later, *Edible Art* was published, a text on the subject of garnishing. Since then, the *art* in the *culinary arts* has continued to be of significant interest to me. I have found it to be less of a dilemma to solve or a question to answer, and more of a concept to understand. Trying to discover the art in cookery was like trying to describe the color blue to someone who had never seen the color blue. It seemed to be there—after all it is called culinary *art*—yet it was critically dependent on so many other elements. Like the Tao in Taoism, it was elusive and intangible, yet everywhere at the same time. Lao Tze wrote that the Tao that can be seen, and heard, and felt, was not the true Tao. The moment it is identified or grasped, it is gone.

Philosophical meditations aside, there is an important axiom which runs through all culinary undertakings, whether perceived as art, sustenance, or the trade one works in. Henri Charpentier recounted these words from his mentor, Jean Camous, in his 1934 autobiography, *Life à la Henri*: "A man should always see what he eats. It is true that the eyes and the nose give the signals for the release of the chemical fluids which are secreted in the body by an intelligence of tremendous significance in the philosophy of a chef—the intelligence of the inner man." That message is perpetually reiterated in every culinary educational curriculum: "People eat with their eyes first."

For the student of the culinary trade, this was simply a guiding dictum to learn how to keep the green vegetables green, and to compose and assemble the food offerings on a plate in a visually pleasing manner, so that the dining patron's first contact with their dinner (visual) would be of a positive nature. (If it looks good, it follows that it will taste good.) Pretty basic stuff. After grasping that basic precept, we can expand further on the elements of artistic creativity. A garnish became a possible addition, yet today, a garnish added just for the sake of including a garnish is not sufficient cause for its use. What are now termed "nonintegral" garnishes reflect the disfavor shed on mock flowers such as a tomato rose, a strand of lemon zest tied into a clever knot, or a scallion cut to resemble a brush. Garnishes have their place, but they must be integrated, harmonizing with the dish they embellish. So the tomato rose has been replaced with a side dish of tomato fondue (diced fresh tomatoes simmered with shallot, herbs, and Armagnac); a lemon uniquely sculpted, serving as a source of seasoning (lemon juice); and a small timbale of scallion royale (very chic).

Sauce Painting

Enter *sauce painting*, the arrangement of two or more sauces on a serving dish, manipulated into a visually stunning design, upon which a prepared edible is placed. It is not clear who "invented" this practice, or how it evolved into common culinary practice. There are some classic motifs employed in pastry and confection work, indicating a crossover influence. And no doubt the practice of sauce painting has been employed simultaneously by many a chef-artiste, representing a sort of collective evolutionary shift. But however it evolved, for the chef-artiste, sauce painting offered a simple and easy way to bring an element of art to this most transient of mediums. It represented a juncture where art and cuisine truly met, in a practical, direct, and stunning manner. No matter that a dining guest perceived food solely as fuel for their body; no matter that a restaurant patron chose to eat solely as a perfunctory activity, something that took them away from their true work of the day; and no matter what the *raison d'être* a culinary practitioner embraced in his or her work. Sauce painting seemed to be the sole juncture of the mechanical and the artistic, the purest and most basic presence of art within the craft of cooking. This was a brief moment when, with very little ado, the culinary craft rose to the level culinary art.

Sauce painting is neither new, nor the latest hot trend. It has been around for some time. But when seen in a cookbook or magazine, there is virtually no description of how to execute it. One can imagine how frustrating this must be to those unfamiliar with the technique. And there has never been a proper term applied to the technique that reflects its elegance. At some point, the artist in the author, seeking a word to describe the pure moment of the intersection of art and cooking, arrived at *Arabesque*, from the Italian *arabesco*, meaning "done in the Arabic fashion." It is defined as: "An ornate design of intertwined floral, foliate, and geometric figures."

GUIDELINES FOR CREATING ARABESQUES

Not all culinary practitioners subscribe to these theories of art and its intersection with cooking, and not all include this technique in their repertoire (see Foreword by Jasper White). But I believe that there is a place for arabesques, when used judiciously, and with good taste. The following is a guide for following such an approach.

The Sauces

Viscosity. The thickness of sauces used to execute an arabesque must be similar. If one sauce varies significantly in its thickness from the other, they will not bind properly. An example is a cornstarch-thickened red wine sauce, which is made with *Poire au Poivre*. I once attempted to use sweetened whipped cream as the opposing decorative sauce, and found myself faced with disaster. The whipped cream is so light, thickened by an air emulsion, that it would not adhere to the base sauce. Fortunately, I had some sour cream, which had sufficient fat content, and resolved the crisis.

Heat. Nothing is worse than hot food served lukewarm. Be certain that the serving plate, the sauce, and the food placed on the plate arrive at the dining guest's table at the appropriate temperature. (The reverse applies for cold foods.) A squeeze bottle, filled with a hot sauce, should be maintained at a temperature of approximately 140°.

Flow. Be sure that a sauce is free from any solid particles that might block the tip, and prevent the smooth flow of sauce from the bottle. The moment of service is not the time to stop production to restrain and reheat sauces.

The Test. Just as a professional culinarian sprinkles a small amount of salt, or pepper, or spice into his palm before applying it to a dish, it is important to test the flow of a sauce from a bottle before it is applied to a serving plate. Rhythm is important in culinary production, and a proper mise-en-place includes being prepared for all unexpected problems. Squirt a little of the sauce onto a small plate to determine the flow of the sauce.

The Squeeze Bottle. Flexible, clear plastic squeeze bottles can be found in hobby and art supply shops, and in some restaurant

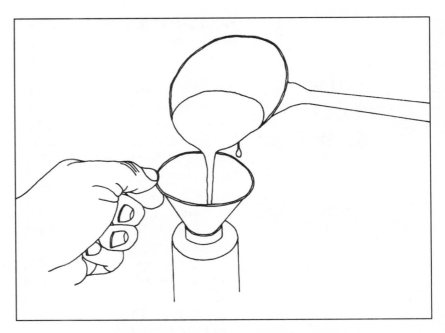

Filling a plastic squeeze bottle with a sauce.

supply houses. Be sure to clean all bottles thoroughly with warm soapy water when new, dry them thoroughly, and store them in a safe location. Maintaining cleanliness and dryness at all times is essential. A long, thin wire brush is the best tool for cleaning.

Since the upper tip of a new bottle requires cutting, experiment with cuts at several different levels, to get a feel for how a sauce will propel from the bottle. It is recommended to maintain an ample supply of several different bottles, with several different openings at the tip, to suit a given design.

The Design

This is a matter of personal preference. I personally do not subscribe to realism in culinary artistry—neither hard-boiled egg frogs, smiling faces, nor sauce paintings of miniature flower baskets on the side of a plate. I prefer the light, undefinable flourish. There is a time element to consider as well. Even in upscale restaurant houses, where an evening's service may not exceed 100 guests, time, *and timing*, are often critical affairs. Stopping to create intricate designs is time consuming, and, in my opinion, missing the point of the exercise. Sauces should be applied with a swift, simple flourish, with as little ado as possible. Design the basic application of sauces in an arabesque *before*

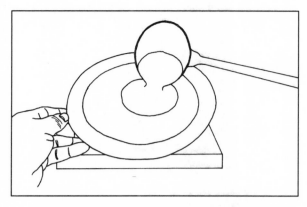

Ladling the primary sauce onto a serving plate.

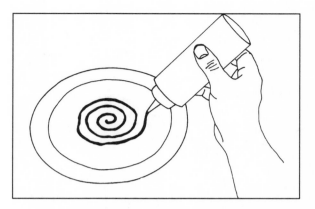

Laying down a spiral, the first step to create a spider web.

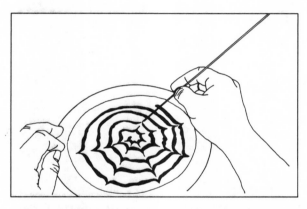

Running a toothpick in radial lines, through the spiral, from the center out.

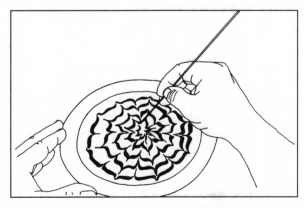

Running the toothpick radially, in the opposite direction, toward the center. (Photo: Boiled Lobster, Bello Giorno)

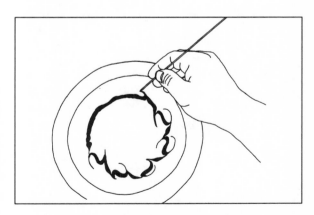

Looped wheel. (Photo: Spinach Ravioli, Crimson Sauce)

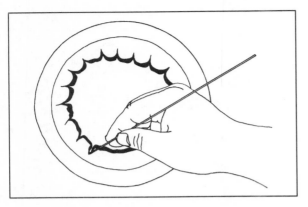

Single-spoked wheel.

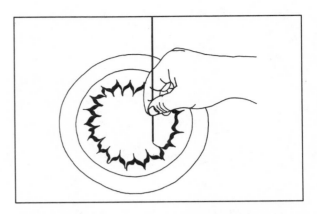

Double-spoked wheel. (Photo: Poached Chicken Ivory)

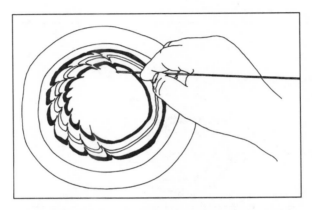

Triple-spoked wheel. (Photo: Poached Shrimp with Scallop Mousse, Lobster Sauce)

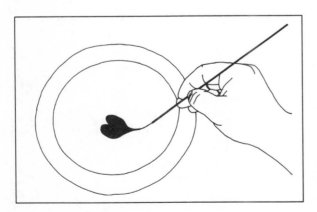

First step to create a floating wing.

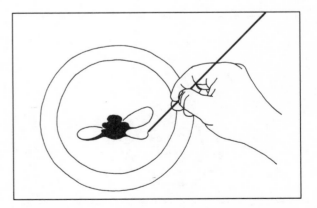

The finished floating wing. (Photo: Grilled Tuna Steak, Black Bean Sauce)

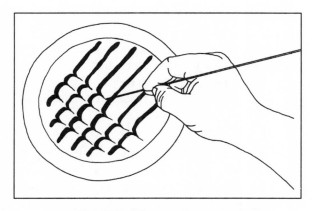

Parallel web. (Photo: Poire aux Poivre)

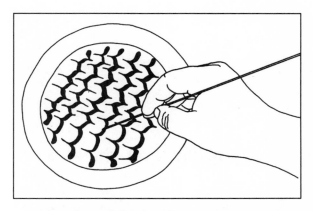

Reversed parallel web. (Photo: Beggar's Purses, Avocado Sauce)

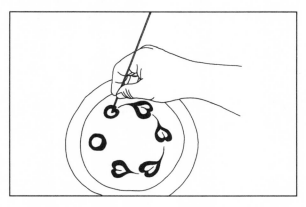

Hollow leaf border.

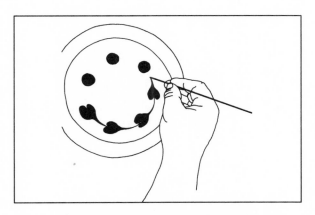

Leaf border. (Photo: Grilled Beef Medallions, Henri IV)

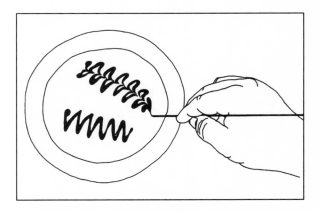

Zig-zag. (Photo: Crab Cakes, Le Central)

service, but execute them in a spontaneous, impromptu, and effortless gesture. Avoid giving a dining patron the feeling that the chef has been hovering over the plate for endless minutes, touching, and arranging, and *playing* with his or her *work of art*. Even the most dedicated culinary artists strive to make their creations visually appealing so that the recipient *wants* to consume it.

Application The when and where of applying an arabesque is significant, in the same way that a writer attempts to write with as few words as possible (brevity). Use arabesques on an occasional item—perhaps a signature dessert printed on the menu, and one or two others among an evening's specials (plat du jour). Overwhelming a kitchen's offerings not only complicates the service organization, but may also overwhelm the clientele, to the point that they become desensitized to the whole genre. Mies Van der Rohe's dictum pertaining to architecture is applicable to cookery: "Less is more."

Appendix A THE BASIC CUTS

Potatoes—Les Pommes de Terre

English	French	Description/Dimension
straw	paille	a thin ribbon
chip	chip	a thin uniform slice
waffle	gaufrette	a crisscrossed slice
matchstick	allumette	$\frac{1}{8}$" × $\frac{1}{8}$" × $1\frac{1}{2}$"
french fries	frite	$\frac{1}{4}$" × $\frac{1}{4}$" × 2–$2\frac{1}{2}$"
steak fries	pont-neuf	$\frac{1}{2}$" × $\frac{1}{2}$" × 3"
medium dice	Parmentier	$\frac{1}{3}$–$\frac{1}{2}$" square
large dice	carré	$\frac{1}{2}$–$\frac{3}{4}$" square
pea	pois	tiny ball or sphere
noisette	noisette	a small ball or sphere
Parisienne	Parisienne	a large ball or sphere

Turned	Tourné	(7-sided oval)
small	château	$1\frac{1}{2}$" long
medium	nature	2–$2\frac{1}{2}$" long
large	fondante	$2\frac{1}{2}$–3" long

Vegetables—Les Legumes

English	French	Description/Dimension
small dice	brunoise	$\frac{1}{8}$" square
medium dice	macedoine*	$\frac{1}{4}$" square
large dice	jardinière	$\frac{1}{3}$–$\frac{1}{2}$" square
julienne	julienne	any variety of small stick, roughly $\frac{1}{8}$" × $\frac{1}{8}$" × 1–2"
large julienne	batonnet	$\frac{1}{4}$" × $\frac{1}{4}$" × 2–$2\frac{1}{2}$"
rough cut	paysanne	a rough, unequal cut
thin sliced	Vichy	a thin circular slice
turned	tourné	a 7-sided oval, 1–$1\frac{1}{2}$" long
shredded	chiffonade	a thin ribbon, usually for green leafy vegetables

Culinary practitioners will forever be debating the true sizes of many of the names of various cut potatoes and vegetables. For this reason, this compendium should be used *only* as a guide.

*An historical reference to Macedonia, the area comprised of Persia, Greece, and Egypt, ruled over by Alexander the Great from 336 to 323 B.C. Common usage: medley or mixture.

Appendix B TOOLS AND SMALLWARES

There is no one single metal which makes the best cookware material. The best cookware combines materials to make the best use of each, but there remain advantages and disadvantages to all varieties. The most important guideline to follow, whatever metal you work with, is to use heavy-gauge cookware. Lightweight metals do not distribute heat evenly, and will leave food burned on the bottom.

Copper is the preferred choice among many professionals, based on its exceptional ability to conduct and distribute heat. And although a minute amount of copper is essential for good health, excessive amounts can be harmful. For this reason, copper cookware has always been plated on the interior with tin. The downside of this is that both copper and tin are expensive. And as the tin wears away, retinning further increases the cost of maintenance. Copper is available with other metals on its interior, such as stainless steel, aluminum, and nickel, and though these do not require replating, they are also expensive. And finally, copper requires continuous polishing to maintain a shiny, tarnish-free exterior. Though this has no effect on its cooking capabilities, the constant polishing may be a labor cost consideration.

Aluminum is also an excellent conductor of heat, second only to copper. It is the most commonly used metal in professional kitchens, and because it is the most abundant metal found in the earth's crust, it is also relatively inexpensive. On the downside, aluminum will discolor light-colored sauces, a clear indicator that aluminum will leach into foods that are prepared in it. And in recent years, there has been speculation of a correlation between high levels of aluminum and Alzheimer's disease. The truth of this hypothesis is still being debated. It is important to point out that we are exposed to aluminum from many sources, not just cookware. Aluminum is found in pickles and preserves, salt, baking powder, baking mixes, nondairy products, processed cheese, aspirin, and deodorant. Common sense would dictate steps to avoid excessive exposure to any metal compound, even if its harmful effects on human health are only speculative. Since aluminum is so cost effective, the best solution is to purchase the dark, anodized variety (Calphalon is probably the most popular brand). Anodized aluminum is ordinary aluminum, exposed to an acid solution, making it virtually impervious to acids in food. Another solution is to purchase cookware with aluminum on the exterior, and nickel or stainless steel on the interior. Stainless steel, though expensive, and a slow conductor of heat, will not react with any foods, while the aluminum exterior promotes the transfer of heat.

Cast iron is also held in high esteem, not just because it is inexpensive, but because its thickness promotes slow, even cooking. Any iron that leaches into food is considered a positive addition to the diet, although there is some debate over how well the body absorbs it in this form. Iron must, however, be kept dry, since it rusts easily. And die-hard enthusiasts also maintain that it should never be washed, instead wiped out with a clean cloth, using only salt as an abrasive when needed.

Ceramic and enameled iron cookware manufactured in the United States is generally considered safe, though imports from outside the United States may be improperly glazed, which when exposed to the acid in food leaches lead, in some cases as high as 1,000 times the FDA-recommended level.

Appendix C SOURCES

For information on specialty food items that may be difficult to obtain, contact the following organizations:

Carolyn Collins Caviar, P.O. Box 662, Crystal Lake, Illinois 60014; (312) 226-0342. Producer of a line of North American caviars. Carolyn Collins, contact person.

Clear Creek Distillery, 1430 Northwest 23rd Avenue, Portland, Oregon 97210; (503) 248-9470. Producer of an exceptional pear brandy. Stephen R. McCarthy, contact person.

Commonwealth Enterprises, Ltd., P.O. Box 49, Airport Road, Mongaup Valley, New York 12762; (914) 583-6630. One of the first United States producers of duck foie gras and related products. Send for catalog.

Epicurean International, P.O. Box 13242, Berkeley, California 94701; (510) 268-0209. For catalogue on hard-to-obtain Asian products. Seth Jacobsen, contact person.

Kimberly Wine Vinegar Works, 290 Pierce Street, Daly City, California 94015; (415) 755-0306. Produces several varieties of exceptionally fine vinegars and olive oils. Ruth Robinson, contact person.

Laura Chenel's Chevre, 1550 Ridley Avenue, Santa Rosa, California 95401; (707) 575-8888. Producer of an exceptionally fine line of goat cheeses. Laura Chenel, contact person.

Maytag Dairy Farms, Inc., Box 806, Newton, Iowa 50208; (800) 258-2437. Call for the closest retail source of "Maytag Blue" cheese.

The Oregon Caneberry Commission, 712 NW 4th Street, Corvalis, Oregon 97330; (503) 758-4043. For information on, and recipes using blackberries, boysenberries, caneberries, loganberries, marionberries, and their availability in various forms. Jan Marie Schroeder, contact person.

Oregon Department of Argriculture, 121 SW Salmon Street, Suite 240, Portland, Oregon 97204-2987; (503) 229-6734. For information on many unique products, including Oregon white truffles, write for catalog.

Russell Harrington Cutlery, Inc., 44 Green River, Southbridge, Massachusetts 01550; (508) 765-0201. Write for catalogs and information on how to purchase cutlery and tools.

Appendix D RECIPES FOR DISHES SHOWN IN PHOTOGRAPHY

Note to the reader:

1. The following recipes are designed to yield four servings
2. Crème fraîche is a more complex-flavored form of sour cream. If time or circumstances make it unavailable, sour cream will work in its place
3. Where meat glaze (glace de viande) is called for, the ideal method is to use a flavor of glaze which matches the dish it accompanies. In actual practice however, veal or chicken glaze are often used across the board, since their flavors are relatively neutral. Saucier's choice applies.
4. When a sauce, glaze, or crème fraîche is called for in creating an arabesque, they need to be kept hot. To accomplish this, after a sauce is transferred to plastic squeeze bottles, it should be placed into a small pot of barely simmering water (double boiler) until ready to use.

APPETIZERS

*B*EGGAR'S PURSES, AVOCADO SAUCE

For the Avocado Sauce

1 shallot, minced
1 mushroom, finely chopped
3 cups fish stock
1 cup mussel (or bottled clam) juice
½ cup dry white wine
½ cup dry vermouth

2 cups heavy cream
½ pound unsalted butter, cut into ½-inch cubes
salt and white pepper to taste
2 ripe Haas avocados, peeled and pitted

- Simmer the shallot, mushroom, stock, and wine until reduced by half. Add the cream, and reduce by half again. Mount with the butter, and season with salt and pepper.
- Purée the sauce with the avocado in a blender. Strain, then return to the saucepan, and bring back to a simmer. Remove from the heat, cover, and keep warm until ready to serve.

The Mayonnaise for the Design

1 cup mayonnaise
2 tablespoons tomato paste

fish stock or clam juice, as needed

- Blend all ingredients together into a smooth even sauce. Transfer to a plastic squeeze bottle, and place into a double boiler to warm.

For the Purses

8 large wonton skins (or 8 6-inch square sheets of fresh pasta dough)
8 fresh oysters, poached in their own liqueur and a

little white wine, and drained
8 tablespoons crème fraîche
8 teaspoons Beluga caviar
8 long thin strips of scallion, blanched

- Cook the wonton skins in boiling salted water for 2 minutes. Drain and set aside.
- Place a poached oyster in the center of each wonton. Top with a tablespoon of crème fraîche and a teaspoon of caviar. Pull the edges of the wonton up into a little bundle, and tie together with the scallion. Heat the purses in a covered steamer for 2 or 3 minutes. Pour 4 ounces of sauce onto each of four serving plates, and execute a sauce arabesque with the tomato mayonnaise. Place two purses on each plate, and serve.

. . . .

CRÈME FRAÎCHE

2 cups heavy cream
½ cup buttermilk
½ cup sour cream

½ cup yogurt
¼ teaspoon salt

- Combine all the ingredients in a clean saucepan, and while stirring continuously, bring to a temperature of 100°F.
- Place into a clean stainless steel bowl, cover, and set into an unlit gas oven overnight (the pilot light supplies enough warmth to permit the buttermilk, sour cream, and yogurt cultures to thrive).

- Refrigerate for 24 hours. Carefully remove thickened top part (this is the crème fraîche), and discard any liquid left at the bottom. Cover and refrigerate until ready to use.

Sautéed Scallops, three bell pepper purées

For the Sauce

2 yellow bell peppers, cut into 8 pieces each
2 green bell peppers, cut into 8 pieces each
2 red bell peppers, cut into 8 pieces each
3 shallots, minced
3 garlic cloves, crushed
¾ teaspoon fresh thyme leaves
9 tablespoons olive oil
3 cups fish stock or clam juice
salt and white pepper as needed

- Sauté the yellow pepper, and one-third of the shallot, garlic, and thyme in one-third of the olive oil, over a medium flame, for about 5 minutes.
- Add one-third of the stock, season with salt and pepper, and continue cooking another 5 minutes.
- Remove to a food processor, purée, and strain. Set aside, keeping warm until ready to serve.
- Repeat the same procedure with the green and red bell peppers, keeping all three sauces separate.

For the Scallops

1½ pounds fresh sea scallops
flour, oil, salt, and pepper as needed

- Season the scallops lightly with the salt and pepper, and dust lightly with flour. Heat the oil in a sauté pan, and sauté the scallops about 2 minutes on each side.
- Ladle a portion of each of the three sauces onto a serving plate, and run a toothpick through it to create an arabesque. Place the scallops in the center and serve.

*L*OBSTER STRUDEL, TOMATO-ARMAGNAC SAUCE

For the Strudel

2 tablespoons unsalted butter
1 garlic clove, pressed
½ cup dry bread crumbs
1 box phyllo dough
¼ cup clarified butter
1 pound lobster meat, cut
  into medium dice
½ pound fresh spinach,
  rinsed, blanched 10
seconds in boiling salted
  water, then squeezed dry
6 ounces chèvre (goat
  cheese)
1 tablespoon fresh basil
  leaves, minced
pinch of salt
pinch of white pepper
1 egg, beaten with ¼ cup
  water

- Sauté the bread crumbs and garlic in the butter, until golden brown. Set aside.
- Preheat oven to 350°F.
- Carefully separate two sheets of phyllo dough, and place onto the center of a clean apron. Brush lightly with the clarified butter. Repeat this step three times (8 leaves total).
- Sprinkle the bread crumbs evenly over the dough. Spread the lobster, spinach, cheese, and seasonings in a 4-inch-wide strip along a short side of the dough, leaving it an inch or more from the edges. Carefully roll the dough around the filling, into a long cylinder. Pinch or close the ends, then brush the cylinder with beaten egg. Bake for 20–30 minutes, or until the pastry is golden brown.

For the Sauce

2 tablespoons olive oil
1 shallot, minced
½ cup + 2 tablespoons
  Armagnac
1 cup ripe tomatoes, peeled,
  seeded, and cut into
  medium dice
1 teaspoon fresh thyme
  leaves
1 teaspoon fresh basil leaves,
  minced
1 cup strong fish stock
salt and pepper to taste

- Sweat the shallot in the oil for 5 minutes. Add the Armagnac, tomatoes, herbs, and fish stock, and simmer until reduced by half. Purée this sauce by running it through the fine plate of a food mill, or in a food processor. Add 2 tablespoons Armagnac, and adjust seasoning. Serve under one or two slices of strudel.

CRAB CAKES, LE CENTRAL

For the Crab Cakes

1 shallot, minced
2 tablespoons unsalted
 butter
¼ cup Pernod
1 cup fresh white bread
 crumbs
½ cup sour cream
1 teaspoon fresh dill,
 minced

½ teaspoon salt
¼ teaspoon white pepper
1 pound fresh crabmeat,
 shredded
4 large eggs, lightly beaten
4 cups fresh white bread
 crumbs
2 cups vegetable oil

- Sauté the shallots in the butter. Add the Pernod, and reduce by half. Add the bread crumbs, sour cream, dill, salt, and pepper, blend in, and remove from the fire.
- Add the crab and eggs, and blend in. Shape into 4 individual oval or round patties, then roll in the bread crumbs, pressing them on firmly. Cover and refrigerate 1 hour.
- Preheat oven to 250°F.
- Pour 1 inch of vegetable oil in a cast iron skillet or heavy-gauge saucepan, and heat to 365°F. Fry the cakes until golden brown on each side. Transfer to absorbent paper, and place in the oven for no more than 15 minutes.

For the Sauce

2 shallots, minced
1½ cups dry white wine
¼ cup white wine (or
 champagne) vinegar

¾ pound unsalted butter,
 cut into ½-inch cubes
salt and white pepper to taste

- Simmer the shallots, wine, and vinegar until reduced by two-thirds.

- Mount with the butter, incorporating into the reduction by stirring continuously until fully emulsified. Season to taste with salt and white pepper, and set aside, keeping warm.

For the Design

½ cup veal or chicken glaze, thinned with a little water, brought to a boil, and transferred to a plastic squeeze bottle.

- Ladle about 3 ounces of the beurre blanc onto a serving plate. Squirt two lines of veal glaze onto the beurre blanc, and run a toothpick through it from side to side. Place a crab cake in the center, garnish with parsley, and serve.

SPINACH RAVIOLI, CRIMSON SAUCE

1½ pounds fresh or frozen spinach ravioli
2 medium beets, scrubbed
1 shallot, minced

1 bay leaf
1 cup dry white wine
1 cup chicken stock
salt and white pepper to taste

For the Design

½ cup crème fraîche

- Preheat oven to 375°F.
- Roast the beets for 40 minutes. Allow to cool. Peel, then grate (by hand or in a food processor), and set aside.
- Simmer the shallot, bay leaf, and white wine, until reduced by three-fourths. Add the stock and grated beets, and simmer until reduced by half. Remove to a blender or food processor, and purée. Strain, and season to taste.
- Beat the crème fraîche until smooth, and transfer to a plastic squeeze bottle.
- Ladle the Crimson Sauce onto a serving plate, and squirt a line of crème fraîche around the outside edge of the sauce. Create an arabesque, then place four or five raviolis in the center.

BEER-BATTERED SHRIMP, APRICOT-GINGER COULIS

For the Coulis

6 fresh ripe apricots, peeled
    and pitted (or 12 dried
    apricot halves, rehydrated
    in boiling water, and
    drained)
1 tablespoon gingerroot,
    grated

¼ cup fish fumet
¼ teaspoon Tabasco
    sauce
¼ teaspoon white
    Worcestershire sauce

- Purée all the ingredients in a food processor, then cover and refrigerate until ready to use.

For the Shrimp

1 quart peanut oil
2 12-ounce bottles dark
    beer
½ teaspoon salt
1 cup flour
3 large egg whites, beaten to
    a soft peak

16 U-12 shrimp, peeled,
    deveined, and tails intact
flour as needed
4 large sprigs flat leaf
    parsley

- Preheat oven to 300°F. Heat the peanut oil in a cast-iron or heavy gauge pan, to 360°F.
- Pour the beer and salt into a mixing bowl. Add the flour and beat until smooth. Add the egg whites, and beat gently until incorporated.
- Dust the shrimp lightly with the flour, then dip them into the batter. Allow excess batter to drip off.
- Carefully place the shrimp, 4 at a time, into the hot oil. Fry until golden brown. Set onto absorbent paper, and place into the oven to keep warm. Repeat until all the shrimp have been fried.
- Serve 4 shrimp per person, accompanied by the coulis, and garnished with the parsley.

DUNGENESS CRAB WONTONS, PLUM CHUTNEY

For the Chutney

1 orange, peeled, segments
  removed from membrane
¼ cup fresh-squeezed
  orange juice
2 tablespoons sugar
1 tablespoon gingerroot,
  grated
1 tablespoon dried currants

¼ teaspoon ground cloves
1 tablespoon water
1 teaspoon curry powder
¾ pound Santa Rosa (or
  other variety) freestone
  plums, pitted, and cut into
  ½-inch cubes

- Place all of the ingredients except the plums into a small saucepan. Bring to a boil, and simmer 30 minutes. Add the plums, and simmer for another 15–30 minutes, or until the plums are soft. Cool, cover, and refrigerate.

For the Wontons

½ cup heavy cream
½ tablespoon unsalted butter
1 tablespoon minced onion
2 tablespoons minced celery
½ pound Dungeness crab
  meat, shredded

1 tablespoon cilantro, minced
¼ teaspoon soy sauce
pinch of black pepper
20 4-by-4-inch wonton skins
vegetable oil for deep frying
4 sprigs flat leaf parsley

- Simmer the cream in a small saucepan, until reduced by half.
- Sauté the onion and celery in the butter for 3–4 minutes. Combine the onion, celery, cream, crabmeat, cilantro, soy sauce, and pepper in a bowl, and blend thoroughly.
- Preheat oven to 300°F.
- Draw an imaginary line across a wonton skin, from opposing corners. Place a small bit of filling in the center, to one side of the imaginary line. Dip a small brush in water, and moisten the edges of the skin. Fold the wonton skin over at the imaginary line, and press the edges together.

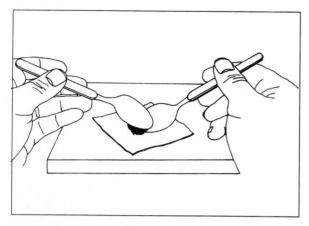

1. *Spooning the filling onto the wonton wrapper.*

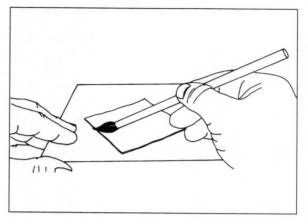

2. *Brushing the edges of the wonton with water.*

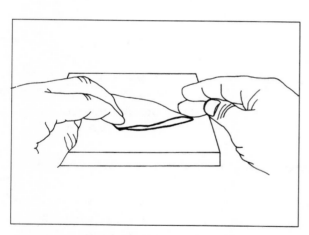

3. *Pressing the edges of the wonton together.*

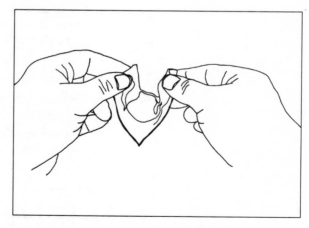

4. *Pressing together two opposing corners of the filled wonton.*

- Moisten the two corners at the ends of the fold, turn them up, and press together. Repeat this procedure with all the wonton skins.
- Pour two inches of vegetable oil into a cast iron skillet or heavy-gauge pan, and heat to 360°F. Deep fry until golden brown. Place on absorbent paper, then into the warm oven. Serve 5 per person, with the chutney, and garnished with flat leaf parsley.

𝒫OACHED SHRIMP WITH SCALLOP MOUSSE, LOBSTER SAUCE

For the Mousse

1 pound fresh sea scallops
½ pound fresh sole fillet, cut into 1-inch pieces
3 eggs
1 pint heavy cream

salt and white pepper
8 U-10 shrimp, shelled, deveined, tails left intact

- Place the scallops and sole into a food processor, and purée coarsely, using the pulse switch. Add the eggs, a little salt and pepper, and while pouring the cream in slowly, purée, again using the pulse switch. Scrape down the sides of the processor, and pulse again, until the mixture is smooth.
- Test the mousse by poaching a small tablespoonful of it in a mixture of simmering water and white wine. Taste the mousse for seasoning, and add additional salt and pepper if required.
- Dip a tablespoon into cold water, and scoop out a heaping spoonful of the mousse (about ⅛ of the whole amount). Wet the palm of the opposite hand, and shape the mousse into a smooth oval. Carefully wrap a shrimp around the mousse, so that the tail sits on top of the oval, and the head of the shrimp wraps around and under the bottom of the oval. Gently press the shrimp into the mousse, then set on a plate, and refrigerate. Repeat with remaining shrimp.

For the Lobster Sauce

1 shallot, minced
1 cup fish stock
¼ cup oyster liqueur
¼ cup mushrooms, finely
    chopped
2 cups fish velouté
2 tablespoons tomato paste

1 egg yolk
¼ cup heavy cream
3 tablespoons lobster butter,
    cut into ½-inch cubes
¼ cup lobster meat, medium
    dice (optional)

- Simmer the shallot, stock, oyster liqueur, and mushrooms, until reduced by three-fourths. Add the fish velouté and tomato paste, and simmer until suitable thickness is achieved.
- Briefly beat the egg and cream in a small bowl. Slowly add the velouté, while beating continuously. Return to the saucepan, mount with the lobster butter, and add the lobster meat. Bring just barely to a boil and set aside, keeping warm.

For the Design

1½ cups chicken or fish
    glaze, thinned with a little
    water, brought to a boil,
    and transferred to a
    plastic bottle

1 cup crème fraîche, stirred
    until smooth, and
    transferred to a plastic
    squeeze bottle

- Fill a sauce pan, large enough to hold the eight mousse-stuffed shrimp, with a mixture of dry white wine and water. (There should be enough liquid to cover the shrimp when placed into the pan.) Bring the liquid to a simmer, place the shrimp in, cover, and poach very gently for 8 minutes. Remove the shrimp with a slotted spoon, place onto absorbent paper, and set aside, keeping warm until ready to serve.
- Ladle enough sauce onto a serving plate to cover the surface of the plate. Squirt two concentric circles of crème fraîche around the edge of the plate, about ¾ of an inch apart. Follow this with a circle of the glaze, in the space between the two lines of crème fraîche.
- Run a toothpick through these three lines, from the outside edge inward, at a slight angle. Place two of the mousses in the center of the plate, and serve.

MAIN COURSES

*S*PRING VEGETABLE RÂGOUT

2–3 pounds fresh miniature
spring vegetables,
scrubbed and trimmed
(such as artichoke hearts,
Brussels sprouts, carrots,
green peas, pearl onions,
new potatoes, patty pan
squash, string beans,
turnips, zucchini, etc.,
sufficient for 4 servings)

3 cups of chicken stock
bouquet garni (thyme,
rosemary, tarragon, and
parsley stems tied
together in a bundle)
¾ pound unsalted butter,
cut into ¼-inch cubes
salt and white pepper to taste

---•---

If baby vegetables are unavailable, a resourceful cook
can take whatever vegeta-
bles are available, and cut
them into a variety of
shapes suitable for this dish.

- Blanch each variety of vegetable, in simmering chicken
stock with bouquet garni, until al dente. Set the vegetables
aside, keeping warm.
- Simmer the chicken stock, until reduced to approximately 1
cup of liquid. Strain the stock, discarding the bouquet garni,
then return to the pan. Mount with the butter, season to
taste, then serve with the hot vegetables.

*P*OACHED CHICKEN IVORY

For the Chicken

1 2- to 2½-pound fresh
chicken
3 quarts chicken stock

1 cup dry white wine
1 bouquet garni
3 cups Suprême sauce

For the Design

½ cup veal or chicken glaze
thinned with a little
water, brought to a boil,

and transferred to a
plastic squeeze bottle

For the Garnish

1 large cucumber, peeled,
seeded, and shaped into 4
small ovals (tournées)

8 mushroom caps
2 tablespoons unsalted butter
2 tablespoons lemon juice

- Rinse the chicken well, and truss with cotton cord. Poach the chicken in the stock, wine, and bouquet garni, very gently, for 1 hour. Remove from the fire and set aside (the chicken can remain in the poaching medium to stay warm).
- Poach the cucumber tournées in some of the poaching liquid, until al dente. Remove from the fire.
- Poach the mushroom caps in the butter and lemon juice for several minutes, and set aside.
- Remove the string from the chicken, and allow the liquid to drain from the bird. Ladle the Suprême sauce onto a large serving platter. Squirt the meat glaze onto the sauce to create a design. Place the chicken in the center of the platter, top with some of the sauce, and arrange the cucumbers and mushrooms around the chicken.

GRILLED TUNA STEAK, BLACK BEAN SAUCE

2 tablespoons olive oil
1 shallot, minced
1 garlic clove, pressed
¼ cup orange juice
¼ cup grapefruit juice
2 tablespoons lime juice
2 tablespoons lemon juice

3 cups chicken stock
1 cup black beans, soaked overnight in cold water, drained, culled, and thoroughly rinsed
2 tablespoons cilantro, minced

For the Design

½ cup Dutch sauce, slightly thinned, and transferred to a plastic squeeze bottle

- Sauté the shallot and garlic in the olive oil for 3 minutes. Add the fruit juices and simmer until reduced by two-thirds. Add the stock, beans, and cilantro, and simmer covered, about 2 hours, or until the beans are very soft. (Add additional liquid during cooking, or when puréeing, if necessary.)
- Purée the sauce in a food processor, and season to taste with salt and pepper. Strain.

For the Tuna

4 6-ounce fresh tuna steaks   oil, salt, and pepper as
                                        needed

- Brush the tuna steaks with the oil, and sprinkle lightly with salt and pepper.
- Grill or broil the steaks, 4 minutes on each side.
- Ladle the Black Bean sauce onto a serving plate. Squirt a large dab of Dutch sauce onto the Black Bean sauce, and create an arabesque. Place the steaks on top, and serve.

SAUTÉED HALIBUT, ORANGE-LIME SALSA

For the Salsa

5 oranges   ½ cup red onion, cut into
5 limes   fine dice
1 tablespoon cilantro,   ½ jalapeño pepper, minced
   roughly chopped   juice of 1 lime

- Pare the oranges and limes with a sharp knife, making sure to remove all the pith. Holding the fruit over a small bowl (to catch the juice), remove the fruit segments by cutting on either side of the skin that separates them.
- Remove any seeds from the segments, add the fruit to the bowl, then squeeze the juice from the remaining pulp into the same bowl. Add the cilantro, onion, lemon juice, and jalapeño. Cover, refrigerate, and allow to marinate refrigerated overnight.

For the Halibut

4 6-ounce halibut steaks   olive oil as needed
salt and white pepper as
   needed

- Sprinkle the halibut steaks lightly with salt and pepper. Sauté in hot olive oil 4 minutes on each side, and serve with the salsa.

$\mathscr{P}$OACHED SOLE, PAN-PACIFIC

For the Sauce

2 tablespoons unsalted butter
1 shallot, minced
1 cup dry white wine
2 cups heavy cream
½ cup parsley leaves,
   roughly chopped

½ cup fresh cilantro leaves,
   roughly chopped
¾ cup shiitake mushrooms,
   cut into julienne, and
   sautéed in ¼ cup unsalted
   butter
salt and white pepper to taste

- Sauté the shallot in the butter for 4 or 5 minutes. Add the wine, and reduce by half. Add the cream, and continue to reduce, until the sauce is thick. Add the parsley and cilantro, salt and pepper, and simmer another 2 minutes.
- Purée the sauce in a blender or food processor, return to the fire, add the sautéed shiitake mushrooms, and adjust seasoning.

For the Sole

8 3–4 ounce sole fillets
salt and white pepper as
   needed

court bouillon (see Poached
   Salmon)

For the Garnish (Optional)

8 heads baby bok choy,
   poached in a little fish
   stock

4 mustard-pickled eggs
20 small flowers sculpted
   from daikon radish

- Sprinkle the sole with salt and pepper, and roll up. Poach in the court bouillon, immersed, for 6 minutes. Remove from the fire.
- Remove the sole, drain, and place on a serving plate. Ladle the Cilantro sauce over the top, arrange the bok choy and daikon flowers on the plate, and serve.

———————— • ————————

The garnish for this dish, as pictured in the color photograph, consists of bok choy, daikon flowers, and a mustard-pickled egg in the background. They are accompaniments to this dish, and their inclusion are not cast in stone. Bok choy (literally "white vegetable") can be substituted with braised cabbage, or any seasonal green vegetable. The daikon flowers are actually fairly simple to create, and can be found in *Edible Art* (by D.P. Larousse, published by Van Nostrand Reinhold). They are tinted red and yellow, by soaking them in hot beet juice and the brine used to make the pickled eggs, respectively. Mustard-pickled eggs can be made by boiling up 1½ cups cider vinegar, 1 cup water, 2 tablespoons Dijon-style mustard, 1 tablespoon turmeric, 1 teaspoon salt, ½ teaspoon white peppercorns, and a clove of crushed garlic. Pour this solution over 4 peeled, hard-boiled eggs, and allow to marinate overnight.

*B*OILED LOBSTER, BELLO GIORNO

For the Lobster

4 1½-pound lobsters   3 gallons boiling salted water

- With the point of a cook's knife, make an incision into the center of the back of the head, at a point about an inch below the eyes (this stuns the crustacean). Drop the lobsters into the boiling water, and cover. When the water comes to a rolling boil, remove from the fire. Allow to sit for 15 minutes. Remove the lobster, and refrigerate for 1 hour.

For the Garnish

16 asparagus tips, about 2 ½-inches long, and blanched in boiling salted water until al dente

2 yellow bell peppers, blanched briefly in boiling salted water

2 large carrots, cut into 2½-inch long julienne, and blanched in boiling salted water until al dente

4 leeks, white part only, cut into 2½-inch long julienne, and blanched in boiling salted water until al dente

2 bunches scallions, green tops only, blanched in boiling salted water for 2 minutes

- Tie up four packages (paupiettes) each, using the blanched scallion, of asparagus, pepper, carrot, and leek. Set aside.

For the Sauce

2 cups mayonnaise, thinned
with a little water, and
transferred to a plastic
squeeze bottle

½ cup tomato paste, thinned
with 1 tablespoon fish or
meat glaze dissolved in a
little hot water

To Assemble

- Ladle some of the mayonnaise onto a serving plate. Squirt
the tomato paste onto the mayonnaise in a spiral design.
Create an arabesque by running a toothpick through the
spiral, in radial lines, alternating away from, and towards,
the center.

- Separate the tail and claws, crack the shells, and carefully remove the meat. (Save the shells for stock or sauce.) Slice the
tails, and arrange the slices down the center of the plate, with
the claw meat extending from either end. Place one of each
of the four vegetable paupiettes to the side of the lobster.

*P*OACHED SALMON, SORREL SAUCE

For the Sauce

1 shallot, minced
2 tablespoons unsalted butter
2 cups sorrel leaves, washed,
dried, and roughly chopped
1 tablespoon all-purpose
flour, kneaded together

with 2 tablespoons
unsalted butter
2 cups fish stock (hot)
1½ cups heavy cream
salt and white pepper to taste

For the Design

1 cup Dutch sauce, thinned
with a little water, and
transferred to a plastic
squeeze bottle

½ cup chicken or fish glaze,
thinned with a little
water, brought to a boil,
and transferred to a
plastic squeeze bottle

- Sauté the shallot in the butter for 3 minutes. Add the sorrel,
cover, and cook another 3 minutes.

- Place the cream in a small saucepan and simmer very gently,
until reduced by half.

- Add the fish stock and pinch of salt and pepper to the sorrel, and simmer briefly. Add the flour/butter mixture, in small pieces, and blend thoroughly, using a wire whip. Simmer gently, stirring frequently, for about ten minutes.
- Remove the sorrel mixture and the cream to a blender or food processor, and purée. Strain through a sieve, return the sauce to the fire, and adjust seasoning.

For the Salmon

4 6-ounce salmon fillets

The Court Bouillon

1 cup fish stock
1 cup dry white wine
1 cup water
juice of 1 lemon

1 small onion, quartered
1 bay leaf
1 bouquet garni

- Bring all the ingredients except the salmon to a boil. Poach the salmon, immersed in this liquid, for 6–8 minutes. Ladle some of the sauce onto a serving plate. Remove the salmon, drain thoroughly, and place in the center of the sauce. Squirt a series of dabs of the glaze around the salmon, and run a toothpick through them to create an arabesque. Drizzle the top of the salmon with the Dutch sauce, and serve.

....

*G*RILLED BEEF MEDALLIONS, HENRI IV

4 3- to 4-ounce beef
   tenderloin steaks
salt and pepper as needed

4 tablespoons butter (if
   needed)

For the Design

4 cups Madeira sauce

2 cups Béarnaise sauce

For the Garnish

4 artichoke bottoms,
   blanched in boiling water,

with a little lemon juice
and salt

| ¼ cup unsalted butter, clarified | 2 cups noisette potatoes (small Parisienne) |

- Sauté the noisette potatoes in the butter, until golden brown. Set aside, keeping warm.
- Season the medallions lightly with salt and pepper, and grill (or sauté in the butter) about 4 minutes on each side. Ladle 1 cup of Madeira sauce on the surface of a plate. Place a steak in the center of the sauce, then squirt a series of small dabs of the Béarnaise sauce around the edge of the sauce. Run a toothpick through the center of the dabs of Béarnaise sauce, in one continuous direction. Garnish with the potatoes served inside the artichoke bottoms.

·  # *G*RILLED VEAL CHOP, FLORENTINE

For the Chop

2 pounds fresh spinach, well rinsed	2 cups Soubise sauce
1½ cups heavy cream	4 6-ounce veal chops
salt and pepper to taste	salt, pepper, and olive oil as needed
2 cups Madeira sauce	

- Steam the spinach in a small amount of water, until wilted (about 5 minutes). Drain, squeeze very dry, roughly chop, and set aside. Simmer the cream in a heavy-gauge saucepan, until reduced by two-thirds. Combine the spinach and the cream reduction, blend well, and season to taste with salt and pepper. Heat thoroughly.
- Heat both sauces, and transfer each to a plastic squeeze bottle. Set aside, keeping warm in a hot water bath.
- Season the veal chops with salt and pepper, brush with olive oil, and grill (or sauté in butter) about 5 minutes on each side. Set aside, keeping warm.
- Place a base of creamed spinach in the center of a serving plate, allowing a 1-inch space between the spinach and the inner lip of the plate. Squirt alternating dabs of the two sauces around the spinach. Create an arabesque as desired, or leave as is. Place a grilled chop on top of the spinach, and serve.

DESSERTS

$\mathscr{P}$OIRE AUX POIVRE

4 firm pears (Bosc or Bartlett)
3 cups dry red wine
2 cups water
½ cup brown sugar
1 tablespoon black
    peppercorns, cracked,

and tied in a muslin
sachet
1 cinnamon stick
4 tablespoons cornstarch,
    dissolved in ¼ cup brandy
4 sprigs fresh mint

For the Design

1½ cups crème fraîche,
    beaten until smooth, and

transferred to a plastic
squeeze bottle

- Bring the wine, water, sugar, peppercorn sachet, and cinnamon stick to a boil.
- Peel the pears, flattening the bottom, and leaving the stem intact, and poach them in the simmering liquid. When tender, but still firm, remove the pears, and set aside, keeping warm. Simmer the poaching medium, until reduced by half. Remove the sachet and cinnamon, and add the cornstarch dissolved in brandy. Bring to a boil, and strain.
- Ladle some of the sauce onto a serving plate. Squirt some of the crème fraîche onto the sauce to create a design. Place a pear in the center, and garnish with a sprig of mint.

$\mathscr{S}$EASONAL BERRIES IN PASTRY
TULIP, THREE FRUIT SAUCES

For the Fruit

Select enough seasonal
    berries to serve four, cull

them, rinse gently in cold
water, drain, and set aside

Since fresh berries are not always available throughout the year, virtually any other fruit can be substituted. Simply prepare a fruit salad with whatever fruit is available, and season lightly with sugar if additional sweetness is needed. This may include apples, oranges, pears, bananas, or kiwis, as well as raisins, dried figs, apricots, prunes, and so on.

For the Tulips

⅔ cup sugar
½ cup egg whites
½ cup unsalted butter, melted

¾ cup, plus 2 tablespoons flour

- Preheat oven to 400°F.
- Beat the sugar and egg whites until the sugar is dissolved.
- Add the butter and flour, and beat until thoroughly blended.
- Lightly butter a baking sheet, and spread 3 tablespoons of the batter onto the sheet, spread out into a 5-inch-wide circle. Repeat until all the batter is used up. Bake for 8–10 minutes, or until the circles are golden brown at the edges. (You may need to experiment with this technique, and may consider preparing a double batch of the batter.)
- With a metal spatula, carefully lift the circles from the pan, and place them immediately over an inverted coffee cup. Gently press the sides down so that it forms a small bowl with wavy edges. (It will become firm very quickly.) Lift the tulip up, and gently set aside in a safe place.

For the Design

Blueberry Sauce

2 cups fresh (or frozen) blueberries
2 tablespoons water
¼ cup sugar
1 tablespoon lemon juice

pinch of nutmeg
½ teaspoon cornstarch, dissolved in 2 tablespoons Kirsch

- Bring the blueberries, water, sugar, and lemon juice to a boil. Cover, and simmer for 10 minutes.
- Add the cornstarch dissolved in Kirsch, and while stirring, simmer for 1 minute. Press through a sieve, and set aside until ready to serve.

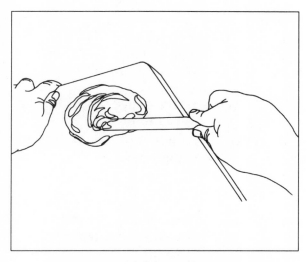

1. *Spreading the batter on the*
   back of a baking pan.

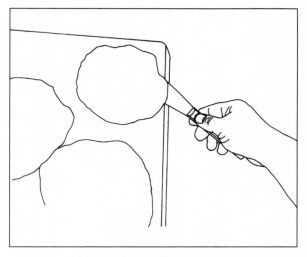

2. *Lifting off the tulip*
   with the spatula.

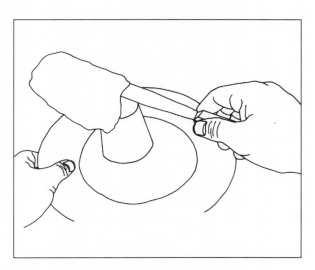

3. *Placing the tulip over*
   a small glass.

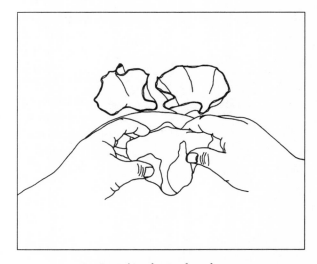

4. *Pressing down the edges to*
   create the finished tulips.

Peach Sauce

4 ripe medium peaches
  (fresh or frozen), peeled,
  pitted, and roughly cut

½ cup sugar
¼ cup water
2 teaspoons brandy

- Combine all the ingredients in a heavy-gauge saucepan, and simmer until thick and syrupy (8–10 minutes).
- Remove to a food processor, and purée. Transfer to a plastic squeeze bottle, and set aside, keeping warm.

Raspberry Sauce

2 cups fresh (or frozen)
  raspberries
3 tablespoons sugar
1 tablespoon lemon juice

½ teaspoon cornstarch,
  dissolved in 1 tablespoon
  Kirsch

- Purée the raspberries in a food processor. Press through a sieve, discarding the seeds.
- Simmer the raspberry purée, sugar, and lemon juice for 10 minutes. Add the cornstarch dissolved in the Kirsch. Blend in, stirring continuously, and simmer for 1 minute. Transfer to a plastic squeeze bottle, and set aside, keeping warm.
- Squirt six to eight 2-inch round circles of the Peach sauce around the edge of the plate. Squirt a small circle of the Raspberry sauce around the inside of these circles, and fill in the center with the Blueberry sauce. Run a toothpick through each of these, toward the center, to create an arabesque. Fill the tulips with the selection of fresh fruit, and place in the center of the plate. Garnish with a sprig of fresh mint, and serve.

GLOSSARY OF CULINARY TERMS AND TECHNIQUES

- -

à la carte: In kitchen parlance, any dish that is prepared at the time it is ordered. Also "à la minute" and "à la command."

al dente: Literally "to the tooth" or "to the bite," this term is used to describe pasta and vegetables cooked until they are tender but not mushy. They should be somewhat firm and resilient when bitten into.

bain marie: A vessel of hot water, used for maintaining the heat of a smaller vessel, containing soup, sauce, or some other food item within the larger vessel. May refer to small vessels placed into a steam table, and can also be used for chilling, placing one cold container into a larger one filled with ice and water.

blanch: To place food in boiling salted water, stock, or other liquid, in order to cook it partially, set its color, or facilitate peeling.

boil: To cook a food in water or other liquid at 212°F. A full rolling boil is essential for cooking some foods (such as pasta), but undesirable for cooking others (such as stocks).

bouquet garni: A collection of herbs and spices, tied together in a bundle with cotton twine, and added to a stock, soup, sauce, or stew, to impart the flavor of those herbs and spices to the dish it is simmered with. A standard bouquet garni consists of parsley stems, bay leaf, thyme, and peppercorns. Variations on this are limitless, depending on an individual's style, and the dish in which it is used. Loose herbs and spices can be added within a tea ball, or can be tied up in a large leek leaf.

caramelize: To cook sugar or another food in a sauté or sauce pan over direct heat long enough to allow the sugar, or the sugar in the food, to begin to brown. Caramelizing imparts a brown color and a nutty flavor to the finished dish.

chiffonade: A leafy vegetable cut into shreds, approximately ⅛-inch wide, and used as a salad base, or as a garnish. (*see* Sorrel Sauce.)

china cap (chinoise): A cone-shaped strainer, with a single handle extending from the wide end of the strainer. China caps come in three basic varieties in reference to the size of their perforations: large (chinoise gros), small (chinoise fin), and very fine (bouillon strainer, or chinois mousseline).

clarified butter: The butter fat remaining after whole butter is simmered, evaporating the liquid's mild solids (the equivalent of skim milk), and leaving their residue.

compound sauce: A finished sauce fashioned from a foundation (mother) sauce as a base, augmented with other specific ingredients, including reductions; aromatic vegetables, herbs, and spices; and various liaisons. Also called small sauces or compound derivative.

croustade: A small farinaceous vessel, made from hollowed-out bread, pastry, mashed potato (Duchess potato mixture), or rice. The vessel is usually deep fried or baked, then filled with a stew, soup, purée, or other viscous dish.

cull: To separate spoiled or substandard food items. Usually associated with small food items, such as dried beans, peas, blueberries, raspberries, and the like.

debeard: To remove the fibrous strands extending from the hinged side of a fresh mussel. Mussels use these strands to attach themselves to shoreline rocks.

deep fry: To fry a food item by immersing in fat.

deglaze (déglacer): To pour a liquid into a sauté or roasting pan, apply heat, and remove particles of food remaining in the pan after sautéing or roasting. This liquid may consist of wine, brandy, juice, or stock, and is used to augment the flavor of stocks or sauces.

drum sieve: A circular metal frame, open on one end, and covered with a screen on the other. Used for sifting flour and other dry ingredients, as well as pressing mousses and various farces through, as a final step in puréeing.

egg wash: Beaten whole egg, sometimes with water or milk added, that is brushed onto a pastry exterior. When the pastry is baked, the egg browns slightly, resulting in a glossy, golden-brown appearance.

emulsion: A liquid slightly thickened by the suspension of minute drops of oil or fat; hollandaise sauce, mayonnaise, and certain vinaigrettes are emulsions.

faggot: (pronounced "feh-go") Literally "a bundle of sticks," it refers to a collection of fresh herbs and spices tied up into a bundle, also called bouquet garni.

fine herbs: A mixture of finely minced fresh herbs, generally parsley, chervil, tarragon, and chives. In actual practice, it may consist of any assemblage of herbs—parsley plus three others.

fold: Generally with the help of a rubber spatula, to combine two foods gently, one being highly whipped. This method of blending allows the whipped product to retain its whipped-in air. It is most often associated with soufflés.

fond: Literally base, or bottom, it is a French term for stock, as well as the caramelized particles remaining in a cooking vessel after roasting or sautéing.

food mill: With the advent of food processors, this ingeniously simple device has fallen on hard times. But it can still be a tremendous aid in puréeing soups and sauces. It consists of a straight-sided, or conical container with a perforated bottom, and a curved flange attached to a crank, which rests in the center of a perforated plate at the bottom. The crank is manually rotated, pressing a soup or sauce through one of three different sizes of perforated plates.

forcemeat (also farce): A seasoned mixture of raw or cooked meat, poultry, game, fish, or vegetables, used to stuff a multitude of dishes, from meat dishes to vegetables to pasta. It also refers to the seasoned ground meat preparations made into pâtés, terrines, quenelles, and sausages. The French term *farce* (from *farcir*, meaning "to stuff"), which also connotes a prank or practical joke, comes from an earlier practice (probably dating to ancient Rome) of playing a joke on one's guests by filling a hen, fish, or some other animal with an unexpected filling.

garlic press: A familiar tool, designed to quickly purée garlic, one peeled clove at a time. (Recipes that include the term "pressed garlic," refer to this procedure.)

glaze (glace de viande): A 90 percent reduction of a meat, poultry, game, or fish stock.

gratin: A technique (gratiner) in which the top of a food is lightly browned, often using a mixture of butter plus bread crumbs and/or cheese, then placed under a broiler.

julienne: A designated rectangularly shaped vegetable cut, generally used for garnishes, measuring from $\frac{1}{8} \times \frac{1}{8} \times 1$-inch to $\frac{1}{4} \times \frac{1}{4} \times 2$ or 3 inches, or any food cut into strips. A large julienne is also referred to as bâtonnet (little stick).

lard: Larding is a technique in which a strip of pork fat is inserted into a piece of meat or poultry, using a "larding needle," in order to add moisture and flavor during roasting or braising. In modern times, other items have been inserted, including compound butters, herbs, vegetables, and truffles.

large dice (jardinière): A designated vegetable cut, measuring approximately $\frac{1}{3}$–$\frac{1}{2}$ inch square.

liaison: A thickening agent used in soups and sauces (roux, cornstarch).

liaison finale: A very rich thickening agent which, because of its delicate nature, must be incorporated into a soup or sauce at the very last moment before it is served (beurre manié, cream, egg yolks, butter).

medium dice (macedoine): A size of vegetable cut, measuring approximately $\frac{1}{4}$ inch square.

mince: To chop a spice, herb, or vegetable very fine.

mirepoix: A mixture of celery, carrot, and onion, commonly used for flavoring a stock or sauce.

mise-en-place: From the verb *mettre*, "to place," in culinary parlance this phrase is translated to mean "A place for everything, and everything in its place." It refers to the importance of being well organized and well prepped, so that kitchen production can move smoothly, and all problems can be handled in the heat of peak production.

mother sauce (sauce de mère): One of five foundation sauces, originally formulated by Antoine Carême, and later revised by August Escoffier. Also called *leading*, or *foundation* sauce.

mount (monter au beurre): From the French verb *monter*, "to lift," this term refers to the technique of incorporating butter into a sauce or soup just before it is served. Stirring in butter in small pieces creates an emulsion that slightly thickens the liquid and improves or "lifts" the flavor of the final product. *Montée* is the past participle of the verb *monter*; *mount* is the colloquial American equivalent.

offal: Edible internal organs (and some external parts) of an animal, considered by some to be gastronomically superior to other edible parts. They include bone marrow, brains, ears, feet, heart, kidneys, liver, sweetbreads (thymus gland), tongue, and tripe (stomach lining).

pan fry: To fry a food item in a sauce or sauté pan in a small amount of fat.

Parisienne scoop: Commonly known as a melon baller, this tool creates spherical garnishes from fruits and vegetables.

pastry thermometer: A high-range thermometer, particularly useful in pastry work, as well as for determining and maintaining the correct temperature when deep-frying a food item.

paupiette: Literally "little package," referring to a rolled fish fillet, bundle of julienned vegetables tied together with scallion greens, etc.

peasant style (paysanne): A common term for both a style of cooking, and a method of cutting food ingredients. As a cooking style, it is characterized by a robust and spontaneous approach, based on available ingredients, and/or refashioned leftovers, often including root vegetables (potatoes, carrots, and turnips) and cabbage. As a cutting technique, it refers to rough and unevenly cut mirepoix for use as aromatics, as well as ingredients used within its style.

poach: To cook very gently in simmering liquid, at between 180°F and 200°F.

pressed garlic: Garlic puréed using a garlic press.

red chili pepper paste: A spicy purée of exceptionally hot chile peppers, blended with oil, and found in Asian and Hispanic food markets. It affords an easily available and consistent condiment to use in recipes that call for this kind of flavoring.

reduce: To decrease the volume of a sauce or stock by simmering or boiling, thus increasing its flavor and thickness.

render: To melt bacon, fatback, chicken fat, or other fat by cooking it in a heavy-gauge pan over medium heat.

roasting pan (plaque à rôtir): A large rectangular metal pan, deeper and heavier than a baking (sheet) pan, used for roasting meats and poultry.

saucepan (sautoir): A heavy-gauge round cooking vessel with vertical sides and a single handle.

sauté: From the French verb *sauter*, "to jump." To cook food in a small amount of fat or oil.

sauté pan (sauteuse): A round cooking vessel with sloping sides and a single handle.

scallop: Though most often associated with the connector muscle of one variety of bivalve mollusk, it is also used in this book as the English translation of the Latin term for a slice of meat, game, poultry or fish, pounded very thin, then cooked. The French word for this is *escalope*, the Italian, *scallopine*.

shallot (eschallote): A unique aromatic vegetable, a separate variety of the onion family, and an essential ingredient in finished sauces. The name is derived from Ascalon, an ancient Palestinian port, and it is believed that they were cultivated as early as the middle of the eighth century. Their flavor is subtler than onion, with a hint of garlic. They are also served raw in salads, and grilled or roasted as an accompaniment to scores of dishes. Because of their ancient and Middle Eastern origins, they are also used frequently in Vietnamese, Chinese, Indian, and Creole cookery.

sieve: A fine-screened strainer through which sauces and other foods are pressed, often with the help of a rubber spatula. Pushing mousses, pâtés, and other finely puréed preparations through a sieve eliminates remnants of sinew or elements not fully puréed.

skillet: A heavy-gauge cast iron pan with a single handle. Sometimes called a Griswold pan, it can be placed in the oven, thus doubling as a roasting pan.

skim (dépouiller): Pronounced "day-pou-yay," literally "to skin, to skim." A technique in which the top of a simmering stock, soup, or sauce is skimmed of fat and impurities. (The substance removed is known as dépouillage.)

small dice (brunoise): A designated vegetable cut, measuring approximately ⅛-inch square.

steel: A long, thin, abrasive tool used to maintain a sharp cutting edge on knives—not to be confused with a sharpening stone, which is used to grind a sharp edge. The end of a steel is magnetized to hold any metal burrs removed from a knife's cutting edge.

stock pot (marmite): A large pot, taller than wide, with straight sides, and two opposing handles near the top edge. In French, a stock pot is called a *fait-tout*, literally "do-all," in reference to its many uses. Stock pots can also come with a spigot attached near the bottom, which can expedite the careful removal of a stock, and particularly a consommé.

sweat: To sauté gently, covered, so that the ingredients sautéed exude their moisture, which does not evaporate, effectively steaming these ingredients in their own moisture.

temper: To combine two liquids, one hot and the other cold, by slowly blending the hot liquid into the cold one. By gradually raising the temperature of the cold liquid, the two can be combined, without adversely affecting either liquid. Applies to the incorporation of final liaisons, in the making of crème anglaise, pastry cream, as well as carefully melting chocolate.

turned (tourné): A vegetable or potato cut into a 7-sided oval or olive-shaped oval, measuring 1–3 inches long.

whip (fouet): Sometimes referred to as a "whisk," it consists of several strands of stainless steel wire, in various thicknesses, bent into loops, and held in place with a metal handle. The very heavy, stiff wire whips are commonly called "French whips," the lighter more flexible ones are "piano wire whips," and the even lighter, large bulbous type are known as "balloon whips." All are indispensable in a well-equipped kitchen. They are used for beating liaisons into sauces, blending baking batters, and whipping air into various foods (such as heavy cream and egg whites).

white pepper: Black pepper that has been soaked in water, then rubbed to remove the skin and thin outer pulp. White pepper is preferred over black pepper in some dishes because of its lighter color. Dedicated cooks often keep two pepper mills, one filled with black pepper, the other with white, and each labeled accordingly.

zest: The outermost skin of a citrus fruit, excluding the pith (the underlying white part of the skin). It is shaved off with a zester, a five-holed tool specifically engineered for that purpose, or with a sharp paring knife or vegetable peeler. Zest contains the essential oils of the fruit, and is used as both a flavoring agent and a garnish.

INDEX OF RECIPES